Founders of the Middle Ages

FOUNDERS OF THE MIDDLE AGES

BY

EDWARD KENNARD RAND

Professor of Latin in Harvard University

DOVER PUBLICATIONS INC.

NEW YORK • NEW YORK

CAROLO HOMERO HASKINS

AMICO CARISSIMO
INTER RECENTISSIMOS MEDII AEVI
CONDITORES PRINCIPI

PREFACE

THE chapters of this book were delivered as lectures before the Lowell Institute of Boston in January and February, 1928. They are here reproduced substantially as they were delivered. Minor changes in phrasing have been introduced, and certain paragraphs not read for lack of time have been included. In the lecture on Boethius (chapter V), I have added an analysis of the *Consolation of Philosophy*. The rest is virtually the same.

The aim of the book is, in the main, to make clear the importance of certain great men and of certain great movements in thought and culture during the early Christian centuries, particularly the fourth, fifth, and sixth, and to point out the significance of these men and these movements as precursors of certain aspects of mediaeval civilization. To those times the men of the Middle Ages looked back as to the epoch of their Founders.

The reader will soon become aware of an attempt to defend the culture of the Church and particularly of the form that it assumed in the West. The Greeks are always our masters, but pupils may learn lessons in an original way, even improving what they learn and finding new truth for themselves. The views here represented are open to criticism at many points. A corrective will be found in the various works cited at the end of the text, which range in orthodox intensity from Labriolle to Lake. *Quot homines, tot sententiae.* We are all bound by small horizons, and even our efforts to escape from one prejudice only land us in another. As Henry Osborn Taylor remarks in his Presidential Address (1927) before the American Historical Association: "To different succeeding ages the past will appear, and even *be*, different." From such considerations it would seem advisable that the historian, in his interpretation of the past, should absorb the spirit of an epoch, so far as he can, before submitting it to the canons of criticism fashionable in his own day, and that in applying these canons, he should put less trust in present-day judgments, however brilliantly or learnedly expressed, than in the abiding traditions of the ages. Emenders of the text of history expose themselves to the predicament of rash editors of ancient books, of whom Quintilian remarked, "Dum librariorum insectari volunt inscientiam, suam confitentur."

Most of the writers to whom I am chiefly obliged are cited here and there in the notes at the end of this volume. I gladly take this occasion to express my special gratitude to Arthur Richmond Marsh, at one time Professor of Comparative Literature in Harvard College, whose course on "The Classical Culture of the Middle Ages" inspired me then and has been the basis of much that I have written and taught on that subject since.

PREFACE

In the preparation of these lectures for the platform and the press I have been efficiently aided by the Harvard Service Bureau and its competent chief, Miss Gladys H. McCafferty. I am indebted to Messrs. Harold Murdock and David T. Pottinger of the Harvard University Press for the beauty of the printed pages and the speed with which they were issued. I owe to Mr. G. B. Ives of the Press the careful supervision of the proofs and the preparation of the index.

Above all, I have been helped at every turn by the spurring encouragements and restraining cautions of my wife, who also read the proofs with watchful eye.

EDWARD KENNARD RAND

CONTENTS

Founders of the Middle Ages

CHAPTER I

THE CHURCH AND PAGAN CULTURE

THE PROBLEM

THE Middle Ages, Rabelais's *siècle Gothique*, need no apology at the present time. We are no longer in the days of Rabelais or of Pope, or of Lilius Gregorius Gyraldus, who in 1545 wrote several dialogues on the history of the poets, ancient and modern, and not knowing quite what to do with Petrarch and Boccaccio, put them in a paragraph after the ancients, remarking of the barbarous poetasters of the dark and middle period that their works were good specimens of what ought not to be read.[1] Boccaccio had himself done something similar in his brief account of bucolic poetry. There was first, he states, Theocritus, who hid nothing under the rind of his verse; then there was Virgil, who hid much there; then came a string of ignoble and unmentioned writers, from whom the Pastoral Muse was happily delivered by his glorious master, Franciscus Petrarca.[2] Poor Boccaccio!

> We think our fathers fools, so wise we grow;
> Perhaps our wiser sons will think us so,

and reduce us to a footnote. Petrarch and Boccaccio, who thought of themselves as running on the heights, —

at least Petrarch would not object to this simile, —
were, in the opinion of the perfect stylists of the High
Renaissance, just pulling their feet out of the mire of
the Middle Ages, *medium aevum, media tempestas*, the
age that marked time between two events.[3] But poor
humanists! The most eminent historian of mediaeval
civilization that our country, or perhaps any country,
has produced in recent times has dared to call the twelfth
century a Renaissance, and to remark pithily that the
humanists of the later Renaissance killed Latin.[4] They
thought their fathers fools. But poor Pope! When
Matthew Arnold, no mean judge of good literature,
pondered on the best five-foot shelf of books with which
to pass his life in solitude, he decided on the *Patrologia
Latina* of the Abbé Migne.[5] It is rather a five-fathom
than a five-foot shelf, and comprehensive enough to
hold St. Jerome's translation of the Holy Scriptures, as
well as the gay trifles of Ausonius, but surely more redo-
lent of Hebraism than of Hellenism, and in the main a
Gothic library — the classics of an age that heard of
none.

Since Arnold's day, we have travelled even farther.
Companion volumes have recently been issued by the
Clarendon Press at Oxford, one on the Legacy of Greece,
one on the Legacy of Rome, one on the Legacy of Israel,
and one on the Legacy of the Middle Ages. It is some
satisfaction that our forefathers did not die intestate,
and that we are the heirs of rich and varied bequests.

In our own country, we less invitingly advertise not legacies, but debts, with a commendable sense of international obligation, — at least to the ancients, — in the series, *Our Debt to Greece and Rome*. We have produced as yet no such series devoted to the Middle Ages, but book-stalls here as well as abroad abound in manuals on mediaeval Latin literature, some of which are used in secondary schools — *horresco referens* — in place of Julius Caesar. We also have what might seem to Matthew Arnold a contradiction in terms, a Mediaeval Academy of America, with a thriving membership of over a thousand, drawn from the most widely separated states and from various lands across the seas.

Now, although it has thus become something of a commonplace that the culture of the present day springs from many a mediaeval root, it may not appear so obvious that the Middle Ages drew their own strength from the past. Was not the ancient way of life effaced when barbarians overran Western Europe, and the light of Greek letters went out for nearly eight centuries? Shall we not call mediaeval civilization for good or for ill a new civilization, crude at first, but, from first to last, independent? No reader of those splendid volumes of Dr. Henry Osborn Taylor on the *Mediaeval Mind* and the *Classical Heritage of the Middle Ages* will fail to protest against such an estimate. In any thorough-going history of the Mediaeval period, one will find material to controvert it. I have nothing radically new or startling on this score to offer in the present lectures.

And yet we may perhaps devote our attention with some profit to precisely this point — what were the antecedents of the Middle Ages, what were the traditions in letters and in thought to which mediaeval men looked back as to the rock whence they were hewn? Who were its Founders? I say Founders and not *the* Founders, that is, not all of them. Hampered by lack of space, time, and information, I cannot speak of all the movements that flourished at the end of the Roman Empire. I can speak only incidentally, if at all, of government, law, and economic forces. I shall not penetrate deeply into theology, which is the life of the times and to which all sciences were eventually reduced. My main concern is literature, with a bit of philosophy, and that the literature and the philosophy of the West. Of course, thoroughly to understand Western apologetics, Western theology, Western culture, one must begin, as usual, with the Greeks. For this last restriction, I must plead, besides the limitation of space and time and information, the fact that the Middle Ages, once more, were deprived of Greek letters. Some knowledge of Greek persisted, but it was a knowledge, a feeble knowledge, of the Greek language and of certain technical works, particularly in the domain of philosophy. But nobody knew Homer at first hand, Aristophanes or the tragedians, Thucydides or Demosthenes, Menander or Theocritus. Even when Petrarch in his eclogue on the poets expresses his rapturous devotion to the Greeks, his raptures take the form of eulogistic scraps from the ancient Latin critics; the Greeks themselves he had not read, and could not read.

Therefore, since our attention is centred ultimately on the Middle Ages, there is no point in examining elaborately, for instance, the use that St. Ambrose made of the Greek fathers, St. Basil, St. Gregory of Nyssa, and St. Gregory of Nazianzus. All that we need consider is what the Middle Ages had at first hand, namely, St. Ambrose himself. Further, we have perhaps heard enough about the tremendous superiority of the Greek fathers at the expense of the writers of the West, those legalistic souls, versed in a mechanical theology and the dull, dead formalism of Rome. That is the point of view set forth years ago in John Fiske's little book, *The Idea of God*, the theological information wherein, if I mistake not, is lifted bodily from a far more significant volume of the same tendency, as fresh and delightful now as in the day when it was written, *The Continuity of Christian Thought*, by Dr. A. V. G. Allen. The same attitude is exhibited, though with reserve, in two recent books of high originality and enduring worth by Dr. Paul Elmer More, leaves in the garland that he has been weaving for Plato; I will say more of them presently. Of course such authorities must be right, yet I own a sneaking sympathy with the young American who, after hearing Professor Norton's lectures, wrote in an examination-paper, "I am tired of the Greeks." I am going to let the Latins speak for themselves, just as if — blasphemous thought! — the Greeks did not exist at all. Even so, I may have to mention the latter now and then.

If the Middle Ages did not know Greek literature at first hand, a goodly amount of Latin literature had filtered in; in fact, the mediaeval monks transmitted most of it to us. Had it not been for the Middle Ages, Pope would have had no Latin classics at all to study, save those of the age that heard of none. Why was the transmission made? What had the Church to do with the Pagans of Greece and Rome? It is the foremost question for us to ask as we examine the foundations of Mediaeval culture, and the answer might seem, at first thought, rather obvious.

The first followers of our Lord were in general unlearned men, fishers and publicans. They made literature, but they knew none, and hence offer no criticism of Pagan letters. There is one notable exception, St. Paul, who, though brought up in the strictest sect of the Jews, a Pharisee, was likewise a Roman citizen and a man of considerable culture. Yet the life of St. Paul was devoted to preaching the Gospel of the risen Saviour and to establishing His Church among the Gentiles. The wisdom of this world, he declared, is foolishness with God; and the wisdom of this world would, I suppose, include a liberal education. One might infer, as various Christians did infer, that an elaborate course in such foolishness was not worth while.[6]

In endeavoring to ascertain the mind of the Church in regard to Pagan culture, I am assuming that the message of Christianity was clear, profound, and new. Anybody can read it in the Gospels, even, I venture to imagine, in the sources that New Testament scholars have discovered behind the first three Gospels, — writers that I must mention as canonized, since they precede the Evangelists themselves, — St. Urmarkus and St. Q. Far be it from a mere Classical scholar to rush into the fields of Sacred History, Sacred Exegesis, and Sacred Higher Criticism, — *procul o procul este profani!* — but when he has followed the course of Homeric scholarship in the last century and seen the disintegrating critics themselves disintegrated, he may be permitted to question the value, not of a scholarly attempt to analyze the composition or to find the sources of the Gospels or of *Acts*, but of an account of the beginnings of Christianity, strewn with epigrams and learned guesses, in which what is great in the Gospels becomes little in the retelling, and in which the frame of the drama is preserved with the protagonist left out.

I am reminded of a remark by the author of *The Continuity of Christian Thought*, whose lectures I was once privileged to hear. He declared that the effort to get back to the primitive core of Christianity — however necessary the historian may find that effort to be — is something like peeling an onion. You begin to remove the accretions, you peel and peel, till nothing is left —

nothing but the knife, the own peculiar knife, of the
peeler. But an onion was there at first. An attitude
more critical, more saving of time, and considerably less
naïf, was adopted by the historian Livy, who remarked
in the preface of his *History* that with regard to the
events that accompanied the founding of Rome he intended neither to affirm nor to deny them. Similarly,
we common folk, οἳ ἀρούρης καρπὸν ἔδουσιν, need not
concern ourselves particularly about modern research
into the origins of Christianity. That research should
be pressed to the utmost, guided by reason and con-
science, but we should be aware that each one of us,
even an historian, is enveloped in the fashion of his
times and his temperament. German investigators have
looked at early Christianity through Lutheran and
Kantian spectacles — a magnifier of high power, according to them, but a darkening glass, according to
Dr. More. There is nothing in all this for humble folk
to fear, as if the failure to accept the "latest results"
immediately classed one as an ignoramus. There is the
authority of scholarship, and there is also the authority
of tradition, based on information not accessible to us
and sanctioned by the Church. When scholars have
discovered a theory of the New Testament as solid as
the Copernican astronomy, the Church will listen; for
it must.

Meanwhile, I think we can discern the landmarks of
early Christianity less clearly in the publications of my

friend Kirsopp Lake than in those volumes of Dr. More, *The Christ of the New Testament*, and *Christ the Word*, where we find a fearless yet reverent discussion of the New Testament by one who knows the literature and the thought of many nations, and who has mastered at first hand the philosophical background of Christianity. Dr. More has some independent notions about theology — he is a Binitarian *contra mundum*, if I read him aright. He is not reluctant to analyze and to tear down. But he also builds. Some of his reconstructions may not stand the test of time, yet they repose on deep study, keen insight, and reverence. I cannot refrain from making one quotation, which will show the spirit of these works. He remarks at the end of the first of them: [7]

Read the fragments of literature left to us by the Orphic and Phrygian and Egyptian and Chaldaean mythologies of the age, consider the monstrosities of Mithra and the fabulous follies of Gnosticism, each in its own fashion seeking, like Christianity, to bridge the gulf between the human and the divine, — and then turn to the Gospel of Mark! It is like coming out into the clear light of the sun from a misty region haunted by

"The ghosts of words and dusty dreams,
Old memories, faiths infirm and dead."

It was natural, then, for the Christian Church, aware perhaps of the difference between its teaching and that of Stoic ethics and that of the Graeco-Oriental mysteries, instinctively to turn away from the culture of the past. Did not Greek and Roman letters harbor indecencies, superstition, and the pomps and vanities of an outworn rhetoric? One may gather from Christian writers vituperations of the ancients in goodly store. There are prohibitions in the decrees of various Church Councils against the reading of Pagan authors, that of the Fourth Council of Carthage of the year 398 forbidding Bishops to indulge in this practice.[8] There is St. Jerome's famous dream, in which he was haled before the throne of the Almighty for being, not a Christian, but a Ciceronian. Immediately before his account of that dream, to which we shall revert in a later lecture, St. Jerome asks, "What fellowship can there be between light and darkness? What agreement between Christ and Belial? What has Horace to do with the Psalter, or Virgil with the Gospels, or Cicero with the Apostle? . . . We ought not drink both from the chalice of Christ and from the chalice of demons."[9] Most disconcerting of all to one of my calling is Tertullian's declaration that professors of Greek and Latin literature are idolaters in disguise — "near neighbors of multiform idolatry" are his words.[10] No wonder that, with these and many similar utterances in mind, scholars so different as Comparetti in his brilliant but biased book on the Mediaeval career of Virgil,[11] and Canon Rashdall in his sane and scholarly work on universities in the Middle Ages,[12] conclude that the tendency of the Church's teaching was to depreciate secular education.

Nor is it difficult to follow such a clue into the Middle Ages. Alcuin, in his youth, had an anti-Virgilian dream to match the anti-Ciceronian dream of St. Jerome, and in the last years of his life, he administered stern reprimand to two of the monks of St. Martin's for reading Virgil on the sly; [13] Abelard wonders why bishops and doctors of the Christian religion do not forbid the city of God to the poets that Plato would not admit to his city of the world; [14] and when a monk wanted an Ovid or a Juvenal during a silent hour in a mediaeval library, he expressed his desire in the requisite sign-language by scratching his ear, "even as a dog, when itching, does, since infidels are not unjustly likened to such an animal." [15]

This testimony would settle the case, if it constituted the truth, the whole truth, and nothing but the truth. It at least points out a tendency toward hostility, natural enough in the early Christian centuries when one thinks of the Pagan shows, the persecutions of the Church, and some of the contents of Pagan books. There is also a deeper consideration at which I have only hinted thus far.

In 1920, the late Professor Bury published a stimulating volume on *Progress*. He found that the idea of progress is in the main a modern affair. So I suppose it is. At least the modern man spends more time in thinking of a society that is advancing onward and ever upward, than of himself as a miserable sinner, lineal de-

scendant of the first offender. But Mr. Bury has not
quoted all that the ancients said about the matter. For
instance, the black verses on the degradation of time
that he cites from Horace could be matched with others
of exactly the opposite color.[16] He has also failed to do
justice to the emphasis on the idea of progress in early
Christian thought. To say nothing of St. Paul and that
birth for which creation had been groaning and travail-
ing till then, I would invite your attention to an episode
of the fourth century, an episode that marks pictur-
esquely the swinging over of the world from the old faith
to the new. It is the affair of the Altar of Victory.

This altar had long adorned the Roman Senate house,
the Curia Julia in the Forum. The statue of Victory
was said to have been taken from the Tarentines, and
was decorated with ornaments that Augustus had
brought from Egypt. The meetings of the Roman Senate were opened with the burning of incense at the altar,
and senators took their oath of loyalty to the emperor
there. The place was thus hallowed with associations
of the past, and seemed an indispensable accompani-
ment of parliamentary procedure. It did not seem like
a meeting of the Senate without the little sacrifice to
Victory, and without the oath on her altar a senator
might have felt free to follow his own devices, unbound
by a sense of duty to authority and the state. Constan-
tius had had the statue removed, but the act did not
occasion much comment at the time; the Pagans may

have felt that amid the general air of tolerance it did not so much matter. But when Julian restored the statue, it gained a new significance, with which Valentinian did not venture to interfere; the problem was complicated by the fact that the majority of the Senate were still Pagans — it was the stronghold of conservatism. Gratian, however, on his accession in 375, had the goddess removed; it may well have been that his old teacher, St. Ambrose, prompted the act. The Pagans were indignant and alarmed. They made various attempts to effect its restoration, particularly in the year 384, when Symmachus, as prefect of the city, presented a report, or *relatio*, on the matter to the Emperors Valentinian II, Theodosius, Emperor of the East, and the latter's son, Arcadius, who was associated with him in the rule. St. Ambrose spoke upon the other side.

By great good fortune, the speech of Symmachus has been preserved. It is one of a very few documents now extant that represent the feeling of high-minded Pagans about Christianity in the hour of the latter's victory. A competent German historian of the decline and fall of Pagan culture calls it the swan-song of the dying religion, and speaks of the moving beauty, which even the Christians could not fail to note.[17] The style is concise, in the manner of a report, but its very abruptness is eloquent. Symmachus's main argument is the appeal to tradition. "Grant, I implore you, that we who are old men may leave to posterity that which we received as boys." He pleads for the sanctity of the altar and its efficacy in safeguarding oaths.

All things [he declares] are full of God, and no place is safe for perjurers, but the fear of transgression is greatly spurred by the consciousness of the very presence of deity. That altar contains in itself the harmony of the members of our order and the good faith of each of them individually. Nor does anything so much contribute to the authority of the Senate's decrees, as the fact that one body, sworn to the same oath, has resolved them.

Symmachus then represents the Eternal City herself, *aeterna Roma*, as pleading with the Emperors.

Let me use my ancestral ceremonies, she says, for I do not repent me of them. Let me live after my own way; for I am free. This was the cult that drove Hannibal from the walls of Rome and the Gauls from the Capitolium. Am I kept for this, to be chastised in my old age? . . . I do but ask peace for the gods of our fathers, the native gods of Rome. It is right that what all adore should be deemed one. We all look up at the same stars. We have a common sky. A common firmament encompasses us. What matters it by what kind of learned theory each man looketh for the truth? There is no one way that will take us to so mighty a secret. All this is matter of discussion for men of leisure. We offer your majesties not a debate but a plea.

This is only a brief extract of this memorable report. The answer made by St. Ambrose is one of his best and most characteristic works. It is the utterance of a calm and noble mind, fair and courteous to his opponent and sure of the victory of his cause. He declares that he is master of no glittering eloquence. He makes straight for the facts. He gives the *relatio* in one of his letters, and in another he takes up Symmachus's arguments one by one, quoting them exactly, and so fully that, even if the document were lacking, we could reconstruct its main points from St. Ambrose; the fortunate transmission of the *relatio* through another channel enables us to check up St. Ambrose and find that his method of dealing with his opponent is fair.[18]

I will reiterate only one of his points, the one most pertinent to my present theme. It is a plea for progress to match that of Symmachus for tradition.

Why cite me the examples of the ancients? [he asks]. 'T is no disgrace to pass on to better things (*nullus pudor est ad meliora transire*). Take the ancient days of chaos, when elements were flying about in an unorganized mass. Think how that turmoil settled into the new order of a world and how the world has developed since then, with the gradual invention of the arts and the advances of human history. I suppose that back in the good old times of chaos, the conservative particles objected to the advent of the novel and vulgar sunlight which accompanied the introduction of order. But for all that, the world moved (*eppur si muove*). And we Christians too have grown. Through wrongs, through poverty, through persecution, we have grown; and the great difference between us and you is that what you seek in surmises, we know. How can I put faith in you when you confess that you do not know what you worship?

Such is the challenge that Ambrose flings back at Symmachus. Christianity is a certain, as well as a growing, faith. The words have the ring of victory — a victory over a noble opponent.

Some twenty years later, when the greatness of this episode stood out in its true proportions, Prudentius saw its fitness for an epic theme. He made an epic of it, brief in bulk but broad in scope, his poem *Contra Symmachum*.[19] It is in the reign of Honorius; the poet can look back from a tranquil place to the scene of the contest. And he looks back farther still. He begins with the lineage of the gods, and the part they play in Roman history. He lingers quite as affectionately on the primitive days of ancient Rome when the gods had humble temples of thatch, as Virgil does in the eighth book of his *Aeneid*. The poet's picture is sympathetic and imaginative; Prudentius almost persuades me to become a Pagan. He comes down to the cults of imperial Rome, not forgetting that of the Sun, till we reach the age of the triumph under Constantine. The mists of superstition now begin to disperse. The remnant of Pagans is small and dwindling, but they turn for one more encounter before they leave the field.

The protest of Symmachus is thus presented on a large background of history. It is an epoch in the story of the eternal city, which is as dear to Prudentius as to Symmachus. That story, however, is not one of decline and fall, or of the gradual betrayal of those gods that have watched over the city; it is the history of the true progress of Rome, like the life of St. Augustine, as Dante has it, from bad to good, from good to better, and from better to best.

The poet now summons God as Symmachus summoned Roma, to speak to the present world. The words imputed to Deity are noble and splendid poetry, which leave us impressed with the majesty and the goodness of God, and with the dignity of man, who by the grace of God is himself exalted to divinity. With these larger issues confronting us, Paganism looks small. The "precepts of our fathers" shrivel into a tiny moment when viewed *sub specie aeternitatis.* The Golden Age, as painted by the poets, — and Prudentius paints it after Virgil to make his point the clearer, — could hardly offer inducements to the cultivated man of the fourth century. "Back to our caves," — *Redeamus ad antra,*— if we are really believers in tradition; your real conservatives are the cavemen. Prudentius, like Ambrose, is on the side of progress and evolution. He asks if, in view of the development of the Roman republic into Augustan monarchy, which both he and Symmachus doubtless accepted as the best form of government, it is not natural to expect some such crowning moment in the development of Roman religion. Augustus brought the empire, and Christ the Church.

But the prosperity of Rome, says the Pagan, is the gift of the Gods. Not so, is the reply. It was not Venus or Cybele or omen of crow or magpie that saved Rome, but her triumphant arms. Rome triumphed, — and here we have a large philosophy of history briefly expressed, — Rome triumphed because God wished to achieve the unity of the human race as a precursor of the Gospel. This is the mission of Rome, whose glory is

not over, but just begun. Prudentius hears her speak,
but in more jubilant tones than those that Symmachus
heard. She rejoices in the renewing of her youth. She
refers to the coming of Hannibal and the Gauls. Her
comfort is that no fate like that can ever happen to her
now —

Nullus mea barbarus hostis
Cuspide claustra quatit.

Alas for this proud boast! Only a few years after Prudentius penned it, the barbarians' spears were flourished
in the streets of Rome.

One of the strongest refutations by the poet is directed against a most attractive part of Symmachus's
argument — his plea that Christians and Pagans have
a common sky, to which there are many pathways.
True enough, rejoins Prudentius. It is indeed common
for all — the pure and the impure, the harlot and the
wife, the priest and the gladiator; they all breathe the
same air. Both the honest wayfarer and the robber
drink of the same brook. Traders and pirates have the
same sea for their ends. The world serves humanity's
purposes but does not judge it. Life is common for us all,
but not our merit. Roman, Dacian, Scythian, Vandal,
Hun, Moor, Numidian, Prussian (*Alemannus*), Saxon,
Ethiopian — these all walk the same earth, have the
same sky, the same ocean. But, surely, Roman, Hun,
and Blackamoor are not quite of the same household.
Let us go a bit farther. Animals drink of our fountains.

The same rains nourish crops for men that make grass grow for the wild asses. The uncleanly sow swims in our streams, and dogs breathe our air. But there is as much difference betwixt the Roman and the Teuton, Prudentius would imply, as betwixt quadruped and biped, mute and articulate, *and* betwixt senseless idolaters and those who, freed from vain superstitions, follow the commandments of God. This makes the reasoning of Symmachus seem small. What appeared at first a beautiful tolerance dissolves, under the action of a penetrating Horatian ridicule, into mere silliness and sentimentalism. The passage might be profitably read by modern sentimentalists who think feeling without belief the essence of religion.

This is a remarkable poem. Could Prudentius have translated it into sculpture, he could have set his monument in the Senate house in place of the Pagan Altar of Victory, to immortalize, as before, the ancient ideals, but also their transmutation into the new and forward-looking programme of the day.

Another factor in the problem that faced the Church was the relish for things modern. This is often, though not necessarily, combined with a belief in progress. The believer in progress, whether he hears the diapason of the ages ending full in his own times, or looks ahead to something still better to come, at least is tremendously concerned about the present. Or, one may be concerned about the present just for the present's sake. The Christians, at any rate, constituted the modern party in the fourth century, as well as the party of progress. And if now we may descend to the extreme end of our period of Foundation, I would invite your attention to an excellent example of a modern in the person of Pope Gregory the Great. I am careful to call him a modern and not a modernist, because he is at the same time a fundamentalist, being one of our Founders, and one of the most influential.

Gregory was born in Rome about 540 and died in 604. One point of interest in his character, next to his talent for organization, and his ambition for the Church, is his essential shyness of disposition. Had not the times called him, he would have preferred to remain a simple monk. And before he was an ecclesiastic, Gregory was a man of the world. He was born of noble parents and received a good education. He was learned in the secular arts; so say writers contemporary, or nearly contemporary, and I have no reason for disbelieving their statements. Like Ambrose, he started out on a political career, and was appointed, by Justin II, city praetor in Rome, when he was about thirty years old. Then, like Paulinus of Nola two hundred years before him, he caught the passion for monasticism. With an ample ancestral fortune at his disposal, he founded six monasteries at Palermo, and one in Rome, where he adapted his father's palace for the purpose and consecrated it to the service of St. Andrew. Here he retired from the

world, but not for long. Gregory, despite his love of se-
clusion, was a born organizer and reformer. He was inspired with the idea of converting England — not to
Christianity, for the British branch of the Catholic
Church was already there — but to the discipline of
Rome. We need not inquire whether or not he saw
in the market-place fair British captives who seemed
rather *angeli* than *Angli*, and whether he was really responsible for all the sacred puns recorded in that story;
this is one of those incidents so interesting and picturesque that it is immediately suspected by a critical
mind. Gregory was prevented from going to the distant Britons himself, but his plans were carried out by
Augustine, a monk of St. Andrew's, in 596. Meanwhile
Gregory had been pulled out of his retirement, made a
deacon, and some time in the eighties was ordered by
the Pope to go to Constantinople as a representative of
Rome in its dealings with the Eastern Church. Gregory
professed to know no Greek, but I should think that he
must have had some slight knowledge of the language
to be an acceptable envoy at the Byzantine court. Perhaps he meant that he was unfamiliar with the Greek
authors. At all events, I think we may detect an
underlying intention to cut loose from Greek — and
that means, as I have already suggested, that the
Middle Ages are in the process of foundation.

Soon after his return from Constantinople, in 590,
Gregory was elected Pope. His term of office thus was

not long, but it was marked by striking reforms. Gregory was one of those retiring and conscientious persons who, when circumstances put them in positions of authority, prove exceedingly active. To get at the heart of this remarkable man, we should think of him as a modern.

First, Gregory possessed one of the virtues especially appreciated in our generation, the talent for administration. He perfected the organization of the Church by gradually bringing all parts of Christian Europe into direct connection with the Roman See and making them feel that their interests were bound up with those of Rome. He had his coadjutors in all the countries of Europe. He was in constant communication with them, and ever ready to correct any practice that interfered with the harmonious working of the Church as a whole. He not infrequently begins a letter to some distant minister of the Church, "It has come to our notice . . ." (*pervenit ad nos*). And whatever had once come to his notice, it is safe to say, rarely came twice. Gregory's zeal for the conversion of England sprang not so much from a romantic admiration of fair-haired angels, as from his ambition to make all roads lead to Rome. He likewise laid plans for bringing the Eastern Church into the fold; but in this attempt he did not succeed.

Gregory's interest in organization was not confined to ecclesiastical polity. He reformed the liturgy. He prescribed the proper garments for the ministers of the

Church, and the very tonsure — a matter on which the British Church submitted only after a debate in which the date of the celebration of Easter was also involved, and which lasted over a full century. Gregory also systematized the use of hymns in the service, made a new collection of hymns, an *Antiphonarium*, and whatever he actually did with the music left his name permanently identified with that chant to which the words of the liturgy were set.

Then Gregory was greatly interested in education — but not in the old-fashioned programme. I am constantly reminded, as I turn the pages of St. Gregory's works, of a very great man of modern times, not inaptly called the first citizen of our country, *de Universitate Harvardiana bene meritus*, the late President Eliot. These two men, eminent in zeal, power, and wisdom, have not often, to my knowledge, been compared, and the suggestion of comparing them may seem startling, for at some points their natures were separated by impassable gulfs. At least in their attitude toward education — their attitude, though not of course their actual plans — they are strikingly akin.

An oft-quoted utterance of St. Gregory's is found in a sharp letter to Bishop Desiderius of Vienne.[20]

It has come to our notice (*pervenit ad nos*) [the Pope remarks], that you, my dear Brother, have been holding conferences on ancient literature. . . . This information we received with reluctance and vehemently rejected. . . . For the same lips cannot sound the praises of Jupiter and the praises of

Christ. How serious an impropriety it is for a bishop to sing what is ill-suited even for a religious layman, do yourself reflect. . . . Wherefore if the report that has come to us later prove manifestly false and if it be certain that you do not devote yourself to frivolities and secular letters, we shall render thanks to our God.

Gregory has had his apologists in this matter, even Comparetti.[21] We must recognize that he admits elsewhere that the liberal arts have their place, though only as an instrument for the exact understanding of the Holy Word.[22] We may also agree that it might be unseemly to-day for a Bishop, or even a College President, to give readings, let us say, from Bernard Shaw, or Restoration drama, although these forms of literature are well enough in their places. But there is an apparent animus in Gregory's language. President Eliot had room for various of the ancients on his five-foot shelf, and his attitude toward the teaching of the Classics at Harvard as one of the approaches to culture was generous and fair. Yet in his momentous essay written in 1884 and entitled "What is a Liberal Education?" in which he laid the foundations for the course of study pursued, in the main, by our colleges to-day, he could declare that "Greek literature compares with English as Homer with Shakespeare, that is, as infantile with adult civilization"; and later, in 1909, in a no less momentous address on "The New Definition of the Cultivated Man," he could ask, "Are not the Greek tragedies means of culture? Yet they are full of incest, murder and human sacrifices to lustful and revengeful gods." [23]

This is not exactly an encomium of the study of Greek literature. It is fair, I think, to say that these two masters of education, the ancient and ecclesiastic, the modern and anti-ecclesiastic, both manifest a vigorous desire to have done with the follies of the past, and to build on what is sound, and useful, and contemporary.

Gregory's literary style is formed on the simplest models. Here is a man educated in the old training, who deliberately threw it away. It often happens, to-day, that advocates of a new education in which the Classics have no part owe their own culture to the system that they would have us abandon. I personally should favor the establishment of a school absolutely without Classical influence, and allow it to compete under the same external conditions with one in which the old-fashioned programme was cultivated — to see what would result. Only it would not be fair to allow anybody who had been brought up on the ancients to operate, or to plan, such a school.

Now Gregory, in speaking of his style, not only does not apologize for his rusticity; he glories in it and blasphemes the sacred name of Donatus the grammarian.[44]

Wherefore [he declares] I have scorned to observe all art of style, in which pupils are drilled in schools of the outer [*i. e.*, lower] training. For, as the tenor of the present letter makes evident, I shun not the collision of *m*'s; I avoid not the disorder of barbarisms; I despise a conformity to constructions and moods and cases of prepositions. For I deem it exceedingly inept to fetter the words of the Heavenly Oracle to the rules of Donatus.

Here there is a difference between the two great men that I am comparing; for there is no bad grammar, and no bad rhetoric, in the Attic style of President Eliot. Still, I may add that, despite Gregory's theory, I have observed in his works few, if any, violations of grammar. He may have tried to deviate into Christian illiteracy now and then; but such was the force of the ancient training and his own clear powers of thought that he did not often stray. Indeed, in the very letter from which I have drawn his shocking aspersions of grammar there is nothing to offend the purist. It is couched in a clear, trim style which President Eliot might commend and which permits at least one rhetorical embellishment — a decent use of metrical *clausulae*.

St. Gregory had a modern programme in education. Just as President Eliot, in a stirring utterance of not many years ago,[25] would appeal to sentiments of loyalty and faith, to the religious nature of the young, through literature of immediately contemporary material, so Gregory sought to touch the imaginations of Christian learners in a work that breathes no suggestion of the past.

This is the *Dialogi* ("Dialogues"), a misleading title. There is only a framework of dialogue, carried on between Gregory and a certain Deacon Peter, but this is only a decoy to the reader, like the setting of various works of the later Empire. It is another of Gregory's concessions to the pomps and vanities of a wicked rhetoric. What these dialogues really contain is shown by the sub-title, *De Vita et miraculis patrum Italicorum et de aeternitate animarum libri quatuor* ("On the Life and Miracles of the Italian Fathers and the Immortality of the Soul"), in four volumes. It is a golden legend of the lives of saints and its outlook is on the life to come. For here is the point where we may sharply distinguish St. Gregory, not only from President Eliot but from those apostles of progress, St. Ambrose and Prudentius. Their ultimate thoughts, too, are of course directed toward the world to come, but the present world, the world of the Roman Empire, is for the moment very dear. One feels in St. Gregory that our existence has just two stages, the immediate human present and eternity. Inattentive to the past, he builds not for human progress on this earth, but for the life everlasting.

The main motive of Gregory's *Dialogues*, then, is to draw Christian readers from the fascinating stories of Paganism to those of the new faith, with its present miracles and its promise of the hereafter. Granted this purpose on Gregory's part and the increasing development of popular superstition, there was every inducement for him, perhaps by a kind of self-deception, which I would not call dishonesty, somewhat to magnify existing accounts. And his work, in turn, which had an exceedingly wide vogue, led to fresh excesses of the marvellous and the weird. In this point, too, I need not add, the analogy between Pope Gregory and President Eliot breaks down.

The second book of the *Dialogues* is devoted to just one life — that of St. Benedict. It doubtless had much to do with strengthening the position of the Benedictine order. It is evidently the earlier type of monasticism that wins the approval of Gregory, not its later stage as modified, in a way that we shall examine later, by Cassiodorus.

The last book of the work is important, not only for its effect on the attitude of Christian believers but for its influence on literary forms. It is full of accounts of visions, which illustrate the final topic mentioned in the sub-title, "the immortality of souls." Such visions were not unknown to Plato and Cicero, but, I need not say, Plato and Cicero are not among the sources of Gregory. He is concerned with such visions of the other world as appeared to Christians of all classes and kinds, men, women, and children, especially those glimpses of the other world that appeared to those about to die. He compasses his argument about with a cloud of witnesses. He depends on material of diverse kinds; not all that he tells had he heard with his own ears. Some of his sources are literary. Thus there is a vision of a soldier stricken with the plague, who, at the point of death, saw a bridge that led over the dark and dingy stream of Hell, to a flowery meadow where white-robed saints were walking. On the bridge bad spirits and good fought over the soul that tried to pass. One is instantly reminded of some of the imagery in Dante's *Inferno*, — especially the description of *Malebolge*, — and also of a similar bridge of souls that appears in Mazdean accounts of the other world. At any rate, Gregory's *Dialogues* is a book that anybody must know who would follow with care the dream-literature of the Middle Ages, of which there were many specimens before Dante. It is the work of a Founder.

Gregory's plan of education included instruction in Christian morals as well as in the correct views about the life to come. This is the purpose of his work entitled *Moralia in Iob*. The title indicates the twofold nature of the book. It is first of all an allegorical commentary on *Job*: Job typifies Christ, Job's wife the temptations of the flesh, — an explanation lacking all gallantry, — and Job's counsellors the heresiarchs. The allegory, however curious, is pointed at the right way of living here and now. This is a modern book. So is the eminently practical "Rules for the Pastor's Office," which guided good shepherds of their flocks for centuries to come.

As we glance over the early Christian centuries, then, we may well ask in the name of progress and modernity, what had the Church to do with an outworn culture? Conscious of a new revelation and of modern needs, what should it do but leave the dead past to its dead and press on? Certain leaders of education to-day, in this modern and progressive age, should hardly find fault with the Church for what is substantially their own attitude. It is at least inconsistent for us to throw Classical Culture overboard, and in the same breath to pronounce the programme of the early Church narrow, obscurantist, and hostile to *belles lettres*. We should rather commend it as a programme of modern reform.

And yet, was this the solution at which the Church arrived? As Prudentius has implied, Christianity was the heir of a not inglorious past which somehow had a meaning for the present. Listen to these voices of antiquity:

Prosperity planted with God man finds the more abiding.

The mouth of God knows not how to speak falsely but fulfilleth every word.

Thy power, O Lord, no man subdueth with transgression nor does all-aging sleep possess it ever, nor the untiring months, but thou art ruler in unaging time.

For God, if indeed he is truly God, is in need of naught.

For whatever mortal is by nature bad, him does heaven punish. How then is it just that you who write laws for mortals yourselves incur a charge of lawlessness?

One righteous man conquers the thousand unrighteous, for he has God and justice on his side.

He prayed God simply to give him the good, since God knows best what kind of things is good.

He maketh all, all that grows from the earth and all living things . . . the earth and the heaven and all that is in them and in the world beneath, he maketh all.

It is God through whose counsel provision is made for this world.

It is he from whom all things are born, by whose breath we live.

To obey God is freedom.

A sacred spirit abides within us, observer of our good and evil deeds.

God comes to men, nay, what is closer, comes into men; no mind is good without God.

For we, too, are his offspring.

These are not quotations from a newly revised version of the Old Testament or the New. They do not come from some book of the Apocrypha seldom heard in Protestant pulpits. They are the sayings of Pagan poets and philosophers, — Pindar and Aeschylus, Sophocles and Euripides, Xenophon, Plato, and Seneca, — and are a mere sample of the moral and religious sentiment found in the ancient authors of Greece and Rome that harmonizes with the Christian faith.[26] In some cases, not all, I have used the word "God" instead of "gods" in translating. For when we are aware that monotheism was as familiar to cultivated minds in Greece and Rome as in Judea, and that the vision of a single and supreme deity was not necessarily eclipsed in antiquity by the retinue of subordinate gods any more than in the Middle Ages by the host of angels and saints, we may be allowed a momentary substitution of singular for plural to make our point the clearer.

Could Christian minds throw all this away? An unescapable problem confronted the Church. I shall next try to show how it was solved.

CHAPTER II

THE CHURCH AND PAGAN CULTURE

THE SOLUTION

OUR first lecture closed with certain quotations from the ancient poets and philosophers, which, if you did not know their source, might easily be attributed to some Christian writer. St. Clement of Alexandria, St. Athanasius, St. Augustine might have said the same things and preserved their orthodoxy without spot or blemish.

The last of those quotations was: "For we, too, are his offspring." You recognize those words, or my older readers recognize them, as a bit from the New Testament as well as from some ancient work. St. Paul in his sermon to the Athenians on Mars Hill,[1] a model of an address intended to attract and convert a hostile audience, did not begin by telling his hearers that they were a pack of idiots, but assured them that the new doctrine which he brought had been proclaimed, in part, by writers whom they would accept as authorities. As certain also of your own poets have said, "For we are also his offspring," — τοῦ γὰρ καὶ γένος ἐσμέν. Luckily this half of an hexameter is found in two works extant to-day. One is a poem on astronomy written in the third century B.C. by Aratus; the other is the noble hymn of the Stoic philosopher Cleanthes.[2] In quoting them thus, St. Paul laid the foundation of Christian humanism.

St. Paul may have been a Pharisee. Dr. Paul Elmer More calls his theology Rabbinical.[3] Perhaps it is; I am no judge. But I rather think that Dr. More is a bit hard on St. Paul — not so much, however, in his second volume as in his first; the influence of the Apostle is insidious. We should reckon not only with St. Paul's Rabbinical training, but with his reading of the Greek authors. His ability to make such appropriate citation from two of the less conspicuous poets like Aratus and Cleanthes indicates that he had roamed rather widely in the field of Greek literature. In fact, we find in the letters of St. Paul verses from Menander and Epimenides the Cretan, and possibly a bit of Aristotle.[4] Such reading effects a man's outlook on life. In St. Paul's temperament and his methods of winning his audiences, I see something Greek. I wonder, when we consider his voyages and his mind, that nobody has given him the title of a Christian Odysseus, πολύτροπος, a man of subtle twists and turns, all things to all men, with of course a difference. St. Paul became all things to all men in the hope that he might save some. Odysseus became all things to all men in the hope that he might save Odysseus. But St. Paul is just as agile, just as infallibly alive to the requirements of the moment. When he talks to the Athenians he is Greek. He is just as fittingly Jewish in his defence before King Agrippa, whom he knew to be "expert in all customs and questions which are among the Jews." [5] I doubt not that, if St. Paul were alive to-day and preached to a Boston audience, he would, in the fashion of our most liberal divines, choose a text from the Swami Vivikanda or Rabindranath Tagore, prefacing the quotation with the words "as certain also of your own prophets have said."

The Mass of St. Paul sung at Mantua as late as the fifteenth century included a hymn that expressed the Apostle's grief at not having lived in Virgil's time.

> Ad Maronis mausoleum
> Ductus fudit super eum
> Piae rorem lacrimae.
> Quam te inquit, reddidissem
> Si te vivum invenissem
> Poetarum maxime.

John Addington Symonds thus rendered these lines.

> When to Maro's tomb they brought him,
> Tender grief and pity wrought him
> To bedew the stone with tears.
> What a saint I might have crowned thee,
> Had I only living found thee,
> Poet first and without peers! [6]

It is a pity that these verses were expunged from the Mantuan liturgy in a more scientific age. For though they are, doubtless, grossly unhistorical, they are true to the spirit of St. Paul. [7]

Now, although St. Paul quoted the Stoic Cleanthes, Christianity is not Stoicism — even though two Scandinavians have recently pronounced St. Paul's famous chapter on faith, hope, and charity a Christian Stoic diatribe.[8] Of all the ancient philosophies, Christianity is most nearly allied to Platonism, though it is not that. The leaders of the Church, at any rate, could not help recognizing that many doctrines had been proclaimed by wise men of old, such as the Fatherhood of God and the Brotherhood of man, that compared admirably with their own traditions. The matter is best summed up by St. Augustine, who had lived through all the schools and spoke of what he knew.

There came into my hands [he says] [9] certain of the books of the Platonists and I read there, with other words but the like meaning, "In the beginning was the Word and the Word was with God, and the Word was God. The same was in the beginning with God. All things were made by him, and without him was not anything made that was made. In him was life and the life was the light of men."

St. Augustine thus goes through the prologue to the Gospel of St. John for the parts that he finds Platonic, and then adds, "But that this word was made flesh and dwelt among us, that read I not there." In the same way, he sifts Platonic teaching from the words of St. Paul. The upshot is that it is the doctrine of the Incarnation that according to St. Augustine, as to Dr. More, is at the heart of the Christian faith.

Here then is the problem that confronted the Church. With its new revelation, it must break off from the past, but how could it break from a past that agreed at so many points with its own revelation? The wider the

Church spread, the more intimate its contacts became with the more cultivated portions of society — the better classes. A new form of defence or apologetics was required, less attack and more negotiation, a reasoned endeavor to convince the cultured that the new faith contained something worth their attention.

The course of Christian apologetics is long and intricate. I am here concerned merely with that aspect of it which presents a programme of reconciliation, an attempt to solve the problem of what to do with Pagan culture in the light of the new faith. Further, as I stated in the first lecture, I can say nothing about the Greeks, though their evidence is, of course, of the utmost concern. I will leave you to read of Justin, Athenagoras, Clement of Alexandria, Origen, and the rest, in Dr. Allen's *Continuity of Christian Thought*, in Dr. T. R. Glover's *Conflict of Religions in the Early Roman Empire*, and above all in More's *Christ the Word*.

I wish I could devote all the time at my disposal to the most interesting of the Latin apologetes, Tertullian, a priest of Carthage, vehement, irate, witty, tender, hater of shams and of culture, cultured himself, learned in letters and the law, scorner of rhetoric and master of its devices, original in thought and style, champion of the Catholic faith and self-constituted prosecuting attorney against all heretics, devotee of a sect so strict and so peculiar that it landed him in heresy. He has been likened in temperament to Carlyle. His paradoxes suggest those of Mr. Chesterton, save that the latter are as thin as watered beer — I use a simile that Chesterton might approve — in comparison with the flaming impossibilities of his ancient prototype.

I am going to interpolate a bit from Tertullian, which apparently has nothing to do with our topic — I will apologize for it in a moment. It is an extract from a work in which Tertullian takes up a subject that mere man should never discuss — *De Cultu Feminarum*, "How Women Should Dress." [10] It reads like a sermon intended for publication. After some very plain words to poor woman, who is called the devil's gateway and the forfeitress of the tree of life, he remarks that, after the expulsion from Eden, her first concern was to invent some covering more stylish than the skins of beasts. He inveighs against the fashionable colors for robes, particularly a shimmering "air-shade" which was evidently the rage in Carthage.

If God could have made these tints [he remarks] and did not, obviously he did not wish to make them. And what God did not wish, surely ought not to be invented. Therefore those things are not good by nature which are not from God, the author of the book of nature. Thus we may be sure that they are of the devil, the interpolator of that book.

And it was not only their dresses that the gay women of Carthage colored.

I see some of you [he thunders], who change the color of your hair to saffron. They are ashamed of their own nationality; they 're sorry they were not born in Germany. That 's why they dye their hair. Aye, they've clapped a bad omen on their fiery locks. They think that's pretty which pollutes. I tell you, those medical concoctions ruin the hair; the constant application of any undiluted lotion ensures softening of the brain in your old age. Even the welcome heat of the sun is injurious to hair thus dried and enlivened. — Will a Christian woman dose saffron on her head as if she were a victim led to the altar? — God said, "How can you make white hair black or black hair white?" Just see how they refute the Lord. "Very good," they retort, "we make it saffron, not white or black, as an easier means of grace." Although they do try to turn white to black as well, when they feel old age approaching. Stupid! The more you try to conceal your years, the more you display them. And that's the real meaning of "eternity," is it? — the perpetual youth of your hair? That 's the "incorruptibility" ye shall put on in the new mansions of the Lord — guaranteed by oil of acacia. A fine "preparation" to make for hastening to meet the Lord and leave this wicked world!

I think I can picture a popular preacher thundering to the fair members of a *fin de siècle* society — *fines saeculorum* he calls it — who love to be scolded in an outrageous vocabulary and to thrill with that emotion which lies halfway between penitence and amusement. And you may be sure that the women of Carthage were decked in their finest when they went to hear Father Tertullian declaim *de cultu feminarum*.

Thus much from Tertullian, merely to show why I do not feel particularly alarmed when he calls a professor of Greek and Latin literature an idolater in disguise.[11] Tertullian is a character. He can say anything. He can even say that the ancient studies have their place, after all. A professor of Greek and Latin, therefore, according to Tertullian, is a necessary evil; that is more courteous than what most people consider him to-day — an unnecessary evil.

Tertullian, however, is not of the party of reconciliation. He is one of the permanently irreconcilables, and we need consider him no longer. I must also pass by Tertullian's admirer and daily reader, the placid St. Cyprian, reverenced in his day and after by writers of the most divergent type, but not, I must confess, particularly stimulating to a modern reader, unless he has a certain ecclesiastical axe to grind. Arnobius and Firmicus Maternus cannot detain us, both of them Pagan men of letters before their conversion, learned, misinformed, virulent, and to us tolerant moderns, somewhat repulsive.

Far more important than these writers is Minucius Felix, who at the end of the second or the beginning of the third century, probably following Tertullian, wrote a little work as unlike to Tertullian in spirit as anything could be.

Minucius Felix was a cultured Roman, whose life had been spent in Gentile circles before he adopted the Christian faith. By profession he was a consulting lawyer, *iuris consultus*. "Aha," says the Hellenist, "another of those legalistic theologians." We shall see. Lawyers are not always legalistic, as anybody knows who remembers the banquets of ΦBK at Harvard in the days of Carter and Choate. Tertullian was trained in the law, but there were oases in the legalistic stretches of his mind, as I think I have shown. Minucius Felix was a lawyer, yet his acquaintance with ancient letters and ancient thought was profound. He quotes the poets and the philosophers with the easy air of an essayist of the eighteenth century.

Minucius writes a dialogue called *Octavius*, from the name of the chief character in it. The conversation takes place between Octavius, who is a Christian, Caecilius, a Pagan, and an indulgent arbiter, Minucius himself. The general plan of the work is modelled on Cicero's dialogue on the nature of the gods, and a good bit of the argument comes from it. Just as there Epicureanism is refuted from a Stoic and Platonic point of view, it is here the Christian point of view that triumphs over — what? We should expect, for really successful apologetics, Stoicism and Platonism. But it is once more Epicureanism that is laid low. In a way, that is disappointing, until we see that the author's purpose is not so much to refute, as to identify Christianity with the best in preceding thought. "As certain also of your poets have said." Minucius has taken his cue from St. Paul. He deals with general and commonly accepted ideas. The subtleties of dogma are left untouched. Let not that be proof that the Church had no dogma at the time. The name of Christ is not so much as mentioned, and there is no allusion to the Old Testament or the

New. But Minucius must have known something about the Scriptures of the Church and its Founder, else he would not have taken the trouble to come to its defence. He is holding something up his sleeve. The skill of the little work dawns on us when we think of what the author has not said. I will give you a brief synopsis of its contents. It is worth our while to give more than a passing notice to the first monument — or at least one of the first monuments — of Christian Latin literature.[12]

Octavius and his friends are walking along the beach at Ostia and watching the boys skipping stones on the water. Caecilius, a Pagan, kisses the hand of a statue of Serapis that they pass. When Octavius rebukes what he calls the superstition of his friend, the latter makes his defence. Man, he argues, is an intellectual weakling, unfitted to reason about the causes of things. His best and simplest course is to resign himself to an Epicurean theory of chance, which is all that experience tells us, and let things have their way. But this spiritual *laissez-faire* does not preclude piety. It is also an easy and a comfortable course to maintain the cults that the holy men of old devised. This combination of a cheerful scepticism and a cheerful traditionalism meets us not infrequently in history. There is something of it in Abelard, in Bayle, and in Mr. Balfour's defence of philosophical doubt. It is a kind of Epicureanism that would have made Lucretius turn in his grave — but then, Lucretius was not an Orthodox Epicurean. Nor is Caecilius, as we shall see.

After rehearsing various miraculous occurrences which testify to the power and the benevolence of the gods, Caecilius turns his defence into an attack — which is always good tactics in argument no less than war — and levies a number of charges, all unfounded but evidently widespread, against the morality of the new sect. These Christians, he asserts, hold infamous love-feasts, or ἀγαπαί, in which they indulge in the grossest superstitions and debaucheries, including the worship of an ass's head. They bow before an awful and a solitary god, *unicus, solitarius, destitutus,* whose attribute of omnipresence, which incidentally involves a logical contradiction of terms, makes him, despite his solitude, the universal bore. He runs about everywhere and is everywhere present — *molestus, inquietus,* and *impudenter curiosus.* This pleasant deity, who attains something of the proportions of a comic character in Caecilius's description, will one day destroy his world by fire. On the basis of such old wives' fables believers promise themselves an immortality after the death of the body. It is a natural conclusion for those who in this life get nothing but poverty and persecution, and feed on a bare and Puritanic religion ungraced by pleasant rites or reminiscence of the past. Aye, they even refuse to put flowers on the graves of their dead. They are wretched folk, indeed, for neither shall they rise again in a new life nor do they live in this one. If they will philosophize, let them obey the precept of Socrates, who admonished us to remember that "That which transcends us is none of our affair."

Caecilius concludes his argument with a broad smile of satisfaction that reminds us of Thrasymachus in Plato's *Republic*. One can foretell that, here as there, pride goeth before a fall. In the latter part of his discourse, it has become more and more evident that the Epicureanism with which he started out is well seasoned with the scepticism of the New Academy — the authorities to whom he appeals in closing are all leaders of that school.

Octavius replies with a gentlemanly courtesy. The gist of his answer, of which I will not repeat all the details, is this. He insists first of all, as Lucretius would insist, on the ability of the human mind to arrive at some sort of truth. We may not, indeed, find out God by logical searching. His existence is manifest, however, in the operations of nature and in the minds of men. His nature must be one and supreme, else he would not deserve the name of God. What theologians to-day call the argument from design and the argument from history, the actual acceptance of a deity in some form by all nations by and large, form the basis of Octavius's proof; it is drawn in the main from Cicero. In appealing to the testimony of all mankind, he does not fail to cite the best and most intelligent representatives of the race, the poets and the philosophers. "I hear the poets, too," he exclaims, "asserting that there is 'one father of gods and men,' and that such is the mind of mortals as the light of the day that the all-parent spreads o'er the earth! And what of Mantuan Maro? [13] Are not his words yet more plain, more apt for our purpose and more true? 'In the beginning,' saith he,

> 'The heavens and the earth and all the frame
> Of this broad universe are fed within
> By spirit and the infusing mind that stirs
> The sluggish mass. Thence comes the race of man
> And every kind of beast.'

And in another place he calls that mind and spirit God. These are his words:

> 'God goeth everywhere throughout the lands,
> The stretching ocean and the skies profound,
> Whence men are sprung and beasts and rain and fires.'" [14]

The other poets cited, besides Virgil, are Ennius and Homer. Octavius then summons the philosophers, a noble army of them, from Thales through the Stoics, but not chronologically arranged, for he gives the final place of eminence to Plato, as he should, and above all to the theology of Plato's *Timaeus* which, thanks also to Cicero's reinterpretation of it, became the essence of Plato's teaching for the later Empire and the Middle Ages.

One philosopher, we perhaps are surprised to see, is not cited. It is Cicero, who has furnished Minucius Felix with much of his method, many of his facts, and a model for his style. This part of the discussion ends with a neat variation of Plato's saying about kings and philosophers. "I have set forth the opinions," the speaker says, "of well-nigh all the philosophers of more conspicuous renown, who denote the one God with diverse names. One might well conclude that either Christians to-day are philosophers, or the philosophers of old were Christians."

I will not further analyze the arguments of this worthy follower of St. Paul. He soon turns to a refutation of the charges of immorality and superstition that Caecilius had raised against the Christians. I think we may take the answers for granted. The treatise ends with a beautiful expression of the immanence of God that makes unnecessary the erection of shrines, and of that brotherly love that animates the Christian community. After the peroration, the friends look at each other for some time spellbound. Then Caecilius graciously declares that both are victors, Octavius over him, and he over his own error.

The *Octavius* is the work of a humanist and a dramatist. Minucius has that necessary dramatic sympathy with an antagonist's point of view without which a literary debate cannot long attract us. He even goes the lengths of permitting his antagonist to paint a picture of Christian theology which, if it stood alone, would come dangerously near blasphemy. The interest of the modern reader does not suffer thereby.

The apology of Minucius has been variously and curiously estimated.[15] Some have regarded him as a recent convert, a catechumen imperfectly instructed in the faith. Some have even thought of him as a second-century Strauss or Renan, who had penetrated to the ethical heart of Christianity and let its metaphysics go. I would rather consider him as a master of persuasion who refrained from telling the whole story all at once. He gives enough to make his Pagan reader exclaim, "Well, if this is Christianity, I might inquire into it farther." This is apologetics on a high plane. The little work is, once more, one of the earliest specimens of Christian Latin literature and one of its best — delightful, sincere, and urbane. Think back to the times when it was written, and its originality, not to say audacity, will impress you. The chief compliment that it pays to Paganism is its Ciceronian character — style, literary form and argument, as was obvious to cultivated readers in those days. The reason why Cicero is not mentioned is that there was no need to mention him. Minucius is not assuming the attitude of the ostrich in an attempt to evade the penalty for plagiarism. He is employing a delicate literary device and paying a delicate literary compliment. An exact parallel is Hume's *Dialogue Concerning Natural Religion*, a treatise written by a rather eminent thinker at a period when Cicero was still considered a philosopher. This work, too, is based in an obvious way on Cicero's *De Natura Deorum*, and yet, as in the dialogue of Minucius, the fact is not so much as mentioned. In both cases the writer hoped, and knew, that an educated reader would see the point.

We now come down the decades to Lactantius, who, whatever the charm of Minucius Felix, is by all odds the most important of the apologetes.[16] Lactantius flourished in the first quarter of the fourth century. He was at first, like so many of his predecessors, a Pagan. Diocletian called him from Africa to a professor's chair at Nicomedia in Bithynia. Later he was the tutor of Crispus, the son of the Emperor Constantine. His aim, like that of Minucius Felix, is to interpret Christianity to the cultured classes; he seasons his apologetics with philosophy and tops it with a Ciceronian style. He is an intense Roman. He seeks to prove that Christianity is not subversive of that temporal order which was symbolized forever, so then it seemed, by the Roman Empire. Lactantius is not a striking personality — mediocre in the Latin sense of the word, and a bit also in the French sense, remarks a Frenchman.[17] But perhaps for this reason he is a more trustworthy index of his times. Without the depth of St. Augustine or the versatility of St. Jerome, he may better illustrate the general mind of the Church in its attempt to solve the problem of Pagan culture.

Lactantius's work, the *Divine Institutes*, is more than an apology; it is the first synthetic treatise on theology by a Western writer.[18] There is no single work, to repeat, from which we can gain a truer notion of the attitude of

the Church to Pagan culture. Its date is somewhere between 311 and 324, virtually contemporaneous, that is,
with the accession of Constantine and the Council of
Nicea, and, like these events, a landmark. It is a tract
for the times, and the first-fruits of established Christianity. It is appropriately addressed to the Emperor
Constantine.

I begin my work [the author declares] [19] under the auspices
of thy name, O Constantine, Emperor Supreme, who, first of
Roman rulers to renounce error, hast known and honored the
majesty of the one true God. For when that happiest of days
shone on the earth in which Almighty God raised thee to the
blessed height of empire, thou didst give a splendid omen that
thy government would be wholesome and desirable for all thy
subjects, by restoring routed and banished Justice and thus
expiating the fearful crime of other men. For which deed God
shall give thee happiness, virtue and length of days, that loyal
to this same Justice which guided thee in thy youth, thou
mayst in old age hold fast the tiller of the state, and receiving
the great charge from thy sire, transmit to thy children the
custody of the Roman name.

We seem to be back in the golden age of Augustus,
and to hear Horace or Virgil proclaim the return of that
earlier age of gold, whence Astraea, Maiden of Justice,
had been routed and banished by the sins of men. Nor
were Horace and Virgil more devout than Lactantius in
their adoration of the Roman name.

In choosing his title, Lactantius is thinking of the
great law books called "Institutes."

If certain wise men of the law [he remarks] [20] arbiters of
equity, have composed and edited "Institutes of the Civil

Law," in which they set at rest the disputes and contentions of litigious citizens, how much higher a task it is to write on divine institutes, in which we treat not of leaks and repairs of waterworks or of defence of titles, but of hope, of life, of salvation, of immortality, of God, that we may set at rest death-dealing superstitions and loathsome errors?

Some centuries before, this endeavor to set at rest death-dealing superstitions and loathsome errors had been the high purpose of Lucretius, who presented with like zeal a very different remedy. Students of Lucretius are well aware that Lactantius was a deep reader of the Pagan poet; indeed, he read some portions of his text inaccessible to us to-day. It is not so generally recognized that something more than an aversion to the traditional mythology bound these brother-spirits together. Despite his flaming radicalism, Lucretius did not, like many radicals, replace order by chaos. He had his own order. The old order changeth, but here was he with the new, with the vision of a universe as definite as that of St. Thomas himself, one in which no cranny of mystery remains — except that fourth unnamed part of the soul. Lucretius proceeds about his business with the orderliness of a systematic theologian and with the same relish of dogma. He reasons about the parts of the soul exactly as a theologian does about the Persons of the Holy Trinity. Warde Fowler, in one of his delightful books, knows whereof he speaks in calling Lucretius an ecclesiastic.[21] I need hardly add that this is not the chief reason why Lucretius is read to-day.

Lactantius comes to his subject with a splendid equipment. He is exceedingly well-read in the old poets and philosophers. Not only Lucretius, Horace, Ovid, Lucan, Persius, Juvenal and, of course, Virgil are at his fingers' ends, but he is intimate with less-known authors, — less known to us, — like Ennius and Lucilius; indeed, we have to thank Lactantius for preserving various fragments of the older writers that else had perished with the most of their works. He even finds it appropriate to use the gayer spirits, Plautus and Terence, for pointing an occasional moral. With the Greeks he shows less familiarity, with one notable exception. Homer and Hesiod are sparingly quoted, but the Greek source to which Lactantius turns again and again is the collection of so-called Sibylline oracles. It is highly probable that the Sibyl owes much to Lactantius for the importance that the Middle Ages gave her in theology, in drama, and in art.

There is one Pagan whom I have not yet mentioned who exerts the most profound influence on Lactantius's style and on his whole way of thinking. I mean Cicero. Lactantius adores him. He pays him a compliment that few critics repeat today — he calls him original. Cicero argues for the existence of divine providence, Lactantius declares, on the basis of the Stoic proof, but *nova ipse afferens plurima*, "adding many points of his own."[22]

We hear a great deal of the interpenetration of Christian theology with Greek philosophy. I would not minimize the importance of that most interesting and fruitful movement in the history of Christian thought, which Dr. More has treated, I believe, better than anybody else. But not enough is said of the contribution of Cicero to this movement. For while Plato and Aristotle acted directly on the minds of various Fathers of the East, those of the West took partly from those Fathers, partly from the fountain-head itself, and partly also from that useful and readable essayist who had summed up many aspects of Greek thought for the Roman world. Dr. More well remarks that not the Neoplatonism of Plotinus, Porphyry, and Proclus, but the Christian philosophy of the great Alexandrians and Cappadocians is the real heir of the Academy.[23] True enough, but we should not pass over, especially when we are considering the Western Fathers, the philosophy of Cicero, to whom the problems of thought had been a vital concern from his earliest years, who through the whole course of his thinking had revered Plato as his supreme master, and who deserves, in the best sense of the term, the title of the first Neoplatonist.

Now Lactantius not only looks to Cicero for fitting words and flowing periods, but conceives his very function to be the same. When Cicero had finished his career as a statesman, not altogether voluntarily, he reverted to the dreams of his youth and undertook what he declares to be the patriotic mission of interpreting philosophy to the public. This is precisely the key-note that Lactantius strikes at the opening of his work. The following words might have been pronounced *ex cathedra* some golden morning at Tusculum. Or rather, this is the way that Cicero would have said it in the age of Constantine.[24]

> So then, I have composed a disputation on religion and things divine. For if certain great orators [Lactantius might have said, "a certain great orator"], veterans in their profession, after running the race of their active occupation, have devoted themselves to philosophy and deemed it a merited respite from their toils, if they have tortured their minds in the search of those things that cannot be attained, finding the hunt more of a distraction than a diversion [more *negotium* than *otium* in it] and much more burdensome than their previous pursuits, how much better a right have I to betake me to the safe harbor of that true and heavenly philosophy whose words are light to utter, sweet to hear, easy to understand, honorable to accept.

The chief criticism that Lactantius passes on Cicero is for his failure to enlighten the Roman public on the spiritual truths that he evidently possessed. He reproaches him for fearing the prison of Socrates. How delighted would he have been could he have called Cicero the first of the Roman martyrs!

One author divides his subject in an orderly fashion into seven books, of which I can give only a meagre outline. The first is entitled "On False Religion." He begins by laying down the principle that the human soul needs both philosophy and religion, *ut neque religio ulla sine sapientia suscipienda sit, nec ulla sine religione probanda sapientia.*[25] We see where Lactantius would stand

in the great battle of Darwin's time between religion
and science. He would be a mediator, one of the party
of Tennyson, and hope that knowledge might

> grow from more to more,
> But more of reverence in us dwell.

The trouble with ancient religion is, according to Lactantius, that it is permeated with false science. The
Pagan instinct to worship is sound, but it is cluttered up
with all manner of myth, which the man of science must
brush away. Lactantius therefore gives an account of
Pagan religion in learned fashion, stringing together a
telling array of the indecencies and absurdities of mythology, and then sets forth the *vera historia* which remains after science has stripped off the accretions. The
writing of "true histories" of men and movements is a
practice not unknown in our own time. We have seen
little books with such titles as "The True George Washington," "The True Abraham Lincoln," whose authors
are to be carefully distinguished from the eminent liars
who preceded them.

In this process of getting down to pure history and
undefiled, Lactantius is much aided by Euhemerus.
Euhemerus flourished in the times of Alexander, and
was the Robert Ingersoll of his day. He declared for a
theory championed by Herbert Spencer not many
decades ago, that the so-called gods were really men,
kings or mighty heroes of earth, who for their exploits
had been deified by subsequent generations. In other

words, Euhemerus reduced the gods to the rank of demigods, who had won their immortality. He set forth his theory in a romantic account of his travels, in which he pretended to have found, especially in the fabulous island of Panchaea, certain records, inscribed in temples, of the true careers of various gods. This romance, bearing the impious title of "Sacred Records," was translated into Latin by Father Ennius about the beginning of the third century B.C., and proved a serviceable handbook of rationalism for the *illuminati* of ancient Rome.

Perhaps you would like to hear the "true history" of Saturn, discovered by Euhemerus, translated by Ennius, and quoted by Lactantius.[26] This is how the onion is peeled.

Then Saturn took Ops to wife. Titan, his elder brother, wished to be king himself. Then their mother Vesta and their sisters Ceres and Ops induced Saturn not to yield the throne to Titan. Then Titan, who was not so handsome a man as Saturn, both on that account and because he saw that his mother and his sisters were bent on having Saturn reign, allowed him so to do. He therefore secured an agreement with Saturn, that if the latter had any male offspring thereafter, he should not rear them. This he did for the purpose that the kingdom might revert to his own sons. Then a first son was born to Saturn, and they killed him. Then later twins were born, Jupiter and Juno. Then they openly showed Juno to Saturn, and hid Jove and gave him to Vesta to bring up, concealing him from Saturn. Likewise Ops bare Neptune unbeknownst to Saturn, and carefully hid him away. In like manner, at a third birth, Ops bare twins, Pluto and Glauca. Pluto in Latin is Father Dis; some call him Orcus. Then they showed Glauca to Saturn, but his son Pluto they hid and concealed. Then Glauca died in girlhood. These are the generations of Jupiter and his brothers as recorded in sacred chronicle.

Lactantius quotes a good deal more of Euhemerus than this, but this will amply suffice for illustration. This "true history" sounds like the story of the early kings of Rome after passing through the sieve of modern criticism, or the life of our Lord as revised by the School of Tübingen or of Lake. And yet, amid the otherwise impeccable rationalism of this account, in which nothing offends the critical sense, kindles the false glow of imagination, or appeals to the human and unscientific heart, one faint touch of irrationality remains. We still may wonder at Saturn's courteous and immediate acceptance of the proposal that he should systematically murder his boys, with the obvious result of clearing the dynasty for his brother's line.

Without pausing for an analysis of Book II, which treats "The Origin of Error" and amounts to a psychological inquiry into the reasons for idolatry, we turn to the third book, which takes us to the heart of the matter. The title, "On False Wisdom," would be replaced today by something more complimentary, such as "A Brief History of Ancient Philosophy"; for that is what the book is about.

Lactantius's review of the philosophers is competent and fairly complete. It would stimulate interest, I am sure, if it were read in connection with a college course on ancient philosophy, particularly one dealing with Cicero and Lucretius. Whether or not one agrees with Lactantius, here are side-lights cast on the subject by an early critic who writes with sympathy in a decent style. Cicero, once more, occupies the highest pinnacle. Lactantius subjects him without hesitation to the inevitable canon, but passes from his cross-examination with a sense of relief. "How can *you* expect to hold to the path of truth," says he to Seneca, "when even Cicero goes astray?" Lactantius's devotion to the old Roman comes little short of that of Erasmus to Socrates, in whose honor the sage of Rotterdam wished to enlarge the litany with the plea, *Sancte Socrates, ora pro nobis*.[27]

One error refuted by Lactantius is of some concern to us who inhabit America. Indeed it concerns our very existence.

What about those people [he exclaims] [28] who think there are antipodes on the opposite side of the earth? Is anybody so silly as to believe that there are men whose heels are higher than their heads? Or that the things that lie about us here, there hang up-side down, that crops and trees grow downwards, that rain and snows and hail fall upwards to the earth? Does one wonder that the hanging gardens are mentioned among the seven wonders of the world, when philosophers can create hanging fields and cities and seas and mountains? This error too, must be tracked to its source. For people are always fooled in the same way.

Lactantius proceeds to belabor those who imagine that the earth is round. This is one of the passages from the Fathers that were levelled at Columbus when he proposed the rash experiment of sailing to lands demonstrably non-existent.[29] But we should not say too much about the hostility of the Church to science until we have reckoned with Lucretius in this matter. For Lucretius also was not convinced of the roundness of the earth.[30] He is inclined to the rival view that the earth is flat, that the sun, worn with his journey, goes to pieces, like the Deacon's one-horse shay, when day is done, and that his place is taken by a brand-new sun next morning. This theory holds large chances for poetry and exciting adventure. It also seemed to Lucretius more scientific. It is rather pathetic that the theory that excited his ridicule for its fancifulness should have become the accepted science. Possibly there is a fable for us in all this. Perhaps some theory fixed as axiomatically sure to-day, like gravitation before Einstein, may seem to a later generation unscientific — or even quaint. However this may be, Lactantius's views on the antipodes are determined as much by Lucretian science as by any dogma of the Christian faith.

In the fourth book, Lactantius passes from the object of his attack to that of his defence. The title is "On the True Wisdom and Religion." It would not be germane to our theme to go deeply into his exposition of Christian belief and practice. You will not find that he identifies Christianity with Stoicism; rather, like St. Augustine and Dr. More, he singles out the doctrine of Incarnation as the central truth of the new faith.[31] Pray note that this is the conclusion of one of these legalistic Latins, the very title of whose book is taken from the law.

The fifth book is in the main devoted to ethics. Its title is "On Justice," which at the outset of the treatment means personal morality rather than political justice. Here is where Lactantius answers the familiar charges against the gross immoralities of the Christians, the perverted accounts of their love-feasts and religious rites.

He next considers justice in its social relations, the principle that underlies any well-ordered community. First comes a description of the Golden Age, in which the accounts of the Pagan poets seem almost to be taken at their face value. For they sang of a time that suggests the Garden of Eden and that prophesies the real age of gold that dawned on the world at the birth of Christ. They also sang of man's fall and of the miseries that attended him in the ensuing age of Jove. Throughout, Lactantius treats the old poets with courtesy and is glad to record their harmony with Christian principles whenever it occurs. Horace's odes supply him with examples. The man who is *integer vitae scelerisque purus* is perfectly adaptable to the Christian code.[32] Of course, the Pagans are attacked when they deserve it. The schoolboy to-day who gets somewhat weary of the piety of the distinguished hero of Virgil's *Aeneid*, and who somewhat doubts whether the ancient piety had the modern meaning, will find his mood anticipated by Lactantius.[33]

If one expects from the title of Book VI, *De Vero Cultu*, an elaborately comparative treatment of Pagan and Christian ritual, such as would interest the student of religions, one will be disappointed. For Lactantius's thesis is that true ritual is not ceremony, but the worship of God in spirit and in truth. The most acceptable offering is a clean and contrite heart. The burden of this book, then, like that of the preceding, is ethical; I somehow miss that ceremonial formalism that we naturally expect from a legalistic Roman. Lactantius is rather concerned with the nature of that virtue which the Christian should cultivate as his best act of worship. This truth, he willingly admits, was proclaimed with eloquence and sincerity by the Pagans. He can even quote Lucretius as a witness to the belief in the fatherhood of God on which depends the brotherhood of man.[34]

The most valuable part of the book, in my opinion, is an onslaught on the Stoic conception of virtue.[35] It should make good reading for those who identify Stoicism and Christianity. Lactantius finds Stoic rigidity as unattractive as Pope does.

> In lazy apathy let Stoics boast
> Their virtue fix'd; 't is fix'd, as in a frost.

Those natural human affections, hope and fear and desire and mercy, which the Stoic would crush and transcend, the Christian retained and purged, not allowing, if I may quote an unpublished phrase of an eminent authority, not allowing the milk of human kindness to sour on the stomach.

The seventh and last book is another act of deference and another challenge, to Cicero. Its title is that of the *Tusculan Disputations*, — *De Vita Beata*, — and its subject is immortality. But whereas immortality, as Cicero conceives it, is only one aspect of the blessed life, to Lactantius it is the whole of it; it is another definition of the *summum bonum*.

As Lactantius scans with the eye of prophecy the fate of the generations to come, one dreadful portent cannot escape him — the fall of the Roman state. He describes it, in the hardest words he ever had to write.[36]

The whole world will be in tumult, wars shall rage everywhere, all nations shall be in arms and fight against each other. Neighboring cities shall go to war, and first of all, Egypt shall pay the penalty of its fond superstitions and be deluged with the river of blood. Then shall the sword traverse the world, mowing down all things in a harvest of destruction. And this shall be the cause of that wilderness of confusion, that the Roman name that now ruleth through all the earth, — my mind shudders to say it, but I will say it because it shall come to pass, — the Roman name shall be taken from the earth and the sovereignty revert to Asia, and the East again dominate and the West bow down. Nor should we wonder that a kingdom established on a mighty foundation, increased by the long labor of mighty men, fortified with mighty resources, should one day fall. For there is nothing built up by human strength that cannot be destroyed by human strength, since the works of mortals are mortal.

Such is the *Divine Institutes* of Lactantius, a work of penetrating criticism and sympathetic interpretation of the past. He has not answered all questions. In particular, he has not quite answered the Neoplatonists, leaving something for St. Augustine and Boethius to do. He is guilty of some misunderstandings of the faith into which he had come. But whatever his faults, Lactantius has written the typical book of his age, and solved the Christian problem. For from first to last the principle is written clear that, while Christian faith finds much in Pagan belief and Pagan morals to avoid, it may, or rather must, draw freely for its sustenance on the thought, the poetry, and the inspiration of the past. There is no better intellectual monument of the reign of Constantine than the *Divine Institutes* of Lactantius. Moreover, it became a standard work for the following generations. We find it in a splendid old codex written at the monastery of Bobbio in the sixth or the seventh century, and beginning with the revival of learning under Charlemagne, a steady stream of manuscripts flows down into the Renaissance. The *Divine Institutes* was the first book to be printed in Italy and, in the sixteenth century, there were thirty-six editions published of the works of Lactantius. In his own lifetime this book was found so useful that an Epitome of it was prepared, possibly by the author himself. Lactantius, for all his errors, is highly commended by St. Jerome, St. Augustine, Cassiodorus, and St. Isidore.[37] No better way could be paved to an immortal and authoritative existence in the Middle Ages. In the Renaissance, his fame shows perhaps even brighter. St. Jerome had paid him the compliment — than which nothing could have sounded sweeter to Lactantius — of calling him a veritable stream of Ciceronian eloquence.[38] Beginning with Petrarch, the humanists caught up this praise and echoed it with various refrains.[39]

Thus were the foundations of Christian humanism laid. One who would follow the subject more minutely will find in St. Jerome's seventieth letter a *locus classicus* on this matter, for there we read clearly that the best in ancient literature and ancient thought can and should be adjusted to the Christian faith. We see there a list of the eminent doctors of the Church, both Greek and Roman, who practised what St. Jerome calls a spoiling of the Egyptians without pollution from the spoils. This letter, and the work of Lactantius, were part of the reading of men of culture in Mediaeval times. Despite inevitable differences in the temperament of individuals, or their moods, or their purposes of the moment, this was the standard to which the Church was true. Just how it was applied by different Christian minds, we shall note in the lectures that remain.

For the moment, I will take as a type and symbol a bit of the Eucharistic liturgy of the Church preserved in one of its most ancient monuments, the *Missale Gothicum*.[40] In the *benedictio populi* in the mass for the eve of the Epiphany, Christ is besought to turn dull hearts to Him, even as at the wedding of Cana He converted plain water into — not just wine, but Falernian. Horace's best! Let this be a symbol of the history of Christian humanism. Though the stricter souls have denounced it and even threatened to break it, that jar of old Falernian has always reposed in the sanctuary of the Church.

It is felt by some that there is an unsurmountable barrier between the Pagan authors, with their delight in this temporal and human world, and those of the Middle Ages, who thought of nothing but the world unseen. But if other-worldliness of this sort is Mediaeval, nothing could be more Mediaeval than Cicero and Plato on occasion. If we found in the binding of some Mediaeval tome a strip of parchment bearing in Latin such sentiments as: "That which you humans call life is really death," or "Let us look for the essence of right living in the strength and nobility of the soul and in the utter contempt of all things human," who would not hunt up these passages in St. Bernard or St. Bonaventure? And yet these are the utterances of Marcus Tully,[41] in the spirit of his master Plato. If we called Plato and Cicero the first Christian humanists, we should not be altogether wrong. The paradox of Christian humanism was present in their natures, which were large enough to solve it.

It has also been maintained by some that the Christian programme is not really humanistic, since the ancient arts have in it a subordinate and merely relative value; they have become handmaids of the Church. "It is this menial position of the arts," an eminent scholar remarks,[42] "that betokens the fundamental difference between the Middle Ages and Humanism." But surely Cicero, the prince of humanists, did not set the arts among the absolutes. For him they led the way either to the active life of the statesman or to the contemplative life of the philosopher — ideals between which he wavered at various moments in his career. In precisely the same way, the liberal doctors of the Church cultivated the ancient studies, both for their own value and for their indispensable connection with the new philosophy that Christianity had brought in.

There is, of course, a difference between Christian teaching and dilettanteism, whether the latter appears in antiquity, or the Renaissance, or later. There is a certain danger in humanism as we see it displayed in the history of the Church. In one of his irresponsible moments, — perhaps then I should say in one of his typical moments, — Laurence Sterne prophesies thus the extinction of the soul: [43]

And next winter we shall find them less again; so that if we go on from little to less, and from less to nothing, I hesitate not one moment to affirm that in half a century, at this rate, we shall have no souls at all; which being the period beyond which I doubt likewise of the existence of the Christian faith, 't will be one advantage that both of them will be exactly worn out together. . . .

Blessed Jupiter! and blessed every other heathen god and goddess! for now ye will all come into play again, and with Priapus at your tails — what jovial times! — but where am I? and into what a delicious riot of things am I rushing? I — I who must be cut short in the midst of my days, and taste no more of 'em than what I borrow from my imagination — peace to thee, generous fool! and let me go on.

Poor Yorick has gone on, the Church abides, and the blessed gods may still be with us in their places. But what if they get the upper hand? They become uneasily important in the Renaissance. Zola, an unprejudiced witness, since he is neither Christian nor humanist, contrasts the pomp of the Papacy of the Renaissance and of modern times with the sweet simplicity of the Catacombs, and wonders whether Rome was ever Christian at all, whether the emperors of the Palatine did not merely transfer their residence to the Vatican.[44] But whatever the excesses of the past, they have induced no narrow reaction on the occupants of the Holy See in our own times. One of the characters in Zola's great novel, *Rome*, His Holiness Pope Leo XIII, whom most of the world would regard as Christian, made various utterances, which though not delivered *ex cathedra*, bear to the mind of a classical scholar most certain signs of infallibility. I believe that they would not be denied by the humanist who is Pope to-day. In a letter to Cardinal Parocchi in 1885,[45] Leo XIII considers the question of the Classics, praising the beauty of the ancient literatures, mentioning his eminent predecessors who were profound in Latin and Greek, and pronouncing an incidental animadversion on the Emperor Julian and his shrewd and iniquitous plan (*callidissimum et plenum sceleris consilium*) of preventing the teaching of the old authors in the Pagan schools. Nor does His Holiness fail to quote St. Paul, though not the passage about that wisdom of this world which is foolishness with God. The matter is summed up authoritatively in Ciceronian cadences that it is a pity to translate.[46]

Perceiving, then, the usefulness of the literatures of Greece and Rome, the Catholic Church, which always has fostered whatsoever things are honest, whatsoever things are lovely, whatsoever things are of good report, has always given to the study of the humanities the favor that it deserves, and in promoting it, has expended no slight portion of its best endeavor.

To which I hope we may add, *Roma locuta est, causa finita est.*

CHAPTER III

ST. AMBROSE THE MYSTIC

WHEN Dante and Beatrice in Paradise mount to the presence of the mystic Rose, only St. Bernard utters human words at such a height; only he pours forth a prayer to the Blessed Virgin. It would almost seem as if Beatrice herself, the incarnation of Theology, had lost her powers of speech, even though she has gone on to join those next the throne. Bernard is the true mystic, who communes with God, as he sets forth in his treatise "How to Love God" (*De Diligendo Deo*), not by ratiocination but by rising above reason and dwelling in the pure sphere of contemplation. I will attempt no further definition of mysticism, particularly since in its essence it scorns to be defined. It is allied to the frenzy of the poet, described by Plato in his *Ion*. It is the ecstasy of the Neoplatonist, who thus communicates with that supreme and unapproachable Being to whom the very ascription of being is belittling. Pantheism is often a part of this rapture, when the mystic, as Goethe has it, swells into divinity and delights to feel all the six days of creation in his own bosom —

alle sechs Tagewerk im Busen fühlen.

Mediaeval mysticism owes much to John the Scot's translation of the works attributed to Dionysius the

Areopagite, and to his own high flight into the super-
sensual realm; he flies dangerously near to heresy,
though, if he were asked "Art thou a Pantheist?" he
would answer with some definiteness, "No!" Besides
the Neoplatonism that came in through John the Scot,
the Middle Ages had also parts at least of the real
Plato, in Chalcidius's translation of the *Timaeus*, and
in Cicero here and there. I am not calling Plato a
mystic, but there has always been food for mystics in
his thought. Plato climbs the mountain of reason before
saying, "Thus far and no farther by this path"; the
mystic soars at once into the blue. The Middle Ages
also had St. Augustine, whose mysticism spurred Dante's imagination, as we shall see.[1] They had St. Paul,
for he, after all, had exclaimed *o altitudo* before Sir
Thomas Browne. He had seen a vision on the road to
Damascus and had known of a man in Christ, how that
he was caught up into Paradise and heard unspeakable
words.[2] And the Middle Ages had St. Ambrose.

St. Ambrose may seem a curious person to select as a
typical mystic. Of course, he was not always that.
Neither was St. Bernard. In that great work to which
I have referred, the *De Diligendo Deo*, he declares that
sacred ecstasy is not always vouchsafed a man.

I should account him blessed and sacred [he says],[3] to whom
it is given to have such experience rarely, now and then, or
even once, and swift in its going, lasting scarcely a moment of
time. For to lose himself as it were, as if he had ceased to be,
and to have no consciousness of himself at all, and to be emp-

tied of himself and almost annihilated is a matter of heavenly conversation, not of human affection. Even when it occurs [he adds] the wicked world envies him, the malice of the hour disturbs him, the body of death weighs him down, the demand of the flesh troubles him, the defect of corruption leaves him without support, and more baneful than any of these, brotherly charity recalls him to himself. Ah me! he is compelled to return to himself, to betake himself to the wonted tasks, and miserably to exclaim, "O Lord, I am oppressed," and again, "Unhappy man that I am, who shall deliver me from the body of this death!"

Thus the vision of the mystic fades into the light of common day — partly owing to the all too charitable solicitude of his friends — and leaves him normal. St. Bernard is normal most of the time, — even in his treatise *De Diligendo Deo*, — normal, practical, and matter-of-fact. He had too many things to do to submerge his soul perpetually in a mystic Nirvana.

And so with St. Ambrose. One thinks of him perhaps first of all as an administrator. He was born about 340, in north-central Gaul, in the city of Treves on the Moselle. This city was the residence of a succession of emperors, owing to the threatening advance of the barbarians. It was adorned with magnificent buildings, including libraries, and schools. Famous teachers and men of learning had been attracted thither. It was a centre of culture well nigh as important as Rome itself.

We are fortunate in having a contemporary life of St. Ambrose, written by his stenographer, Paulinus, at the request of St. Augustine. The art of the stenographer is

not a modern institution. In a later chapter,[4] I shall
quote from a poem of Prudentius, which will amply justify this statement in a rather horrifying way. Cicero had
an amanuensis, his faithful Tiro, whose life of his master
has unhappily been lost. What would not scholars give
to have it! The little biography of the Christian Cicero,
St. Ambrose, by his private secretary, has happily been
preserved. You will find it in volume XIV of the *Patrologia Latina* of the Abbé Migne — Matthew Arnold's
favorite five-fathom shelf, you remember.[5] If you are
looking about for a bit of not too difficult Latin to read
in connection with these lectures, I would recommend
the life of St. Ambrose by Paulinus, his secretary. It is
done in an easy and delightful style, with pretty little
trimmings of the mythical that do not interfere with the
credibility of the story. In those days, a scientific biographer dwelt on the marvels which, whether true or not,
were truly expressive of a saintly character. Present-
day biographers, with their passion for truth, and quick
sales, magnify whatever scandals, whether true or not,
have attached themselves to an honored name. *De
mortuis nil nisi malum*. But this is not the higher science. I suppose that in every human being there is a
mixture of good and evil. When a man has won in the
battle of life, it is quite as scientific to applaud the victory as to deride the partial defeats that may have preceded it. It is all a question of emphasis and of the
aspect of human character in which the biographer him-

self is most deeply concerned. Some day, scandal-mongers and disintegrating critics may become aware that they have produced most accurate autobiographies.

Ambrose's father was a high political personage, the praetorian prefect of the Gauls. The family was noble, and had been Christian for several generations. After the early death of his father, Ambrose removed, with his mother and one of his sisters, to Rome, where as befitted his rank, he was carefully trained in the liberal studies. The youth's first ambition was not the Church, but the career that his father had adorned. He began, in the good old Roman fashion, as an advocate. He is thus another of these legalistic theologians who, according to the eminent authorities cited in my previous chapters, have brought the theology of the West into such disrepute. Once more, it is my purpose to present the brighter sides of that theology. The Roman dogs have been given a bad name and hanged — not by due process of law. To the Roman of Cicero's day, to repeat, training in the law was virtually a part of a liberal education and a necessary avenue to success in that career to which most young Romans looked forward — the life of a statesman. So far from lamenting that so many of the Roman theologians were lawyers, I am sorry that so many of the Greeks were not. Most of them were professors. And if there is one subject on which a professor should not talk, as I am amply demonstrating, it is theology.

Ambrose advanced rapidly in his career. Like Cicero, he was an eloquent lawyer. His eloquence attracted the attention of Probus, the Praetorian Prefect, who eventually, in 372 or 373, appointed him governor of Liguria and Aemilia. These provinces also included an archiepiscopate, in which the most important centres were Milan, Turin, Genoa, and Bologna. Probus admonished him to consider himself rather a bishop than a judge, meaning that he should temper justice with mercy. Ambrose ruled with firmness and wisdom and won the confidence of his subjects.

In 374, an event took place that changed the course of his life. On the death of Auxentius, Bishop of Milan, a sharp contest arose between the Arian and the Athanasian factions in the Church. Auxentius had a leaning toward Arianism, and the Arians claimed the right to elect the new bishop. At the election, the contestants came to blows, there was a general riot, and finally Ambrose was summoned. Ambrose was a born ruler. He had no particular theological interests at this time, but he was going to keep the peace. He started to speak to the crowd, when a child's voice cried out from among them, "Let Ambrose be bishop." Out of the mouths of babes and sucklings. The multitude with one impulse took up the cry, as though it were the inspiration of God. There he stood, with the will of every man before him his to command. Someone later said of St. Ambrose, "If he says to the sun 'Stand,' it stands." Tired with their feuds, the people of Milan turned to one who could control. There was their bishop, fore-ordained. It mattered not that he knew little of the mysteries of the sacred calling; at the time, he was a catachumen, a member of a confirmation class, and still unbaptized. But he would learn; he was the man. To Ambrose the call was most unwelcome. Never was *"Nolo episcopari"* spoken by sincerer lips. He tried to bring Milan to its senses. He increased the severity of his administration; he retired to his study and plunged into philosophy; he cultivated extremely mundane, and even demi-mundane society; he attempted to flee the city. All in vain. The Milanese knew a good bishop when they saw one. "Thy sins be upon our heads," they cried. So Ambrose, like a good soldier to whom some impossible task has been assigned, saluted and obeyed orders. He was baptized, and a week later ordained bishop — a record in ecclesiastical advancement that even our enterprising age has never yet surpassed.

Ambrose at once got down to work. He devoted himself intensely to sacred studies, and he organized his charge. To apply to himself a verse from one of his hymns, he proved *usus minister publici*, "good servant of the public weal." No Arian disturbances in the diocese of Milan. It became a model of discipline for the whole Latin world. Ambrose's talent for administration was the largest practical contribution, in his district and elsewhere, to the settlement of the theological controversies that were rending the Church. Dr. More, in discussing Athanasius, speaks of "the restraining influence of the Roman courts with their inherited sense of legal procedure, upon the tumultuous Orient." [6] This is an unexpected compliment from Dr. More. I wish that we might also hear, now and then, something about Roman common sense, Roman balance, *aequa mens* and *aurea mediocritas*. Whether it was instinct or well-grounded deliberation that led Ambrose to uphold the Orthodox party and the doctrines of Athanasius, it was a lucky thing for the good people of Milan, who would have followed their Bishop into the mire of Arianism or the sands of Sabellianism if he had ordered "Forward, March!"

Ambrose was a commander, then, as well as administrator, a Christian Julius Caesar and more. Emperors bowed before him, Valentinian the Great, in response to an outspoken criticism that the Bishop had sent him, replied, "I was always well aware of your freedom in speech, but for all that, I not only did not oppose your ordination but expressly enjoined it. Wherefore proceed to apply thy medicine to the failings of our soul, even as the Divine Law prescribes." [7]

Ambrose also reproved and modified the acts of the great Theodosius in the affair of Callinicum, a town in Mesopotamia where monks had burned a Synagogue; and he also forced him to do penance for the massacre of Thessalonica.[8] This is a noteworthy anticipation of a later imperial humiliation at Canossa. Ambrose declares the principle, and upholds it, that in matters of faith the bishops are judges of the Christian emperors, not the emperors of the bishops.[9] Possibly some voices across the sea are ready just now to cry, "Ambrose, thou should'st be living at this hour — England hath need of thee." Furthermore, Ambrose's power to compel other people's wills, was combined with a diplomatic ability to persuade. That we have seen in the matter of the Altar of Victory,[10] in which his fair dealing with his opponent is no less conspicuous than his success in maintaining the Christian cause.

Now the rest of the acts of the Bishop of Milan, the miracles that his presence wrought, the heresies that he suppressed, the victories that he won over Pagan reactionaries, the punishments that befell those who derided him — are they not written in the book of the stenographer Paulinus? Our concern is with his mysticism and with his attitude toward that ancient culture with which he had become imbued in his youth. I will merely add here the date of his death, 397, and remark that his funeral was attended by a vast concourse of both sexes, all ages and classes; and not only Christians came, but Pagans and Jews.

Ambrose was too busy with problems of administration to accomplish anything really great in either scholarship or theology. And yet he was a man of no mean intellectual training. He had read the authors in his youth, and one of the episcopal duties that he faithfully performed was the constant searching of the scriptures. He also declared it the function of a bishop to teach. All his writings indicate this desire to live up to his part, to play the game into which he had been hurried against his will. He is a modest teacher. "When I was rushed from the bench of justice into the priesthood," he says, "I began to teach what I had not learned myself. — The result is that I now must learn and teach at the same time." [11] This confession of Ambrose's must be made by any teacher of any subject at any stage in his career. Sometimes, at the outset, one makes the confession with a certain glee, as if it involved a kind of crime against society which one committed without detection. Later, one perceives that it is the normal condition of the teacher and the vitality of his art.

The ancient philosophers most frequently quoted in Ambrose's works are Plato, Aristotle, Socrates (that is, both Xenophon and Plato), Stoics, and even Epicureans. Of Greek poets, he cites Homer and Euripides; of the Romans, Virgil, Horace, less frequently Lucan, Statius, and various minor poets. The influence even of Terence, Martial, and Ovid may occasionally be detected. We note that he was far better versed in Greek than either Lactantius or his illustrious contemporary Augustine. Ambrose was also up-to-date in his reading. He went through the Greek fathers, not only authors like Clement of Alexandria and Origen, but contemporary writers, with some of whom he corresponded — St. Didymus, St. Basil, St. Gregory of Nyssa, and St. Gregory of Nazianzus. He also made a very deep study of Philo Judaeus; indeed, perhaps the two chief formative influences on Ambrose's views and method were Philo the Jew and Cicero.

Cicero is suggested by more than one feature in the career of St. Ambrose. As we have seen, both were Roman orators; both were men of state. Likewise in their philosophical studies, they performed a somewhat similar service of interpretation. As Cicero translated Greek thought into Roman, so Ambrose translated it into Christian. His scope was not so large, but his purpose was the same. He likewise was an interpreter of Greek theology to the west. In point of style, Ambrose is less Ciceronian than Lactantius. His periods are more loosely constructed and too frequently marred by redundancy and prolixity. Ambrose was a teacher rather than an artist; he intended that his utterances *ex cathedra episcopali* should be understood at the risk of repetition. But Ambrose has more poetry in his nature than either Lactantius or Cicero had. He is at his best in a musical and richly colored prose that borders on poetry and liturgy. Though let me modify this estimate of Cicero — I was thinking of his attempts at verse. The prose of his *Dream of Scipio* is like that of Ambrose, only finer — liturgical, resonant, and rich.

Ambrose's interpretation of Cicero is most conspicuously set forth in his famous work *De Officiis Ministro-rum.*[12] This is one of the monuments of Christian humanism that illustrates the principles set forth in that standard work, the *Divine Institutes* of Lactantius. It is at once an act of homage and a challenge to Cicero. Both the challenge and the homage are obvious in the title chosen by Ambrose — *De Officiis Ministrorum,* for we think at once of Cicero's *De Officiis.* Cicero wrote his treatise for the benefit of his son Marcus, to hold up before him the ideals of conduct that a young Roman about to enter a career of statesmanship should follow. We should not translate the title "On Duties"; the subject is broader than that. It is the art and science of right living. The title of the work of Panaetius that served Cicero as model suggests better what they were writing about — περὶ τοῦ καθήκοντος, "On the fitting," "On what one should do," "On the proper conduct of young gentlemen." It is one of the mirrors of conduct of which the ancient world had seen a number and the mediaeval world was destined to see more. Now, Ambrose's young gentlemen are candidates for Holy Orders; he adds *Ministrorum* to the title. "And just as Tully wrote for the instruction of his son," he declares, "so I for the informing of my sons. For I love not less those whom I have begotten in the Gospel than if I had reared them in wedlock. For nature is not more strong to love than grace." The plan of Ambrose's argument shows the nature of his challenge. It is, in brief, to take

the scheme of the Pagan virtues, the Pagan definition of
decent conduct, and show that its excellent precepts are
aboundingly illustrated in the Old Testament, the New
Testament, the history of the Christian Church from its
inception, and in Christian living at the moment when
the Bishop was writing.

There is also something like a criticism of the Pagan
ethical structure which underlies his own treatment.
That structure, I may incidentally remark, is not only
Stoic but Platonic, for even in the *De Officiis* Cicero
makes it clear that his sovereign master is Plato. Ambrose starts with the four cardinal virtues as the Greeks
had defined them — wisdom, moderation, justice, and
bravery. This very system had been subjected to a
powerful and subtle attack by Plato, who devoted his
earliest dialogues to this purpose. There are glimpses of
such a general criticism in Ambrose. He points out, for
instance, that Christianity has, of course, transcended
the old law of retaliation — held by most Pagans — of
giving your enemy as good as he sends.[13] Or again, Ambrose alters the ancient scale of duties, in which duty to
the state came first, duty to the family next, and duty
to individuals last. For Ambrose a new duty heads the
list, the duty toward God. We might expect that he
would also enlarge the four Pagan virtues with the three
Christian virtues, which Mr. Chesterton calls the gay
and exuberant virtues, of faith, hope, and charity.[14] He
is of course aware of their existence, as he elsewhere

shows abundantly; and elsewhere, in the treatise *De Paradiso*, he interprets the four rivers of Paradise as symbolic of the four cardinal virtues, flowing from Christ the fountain-head, even as Plato had derived them from the idea of the Good. The main purpose of the *De Officiis Ministrorum*, however, is not to reconcile ancient theory with Christian truth, but to show the Pagans that the new faith has as many exemplifications of their best virtues as they themselves have. Tertullian had suggested something of the kind.[15] Ambrose has an ethical programme that sweeps over Pagan principles and Christian deeds. As a French critic remarks, it was an intellectual *coup d'état*.[16] Ambrose is treating Cicero precisely as Cicero treated Panaetius, translating his predecessor's system into contemporary terms.

Professor Lake observes, in his "Landmarks in the History of Early Christianity,"[17] — and he is not alone in this observation,—that "Probably the culmination of this conquest of the Christian Church by the ethics of the Stoa was reached by Ambrose, who gave to the Christian world Cicero's popularization of Panaetius and Posidonius, in a series of sermons which extracted the ethics of Rome from the scriptures of the Christians." This is just upside down; the horse follows the cart. The Church did not surrender its ethics to Stoic ethics: it included the latter in its own larger and purer thought. This conquest of the Church by the Stoa may be exactly paralleled by the conquest of Waterloo by Napoleon.

The *De Officiis Ministrorum* is, in a way, a new sort of apology. The danger is, not that the author will submerge Christianity in Stoic ethics, but that, although he is well versed in the ancient writers, both Latin and Greek, he may turn his new weapon with deadly effect against Pagan culture, if such be his desire. "Let us return to our Moses," says Ambrose, after recounting the chivalrous conduct of Pyrrhus to the Romans, "and cull examples as superior in point of nobility as they are in point of time." [18] One might well feel that if the Church possessed the treasure of fine lives, high thoughts, and great art that Tertullian and Ambrose claimed for it, the world would profit by lopping off the whole record of Paganism, which, whatever its excellencies, contained much that was harmful to the progress of Christian civilization. But another conclusion is possible from the evidence gathered by Ambrose, namely, that the contemplation of the two pictures side by side was no bad thing, and that the enjoyment of the best in Pagan thought and Pagan art would help, not hinder, in the forming of Christian character. This last attitude is Christian humanism, and to this, as we shall see, St. Ambrose subscribes.

I am slow in arriving at my proof that St. Ambrose was a mystic. In fairness to all sides of his temperament, I must present yet another that is not at all mystical. For he deserves a place, a modest place, among the Roman satirists. It is particularly in his sermons, which could be livelier than most modern sermons, that we note a series of little pictures that might have come out of an ancient satire, or an ancient diatribe, or such a work as the "Characters" of Theophrastus. There are the money-lender, the debtor, the society-woman, the tavern-loafer, the miser, and many others. A set of sermons on Naboth's vineyard includes a picture of the misery of exceeding wealth that has the full flavor of Horace, and a view of land-ownership that would find approval with Tolstoy and Henry George.[19]

As a specimen of these sketches, I will translate St. Ambrose's description of a drunken man, a very drunken man.[20]

Strong drink alters the senses and the forms of men. By it they are turned from men into neighing horses. A drunken man loses voice, he changes color, he flashes fire from his eyes, he pants, he snorts, he goes stark mad, he falls in a foaming fit. . . . Hence come also vain imaginings, uncertain vision, uncertain steps; often he hops over shadows thinking them to be pits. The earth acquires a facial expression, and nods to him; of a sudden, it seems to rise and bend and twist.[1] Fearful, he falls on his face and grasps the ground with his hands or thinks that the mountains close in about him. There is a murmur in his ears as of the surging sea; he hears the surf booming on the beach. If he spies a dog, he imagines it a lion and takes to his heels. Sometimes he shakes with laughter unquenchable; sometimes he is plunged in inconsolable woe; sometimes he is seized with senseless fears. He dreams when awake and quarrels when asleep. His life is a dream, his sleep is a death. No voice can rouse him, and until the fit pass off, no shaking bring him to.

No wonder Ambrose adds that such a person is a "*superflua creatura*" — a non-essential member of society.

There is a touch of Horation ridicule in this picture — though much less subtle than in Horace. There is a bit of poetry and there is a vivid imagination; for we cannot think that the good Bishop is drawing from reminiscence.

A sure path to mysticism is through allegory, and St. Ambrose was the first, if not to introduce, at least to popularize the allegorical method of interpretation in the West. It had flourished vigorously among the Eastern writers, Justin and Clement and Origen, who applied to the New Testament what Philo the Jew had already applied to the Old; and before that time it had had a lengthy history ever since Theagenes of Rhegium, in the sixth century B.C., saved the morality of the Homeric poems by this somewhat desperate remedy.[21] The allegorical habit is absolutely alien to the modern mind, which tosses it over as so much rubbish; but whatever its validity, something may be said for the impulses behind it. St. Hilary, who probably preceded St. Ambrose as an expounder of this system in the West, declared that the Old Testament proclaimed Christ, in order that posterity might contemplate the present in the past and venerate the past in the present.[22] This is a view of history fatal to the idea of development; but it makes for the solidity of human experience and encourages man to feel at home in any age. St. Hilary and St. Ambrose have pointed the way to the familiar Mediaeval view of our little world *sub specie aeternitatis*.

Here again we have a great foundation laid in the fourth century. St. Thomas Aquinas and Dante give what looks like a final and scientific statement about allegory, with the four varieties of meanings that might attend a verse of scripture or a poet's verse — the *sensus literalis*, that is, the obvious or historical meaning of the words; *sensus moralis*, their application to human character; *sensus allegoricus* or *mysticus*, the prophecy of the Gospels in some passage of the Old Testament; and the *sensus anagogicus*, which revealed something about man's experience in the life to come. Dante, for instance, in his famous letter to Can Grande, which will concern us later when we get to St. Augustine, shows how these four meanings are implicit in the verse of the Psalm: *in exitu Israel de Aegypto, domus Iacob de populo barbaro*.[23] This fourfold search for meanings might seem the final elaboration of the art of allegory, but it is all found in the work of a contemporary of St. Ambrose, John Cassian, who will appear as one of our Founders when we arrive at our seventh topic, "The New Education." In one of his *Collationes*, or *Sacred Conferences*,[24] Cassian sets forth precisely the same four varieties, with only one difference in terminology, namely that for *sensus moralis* Cassian has *sensus tropologicus*, which sounds even more scientific. When Ambrose and Cassian read the Scriptures, which was often, they read with care. Some of us, I am afraid, do not read them at all. Those who do, read a passage only once at a time; Ambrose and Cassian read it four times at a time, literally, morally or tropologically, allegorically or mystically, and anagogically. Whatever you may think of such a practice, it kept the mind quadruply awake.

Not to put your attentions to too severe a strain, I will begin with a simpler instance of allegory in St. Ambrose's treatise *De Abraham;* but you have only to open his commentaries at random to see that he had been through the Old Testament and transformed its meaning in the light of what was then the latest and most scientific method in Biblical interpretation, quite as necessary then as disintegrating or decomposing criticism is to-day.

The introduction of the *De Abraham* broaches another matter of much concern to the student of the Middle Ages and of ancient thought.

If the wise men of this world [Ambrose declares],[25] for instance, Plato himself, the chief of philosophers, described not a real, but an imaginary and shadowy republic, a city that he had never seen or heard of, to be an ideal for those who were to govern in the state; if his fellow-pupil in the school of Socrates, Xenophon, himself using fictitious material, painted a picture of a sage in his book entitled Κύρου παιδεία, that the pattern of the training of a just and philosophic king might be taken from the very heart of philosophy, how much more intently ought we to contemplate, not the imagined ideal of wisdom, but its actual expression set forth by divine authority, and follow in the path of him whom Moses so describes, that his story seems a retrospect of his own career?

Ambrose is interested in the portrayal of the ideal character of a leader for the benefit of those particularly who were vouchsafed a similar career — this is one of the mirrors, one of the true mirrors. Cicero's programme in his "Republic" is precisely that of Ambrose here; Cicero would point to no visioned state, a city not made with hands, but to the actual history of the glorious government of Rome.

The *De Abraham* is addressed to Bishop Ambrose's confirmation class, his catechumens. Besides holding up to their contemplation the ideal man exemplified in the actual Abraham, he wishes to introduce them to the proper way of reading the Old Testament.

I will give, as promised, one of the simpler examples.[26] Ambrose is commenting on the presents that Isaac made to Rebecca when he met her at the well — the ear-rings and the bracelets of gold. It then occurs to him that the mention of this finery may put bad ideas into the heads of some of the fair members of his class.

Perhaps, when you hear this, my daughters, you who are tending towards the grace of the Lord, you may be tempted to get you ear-rings and bracelets and say to me, "Why do you forbid us, Bishop, to have what Rebecca accepted as a gift and yet exhort us to be like Rebecca?" Ah, yes, but Rebecca did not have the kind of ear-rings and bracelets that are wont to sow disputes in the Church, the kind that often slip off. She had other ear-rings — and would that you had them too! — and other bracelets. The ear-rings of Rebecca are the symbols of pious attention. The bracelets of Rebecca are the ornament of good works. She had the kind of ear-rings that do not oppress the ears but soothe them. She had the kind of bracelets that do not burden the hand with material gold but lighten it with spiritual deeds. That is the reason why her brother and her parents were so well pleased with her adornment. Very well, then, you *may* have the earrings that Abraham left you. And here are the bracelets that he bequeathed you.

One cannot blame the Bishop for cultivating the allegorical method when it gave results like these. Even feminine repartee could not stand against it.

This is the simpler, moral sort of exposition, and eminently practical. But the account of Isaac's journey is also a prophecy of the mysteries of the Church.[27] For where did he go but to Mesopotamia? And where do we look for the Church but in Mesopotamia? *Between the two rivers* — to wit, the bathing-place of grace and the pouring tears of penitence. "For unless you bewail your own sins, unless you accept the grace of baptism, you do not acquire the faith of the Church or the marriage-union with her." This is subtle. First we have an apparently innocent geographical name, a Greek word, resolved into its component parts. Thus we get two rivers, one signifying (here we should like to know why) baptism, and the other (we should also like to know why) penitence. These two acts indicate the presence of the Church, which is the ultimate allegory.

I will let Mesopotamia, which has become indeed a blessed word, serve as a specimen of the more abstruse allegory of St. Ambrose, though much could be added on this score. Many curious bits of mystic discovery

will be found in the treatise "On Flight from the
World" (*De Fuga Saeculi*).[28] That on "Noah and the
Ark" is worth reading in the light of that most intricate of Mediaeval mystics, Hugo of St. Victor, who
likewise wrote two little works on the ark of Noah, *De
Arca Noe Morali* and *De Arca Noe Mystica*.[29] The allegorizings differ. Hugo has introduced many modern
improvements in the ancient craft, but it is the same
old boat, patiently carrying whatever spiritual cargo
was put aboard.

Allegorical interpretation, in which perversity of imagination is not always accompanied by intensity of
soul, may not be so sure an index of mysticism as are
certain moments of devotion in which the spirit of the
preacher rises in contemplation to the eternal good and
to the peace that passeth understanding. *Pax autem
supra omnem mentem est, et supra omnem sensum.*[30] The
angels on the ladder in Jacob's dream are, in the Saint's
fancy, the holy men of God, whom sometimes the love
of God through the grace of contemplation exalts to
high places.[31] Such mystic moments occur also in Ambrose's hymns and they occur in one of the most remarkable of his commentaries on Sacred Scripture, the
Hexaemeron, a series of nine sermons on the first six
days of creation.[32]

This work, for which our author took the plan and
much of the information from St. Basil's commentary of
the same name, is full of varied interest. Its substance

is connected with the Biblical epic, to which we shall come in a later lecture. Tasso in his *Sette Giornate*, and Du Bartas in *La Semaine* have chosen similar titles and were apparently acquainted with St. Ambrose's treatise. This work also gives us excellent proof, which I had promised to furnish, that St. Ambrose preserves his fondness for the old authors. This he shows not only by direct citations, but by a more subtle kind of imitation, the weaving of their phrases or sentences into his own descriptions. In his very reply to the Pagan Symmachus, part of which was quoted in the first lecture,[33] there are sprinklings of Virgil. It is as if he wished to show his opponent that the new order would not annihilate the old, but absorb it. So in the *Hexaemeron*, when he speaks of the delights of the farmer's life, the joy of green fields and bursting crops, and the glory of gardens, he weaves one tapestry from his own language, from bits of *Genesis* and from bits of Cicero's famous panegyric of agriculture in his essay on "Old Age." [34] I cannot think that Ambrose was attempting to hide his tracks by making no mention of Cicero's name. He is doing what Minucius Felix did — paying a delicate compliment that any educated reader would understand. It all depends on the spirit of the age. The late Senator Lodge, a dozen years ago, at the dedication of the Widener Library at Harvard, quoted Cicero's praise of literature in the *Archias*. He apologized for the quotation, adding that thirty years before he would also have apologized for it, but for a different reason — then because the passage was too trite, now because nobody would understand it. Ambrose was writing in an age when people knew their Cicero. Indeed, as I hope I am making clearer and clearer as we proceed, Cicero held, in the estimation of the fourth century, well-nigh a sovereign place.

We also see in Ambrose's discourse on the first six days of creation a commendable interest in science, at least of one kind. Some have denied that St. Ambrose had the slightest regard for physical phenomena or their causes,[35] basing their assertion, it may be, on some such passage as the following, in which Ambrose is speaking of the different theories about the position of the earth in the universe.[36]

Many say that the earth is in the midst of the air, and that it remains immobile because of its own weight, seeing that it exerts an equal pressure in this direction and in that. On that point we think that enough was said by the Lord to his servant Job, when he spake from the cloud and said: "Where wast thou when I laid the foundations of the earth? Declare if thou hast understanding. Who hath laid the measures thereof, if thou knowest? or who hath stretched the line upon it?" and below, "I have shut up the sea with doors and said, 'Thus far shalt thou come but no farther: and here shall thy proud waves be stayed.'" Did not then God manifestly declare that all things are established by his majesty in number, weight, and measure? For the creature did not assign law, but accepted it, and accepting it, maintains it. It is not, therefore, that the earth is in the centre of things because hung there by "equilibrium," but because the Majesty of God constrains it by the law of his own will.

Doubtless this passage savors more of mysticism than of science, and as such, it is grist to my mill.

If you will read a little farther in Ambrose, however, you will find that such an utterance is not a protest against the idea of natural law, — that, indeed, he has asserted, — but rather against certain scientific hypotheses. Ancient science lacked the laboratory and, without experimentation, was the prey of arbitrary speculation much more than to-day. It would generate a kind of mythology, less interesting and picturesque than the ordinary kind, and no whit more valid, something like "true history" according to Euhemerus or the decomposing critics of to-day. An intellectual Christian like Ambrose rejected such science precisely as he rejected the history of the Olympians, not because it was Pagan and wrong, but because it was stale and untrue. I can quote you from Plato and Cicero passages of essentially the same tenor as that which I have just read from Ambrose.[37] But while there is little sympathy for excogitated science in Ambrose, his work is full of observation of the facts of the natural world. He has minute descriptions of quails and storks and swallows, of bees and crickets, of trees and their modes of reproduction, of evaporation and the action of rain, of human anatomy and physiology.

But this science, I must add, is not always simple. St. Ambrose appends lessons of reproof as he describes the birds of the air, the fish of the sea, and the beasts of the field. The humbler creatures obey the laws of nature that God had appointed for them. They set us human beings examples of virtues which we know but do not always practise — take the hospitality of crows, the gratefulness of dogs, the parental devotion of storks, the canny foresight of the sea-urchin who reads the signs of the future far more surely than any Chaldaean sage, the exquisite chastity of the widowed turtle-dove who, by refusing to mate again, sets a standard, — too high, alas, — for widowed Christian dames.[38]

This praise of the higher life of beasts, in which St. Ambrose anticipates various romanticists of later ages, and in which he was anticipated by Lucretius,[39] readily passes over into allegory. The polypus is a type of the fraudulent, the phoenix is symbol of our resurrection, fishes, both good and evil, are men, and the good fish should not fear the hook of Peter. The sea is the Gospel, on which Peter tottered, but was supported by the right hand of the Lord. The sea is the Gospel, in which are figured the mysteries of Christ.[40]

From such a view of nature, it is not a long journey to the mediaeval bestiaries in which all the humble creatures become types of some ideal. Even the mosquito is a good, not an evil, in this imaginary universe; for he is nothing but the type of the heretic, who, all unperceived, inflicts upon the body of the Church a hideous sting.[41]

Let me indicate this mediaeval quality of St. Ambrose's descriptions, as well as their admirable attention to details and their sympathy with the inner workings — I had almost said the minds — of the dumb creation, by translating his account of the crab, who like the polypus is a type of the fraudulent.[42] I will not vouch for the truth of St. Ambrose's story, in fact an eminent authority on zoölogy assured me that it is highly unscientific — but at least it would be welcomed by Uncle Remus, and by the author of the *Jungle Books*.

Then take the crab — what magic craft does he devise in his quest of food! For he, too, is fond of oysters, and seeks for himself a banquet on their flesh. But he is as wary of danger as he is eager for food; for that hunting is both difficult and dangerous. Difficult it is because the inner morsel is enclosed in exceedingly stout scales; for nature, as though interpreting a general's command, fortified with veritable walls the tenderness of the flesh, which it guards and nourishes in a hollow cup between the shells and spreads in a kind of valley, and therefore all the attacks of the crab are in vain, since no force of his can open the oyster. And the hunting of the oyster is dangerous for the crab, if he gets his claw caught in the oyster's mouth. He therefore lays schemes and devises a ruse as novel as it is sly. Since all creatures enjoy comfort, he watches for the time when the oyster, finding a quiet nook, sheltered from the wind and facing the sun's rays, opens his bivalve and unbars the portals of his shells, to feel the pleasure of the free air playing about his insides. At that moment the crab surreptitiously inserting a pebble, prevents the oyster from closing up again and thus finding the portals wide open, he safely inserts his claws and feeds on the oyster's interior. So then, there are men who in the style of the crab creep into another's precincts and, supporting by a kind of craft the weakness of their own powers, weave toils about their brother and batten on another's woe.

I venture to state, if I may sing the praises of allegory once more, that it presents us with a solution of the problem of evil which, so far as I know, has escaped the attention of philosophers. It is not hard to explain moral evil, theologically; it is a consequence of freedom of the will, which is a good. The stumbling-block is physical evil. But if all apparent manifestations of physical evil, — like the mosquito, who has at least drawn upon himself sufficient remarks, ejaculations, and even imprecations to indicate that he is an evil, — if he and all his like are but symbols of moral evil, useful reminders of what we should avoid, we will grin and bear them and look with more content upon a world in which all that is, is good. Isolated examples of allegory may seem distressing and absurd. But the universe of allegory, as wrought out by the mediaeval mind, with assistance from the Founders, is a permanently satisfying abode, in which the imagination of the allegorizer is alertly on the hunt and is always satisfied with the spoils. Science and history suffer when the intellect is under such a spell, but free thought thrives. Alas, this fairyland of illusion has melted into the unsubstantial air.

> Our dazed eyes
> Have seen a new tinge in the western skies,
> The world has done its duty.

For the allegorical element in the *Hexaemeron*, St. Ambrose is largely responsible. It is present, but only rarely, in the work of St. Basil that served him as source. Something, our author declares, he had learned from the rustics.[43] Surely the breath of poetry that at times lifts allegory to mystic heights is all his own.

Ambrose is specially fascinated by the sea. To Lucretius it was an evil power, a crafty monster luring men to their bane.[44] To Ambrose it calls with a voice of joy and romance and mysticism. As he comes in his account of creation to the Atlantic Ocean, he rises like an epic poet when the theme commands a loftier style.[45] He loves the colors on the waters more than the flowers of the field. He can see the leaping fishes and the dolphins at their play, and the sound of the booming surf is pleasant to his ears. Sails are the lilies of the sea, and more necessary for man's welfare than those white, fragrant flowers. None of the ancient curses on navigation in St. Ambrose![46] The speeding ships, contending in no vain race like that of the Circus, bring cargoes of corn to land. Again, he speaks of the beauty of the sea [47]

when it whitens with the caps of its rising waves and bedews the cliffs with snowy spray or when on its crisping surface, as gentler breezes blow and the sky is calm and cloudless, it takes on purple colors which spread and merge as you see them from the distance. And when it beats the neighboring shore not with the madness of its billows but with quiet salutations and peaceful caresses, how sweet is its sound, how pleasant the breaking surf, how grateful and harmonious its ebbing flow!

This is the actual sea, but there is a spiritual sea, which the eye of allegory can behold.[48]

It is the secret strength of moderation, the practice of re-straint, the retreat of seriousness, the port of security, the tranquillity of the age, the sobriety of this world, the incentive of worship to devout and faithful men, so that when the sing-ing of psalms chimes with the sound of gently breaking waves, the isles clap their hands at the tranquil choir of the sacred waves and echo with the hymns of the saints. . . . Aye, the Sea is the Church, which pours forth from its doors in waves the crowds of the faithful, and echoes with refluent waves of the people's prayer, with the responses of psalms, the singing of men, of women, of children, a crashing surf of concordant song. And what of the wave that washes sin away and the life-giving breezes of the Holy Spirit?

There is the stuff of poetry in this rhapsody on the sea. There is also here a familiar call from the heights, which a mystic's ear will not fail to catch. It is not sur-prising that a passage of similar exaltation was later worked by the author into one of his familiar hymns — *Aeterne rerum conditor*.[49]

One of the finest bits of poetry in the making occurs near the end of the treatise.[50] The creation of man is accomplished. It remains to describe his nature and his needs. Ambrose addresses the poor man to show him that a great treasure is his.

Give ear, ye poor. For your life is precious, and if your flesh is mortal, your soul shall never die. If money fails you, grace is abundantly yours. If you have no roomy house, no stretching lands, the heavens spread above you, the earth is free. The elements were given to all in common; rich and poor share equally the adornments of the sky. Is there more beauty in the gilt-panelled ceilings of costly houses than in the face of heaven, studded with glittering stars? Are the fields of rich men broader than the stretches of the earth?

Wherefore it is said to those who join house to house and villa to villa, "Will ye be placed alone in the midst of the earth?" You have a greater house, oh ye poor, in which you cry and are heard. "Oh Israel," saith the prophet, "how great is the house of God and how mighty the place of his possession!" — But you deem it a luxury to lie down on an ivory couch, and consider not that the earth is greater luxury which spreads for the poor a couch of grass, on which there is sweet repose, pleasant slumber, which he who is settled in a bed of gold, tossing the night through, seeks, and does not find.

An echo of this sentiment comes from India, in a poem translated by our American critic, and now our American theologian, Paul Elmer More.[51]

> One boasted: "Lo, the earth my bed,
> This arm a pillow for my head,
> The moon my lantern, and the sky
> Stretched o'er me like a purple canopy.
>
> No slave-girls have I, but all night
> The four winds fan my slumbers light."
> And I, astonished, "Like a lord
> This beggar sleeps; what more could wealth afford?"

The thought is also common in the Classical authors. In Ambrose's mind, there were echoes, perhaps, of Baruch and Isaiah and Lucretius, but the poetry is his own, with its majestic elevation. To St. Ambrose, as to the ancient seer, the poor man's couch of grass, his pillow of stones, is none other than the house of God and the gate of heaven.

These, then, are mystic moments in the life of a man of action, who when he preached, said St. Augustine, talked to himself and to God.

And when he read, [and again I quote Augustine] [52] his eyes were rivetted on the pages and his mind tore open the meaning of the words. But no sound escaped his lips. Often when we had come to see him, — for access was never denied us, nor was it his fashion to have visitors announced — we would observe him reading there in silence, and after sitting there quietly for a long time, — for who would venture to intrude on so intent a reader? — we would noiselessly withdraw.

I could cite other contemporaries besides Augustine and a host of those who came after, to show that to them St. Ambrose was not merely a strong executive, but a holy man of God, one in whom human nature had been refashioned in the likeness of the divine. [53] The secretary, Paulinus, as we have seen, though writing from the very house of Ambrose, does not refrain from a few touches of myth. What wonder, when he had to record actual marvels that the presence of the Saint had wrought? Of his birth Paulinus relates [54] that, when the infant Ambrose was asleep in his cradle, a swarm of bees flew harmlessly about his face and in and out of his mouth, and finally soared straight aloft beyond the reach of human eyes. A similar story is told of Plato and other masters of honeyed speech. Possibly the bees, a sagacious race, visited them all. Paulinus, at any rate, finds in the incident not only an omen of the future, but a fulfilment of past prediction. "Even then," he declares, "the Lord was working in the infancy of his little servant, that the saying might be fulfilled, 'Pleasant words are as an honeycomb, sweet to the soul and health to the bones.'"

If, then, we break through the daily round, the outer triumphs of the great Bishop of Milan, we find in the inner soul of him a child of the Muses, one of the Saints that know the mystic rapture, one of the pure in heart that see God. No wonder that the mystic Bernard called St. Ambrose and St. Augustine the two pillars of the Church, and declared that, having their truth or their error, he would not ask for more.[55]

CHAPTER IV

ST. JEROME THE HUMANIST

WHAT is a humanist? I have been using the term
humanism rather freely. It is one of those terms,
like mysticism, that are best left undefined. But it is
easy to describe a humanist. We may begin with the
familiar theological method, the *via negationis*. I am
not using the term humanist to signify a member of the
left wing of the Unitarian Church or a disciple of Mr.
F. C. S. Schiller of Oxford. I would not — and here I
have the sanction of my colleague Irving Babbitt —
I would never confuse a humanist with a humanitarian.
A humanist is one who has a love of things human, one
whose regard is centred on the world about him and the
best that man has done; one who cares more for art and
letters, particularly the art and letters of Greece and
Rome, than for the dry light of reason or the mystic's
flight into the unknown; one who distrusts allegory;
one who adores critical editions with variants and vari-
orum notes; one who has a passion for manuscripts,
which he would like to discover, beg, borrow or steal;
one who has an eloquent tongue which he frequently
exercises; one who has a sharp tongue, which on occasion can let free a flood of good billingsgate or sting an

opponent with epigram. You will recognize the aptness of all these characterizations by thinking of some of the great humanists of history—Cicero, Lupus of Ferrières, John of Salisbury, Poggio and Filelfo, Budaeus and Casaubon, Erasmus and Heinsius, Gildersleeve and Jebb. Not all humanists possess all the features of such humanism. You will note certain deficiencies in those that I have named. Most of these eminent men did not steal manuscripts or indulge in cultivated billingsgate, but they were humanists for all that.

One point deserves emphasis above all that I have mentioned. It is this. The humanist, though his sympathies are deeply rooted in the past, concentrates his energies on the present. If he wraps himself up in the past and is not aware what age he is living in, he is a pedant. His works may be useful books of reference, but they will convey no message to his generation. All the great scholars that I have mentioned were true humanists, because they were true servants of their own times.

I will illustrate incidentally the points that I have mentioned, some of them, in sketching the works and character of St. Jerome. We must remember that, if a humanist, he was a Christian humanist, and that he was too much occupied with other things to be a humanist all the time. Even a mystic, as we saw, is not always a mystic. St. Jerome's main object in life, if I interpret it correctly, was to put his scholarship at the disposal of the Church. He did not always have time to be a humanist; for I also should have mentioned leisure as one of the traits of humanism — academic leisure, the σχολή, or *otium*, of the blessed ancients. Moreover, Jerome's temperament was compounded of elements so diverse that the blending of them hardly promises the easy urbanity of a humanist. A learned Benedictine, in a very recent article, calls him an irascible hermit.

St. Jerome was born at about the same date as Ambrose, A.D. 340, in the city of Stridon, on the borderland between Dalmatia and Pannonia, in Illyria. He came of well-to-do Christian parents who did not, however, occupy so high a social position as those of Ambrose. I think one feels that Jerome was of the equestrian rather than of the senatorial order. The lad's education was completed at Rome under the famous scholar Aelius Donatus. He was a baptized Christian at the time, but his conduct was hard telling from that of the young Pagans with whom he consorted. He then went for further study to Treves, which, we saw,[1] was one of the great seats of culture in the fourth century, and there for the first time he became genuinely interested in theology. For he read the works of St. Hilary, the most eminent writer in Gaul, and was attracted by his reasonable and philosophical presentation of Christian doctrine. From Treves, he went to Aquileia, in the northeast corner of Italy, in Venetia, also a most important centre of learning.

At Aquileia, Jerome became acquainted with a group of youthful Christian reformers, Rufinus among them, whose chief interest was the ascetic life and the institution of monasticism. The church, in their estimation, was becoming worldly; "greater in power and in wealth and less in virtue," are Jerome's words.[2] Many good men thought it necessary to escape from the Church in order to escape from the world. Monasticism had been prevalent in the east before, but had only recently made its appearance in the west. Jerome was attracted by the new theory, — it was the last word in education as in religion, — and it was due mainly to his support and that of Augustine that the western church accepted monasticism. In trying to promulgate his ideas at Aquileia, Jerome got into some difficulty, the nature of which we do not know; and he was forced to leave. He was of a restless, inquisitive, reforming temperament, and something of a trouble-breeder; he liked to go round doing good to those who did not like to be done good to. In this he proved himself an excellent humanitarian, but not an excellent humanist; for a humanist preaches, if he preaches at all, contentment with one's lot and the enlargement of one's imagination. Jerome left Aquileia with a friend, and made for Syria, intending to study monasticism at first hand. There he fell ill of a serious disease that kept him many months an invalid. It was then that he had his famous dream, sent to rebuke his excessive fondness of reading the classics.

I could not altogether give up my library [he writes],[3] which I had collected at Rome with much zeal and much labor. And so, poor wretch, I would fast, in preparation for reading Tully. After the long vigils of the night, after the tears, which the remembrance of my past sins drew from the depths of my heart, I would take Plautus in hand. If ever I recovered my senses and tried to read the prophets, their uncouth style rubbed me the wrong way; and because with my blind eyes I saw not the light, I deemed it the fault not of my eyes, but of the sun. While thus the old serpent was beguiling me, one day, about the middle of Lent, a fever flooded me to the very marrow and wracked my weary body. Pausing not, — incredible as it may sound, — it so fed on my hapless limbs that I could scarce cleave to my bones. Meanwhile they made ready for my obsequies. The vital heat of my soul, as my whole body turned cold, was quivering on the surface of my breast, which, in a tiny spot, was still tepid — when, of a sudden, I was caught up in the spirit, and haled before the judgment-seat of God. Blinded by its light and by the brightness of those who stood about it, I fell prostrate to the earth, not daring to look up. When the voice asked me concerning my condition, I replied that I was a Christian. "Thou liest," answered He that sat upon the throne. "Thou art a Ciceronian, not a Christian; for where thy treasure is, there shall thy heart be also."

Then followed Jerome's repentance, a thorough flagellation, and a vow that he would never own or read a secular book again.

After taking oath to that effect [he adds], I came back into the land of the living, and amid their wonder, I opened my eyes that were flooded with such a rain of tears that my grief convinced even the scoffers. Nor was that a sleep, or a vain dream such as often beguiles us. My witness is that judgment seat before which I lay. My witness is that awful judgment that I so feared. May it never be my lot to pass through a like ordeal again. I testify that I wore livid marks upon my shoulders, that I felt the blows after sleep left me, and that I studied divine books thereafter with a zeal far greater than that with which before I had read the works of mortals.

These are not the words of a humanist. They are the words of a converted humanist, and not a perfect humanist at that; for the humanist would pick up his Plautus, not after fasting and tears, but after a decent dinner. Jerome was not normal at this time, and humanists are always normal. The letter that contains the story of his dream is one of his best known works, a little treatise *De Custodia Virginitatis*, written in utter frankness to Eustochium, a young lady in Rome who had taken the vows of a nun. He does not refrain from describing the temptations with which he was beset while essaying the life of a hermit.

O how often [he declares],[4] when I dwelt in the desert, in that vast wilderness, scorched with the heat of the sun, in which monks have their dreadful home, how often would I imagine that I was enjoying the luxuries of Rome. I would sit alone, filled with bitterness of heart. My unsightly limbs were rough and squalid and my shrivelled skin was of the color of an Aethiopian. Daily were my tears, daily my groans, and whenever sleep threatened to overcome my struggling spirit, I would bruise my naked bones, scarce clinging to my flesh, and beat them on the ground. Of food and drink, I say naught, since it is a luxury, even if a monk is ill, to take a sip of cold water or to eat anything cooked. But it was that self-same I, who for the fear of hell had damned myself to such a prison, with none but scorpions and wild beasts for my companions, yes, it was I, who often imagined myself present at the revels of dancing-girls. My face was pallid with fasting, but my heart was hot with desires in my cold body, and before the mind of the man, whose flesh was dead e'er its time, hovered the fiery visions of passion. And so, reft of all aid, I would fall at the feet of Jesus, wash them with my tears and dry them with the hair of my head, and subdue my rebellious flesh with a fast of weeks. Nor do I blush to confess the misery of my woe. Aye, rather do I mourn that I am not now what once I was. I remember that I would cry aloud by night and day, and not cease from lashing my heart till, at the rebuke of my Lord, peace would return. I then would even fear my little cell, inasmuch as it had shared the secrets of my thoughts. So, angry with myself and stern, I would again go alone to the desert. Wherever I saw retreating valleys, rough hills, precipitous cliffs, there was my place of prayer, and there the pillory of my wretched flesh. And there, — the Lord is my witness, — after shedding many tears, after fastening my eyes on the sky, I would seem to be set amidst a choir of Angels, and glad and joyful I would sing, "After thee will we run for the savour of thy good ointments."

This is not the language, or the experience, of a humanist. A modern would say that there is matter here for a psychoanalyst, an obvious case of some sort of complex. El Greco's painting of St. Jerome is not more startlingly uncanny than the saint's own words. Jerome's practices suggest the autohypnotic meditations of Brahmin monks, their meditations on color and the syllable OM. The passage is a nauseous draft for a healthy soul, but may have been good medicine for the case with which St. Jerome was dealing. We must mitigate his language with what he says elsewhere on the subject.[5] He commends the monasticism of the cenobite, not the anchorite, the common, not the solitary life, as normal and best for the soul. Indeed he advises moderation in asceticism, agreeing with Aristotle that virtue is measure and vice excess.[6] Here speaks the humanist once more; for nothing is more humanistic than the observance of the Aristotelian mean and that golden maxim of both Greeks and Romans, *ne quid nimis*.

After five years, Jerome found the desert uncomfortable on account of his fellow-anchorites. They were a nervous and contentious lot, ready to charge each other with backsliding. He accordingly returned to Antioch, was made a Priest, and in 380 went to Constantinople, where he devoted himself to the study of Greek and of Biblical exegesis under St. Gregory of Nazianzus. It was there that he performed the useful task of translating the World Chronicle of Eusebius and of bringing it up to date. Thus Jerome had a triple equipment of languages. He was a *homo trilinguis*, as he modestly states,[7] *Hebraeus, Graecus, Latinus,* and a few other things too — *philosophus, rhetor, grammaticus, dialecticus*. This unhappy display of vanity, — characteristic of some humanists, alas, — occurs in a work that is also unhappily flavored with the *theologicum* or, shall we say, *humanisticum odium*, at the expense of his former friend Rufinus. The two had devotedly studied Origen together in their youth; but when an unfavorable judgment had been pronounced on Origen in a council of the year 400, Rufinus remained loyal to the memory of their master, while Jerome, properly enough, accepted the verdict of the council, to which his own deliberations had also brought him. He also strengthens his orthodoxy by venting his feelings on Rufinus. Jerome had a sharp and humanistic tongue; "a writer of satires in prose," one of his enemies calls him.[8] He fires Cicero's apothegm at Rufinus, "You have the will to lie, good sir, but not the skill to lie."[9] Even after the death of his old friend, he can say,[10] "The Scorpion lies buried in Sicily, half-way between Enceladus and Porphyry" — Enceladus, the giant, whose subterranean squirmings caused eruptions in Mt. Aetna; Porphyry, the Neoplatonic philosopher, who had bitterly assailed the Christian faith. *Requiescat in pace.*

You cannot imagine Ambrose or Augustine saying things like that. Jerome can be nasty if he so chooses. I rather infer that he had no warm admiration for Ambrose. He refers to him several times in various writings, citing his opinions in a non-committal way; but the only time that he expresses a judgment, or comes near to expressing a judgment, is in his work, *De Viris Illustribus.*[11] All that he says is "Ambrosius, Bishop of Milan, is writing at the immediate present. As he is alive, I will refrain from comment, lest I be criticized either for flattery or for truth." The language is ambiguous, but the inference might be that the truth would not be flattering to St. Ambrose. It is one of those compliments which, as *Punch* would remark, might have been differently expressed. In the entire collection of his letters, not one is addressed to Ambrose. Turn for contrast to Augustine — or to Rufinus.

They never mention Ambrose's name save with affection and reverence, almost with adoration, as of some sacred presence with whom they had been vouchsafed to dwell.[12]

With Augustine, Jerome was on much better terms. They exchanged letters on a variety of topics. Augustine speaks freely on occasion, but Jerome, whatever his feelings, answers with unvarying courtesy, despite the fact that one of Augustine's letters of criticism had unfortunately been circulated in Italy before reaching him.[13] He addresses Augustine[14] as "my most beloved friend, my son in years and my peer in eminence." At the end of one letter, referring to a vexed point in his translation of the book of Jonah, he begs that, as an old man and veteran of some years' standing, he be allowed to rest from his labors. "Do you," he says to Augustine,[15] "who are young and established on the pontifical heights, continue to teach the nations and enrich the houses of Rome with the new crops of Africa. Enough for me with one poor hearer or one poor reader to mutter in a corner of my monastery." This is a neat thing to say to the Bishop of Hippo. With his eloquence as its chief product, Jerome implies, Africa was still the granary of Rome. Humanists who can be nasty can also be nice. When they are nice, they are very, very nice, and when they are bad, they are horrid.

In the year 382, Jerome returned to Rome, at the invitation of Pope Damasus, an active pontiff, who was

bent on the reform of society by the establishment of
monasticism. By this time, Jerome had the right to the
title of expert in that subject. And society needed reform. Human nature was human nature, even in the
fourth century. There were sinners among the saints.
There were hypocrites and backsliders. There were
aimiable dames of fashion to whom Christianity was
the latest *ism*, who flocked about St. Jerome, the noted
monasticist, as the good women of a city, thousands of
miles remote from here, flock about the newest Swami
from Hindustan. There were false leaders in the Church,
popular young priests, immaculately dressed, agreeably
perfumed, and fond of society, particularly the society
of the fair communicants just described. In the midst
of this world Jerome now appeared as a new Juvenal.
The *satiricus scriptor in prosa* found plenty of subjects
at hand. As you dip into his letters here and there, you
think you are in the age of Domitian again, or in the
times of George Buchanan and the Franciscan friars
whom he served up in the same style. Perhaps Juvenal
is not the best parallel in either case. For Jerome and
Buchanan, both of them master satirists who deserve
more mention by those who treat of satire, can control
their moral indignation better than Juvenal could. It is
not indignation, or Horatian urbanity, that makes their
verses, but the faculty of pungent epigram that allies
them rather with Cicero and with Pope.

Here are a few of Jerome's pictures of society; you

will find them of a tarter flavor than those of Ambrose. I quote again from the letter to Eustochium. With other pieces of wholesome advice, Jerome warns his pupil to beware of false widows.[16]

Give a wide berth to those who remain widows from necessity, not inclination. Though they change their raiment, their schemings are as of old. Their Basternian litters [the Basternian was the latest model of litter — the fourth-century Rolls Royce] are preceded by a cohort of eunuch couriers. They redden their cheeks and fill in the skin so neatly that you would think they had not lost husbands but were on the hunt for them. Their houses are full of flatterers, full of feasts. The clergy, too, are there, who ought to have been employed in their duties. They kiss the heads of these matrons, and then hold out their hands — to pronounce a benediction over them, you would imagine, if you did not know that they receive in their palms the tip for their sacred salutation. Our good ladies, therefore, seeing that priests depend upon their beneficence, are puffed up with self-esteem. Having got rid of a husband's sovereignty, they prefer the independence of widowhood. They are called chaste and nuns — and after a seven course dinner, they dream of apostles.

Et post cenam dubiam somniant apostolos. Readers of Terence will remember the phrase *cena dubia* (a perplexing dinner), applied by the hungry parasite to a banquet packed so full of good things that you don't know where to begin.[17] Jerome often smears his barbs with a little of the ancient virus, as humanists are wont to do.

And now let us observe my Lady on the way to Church.[18]

You can see most women nowadays pack their wardrobes with garments, change their dress every day, and yet not get the better of the moths. She who is especially devout wears out only one robe at a time, pulling her rags out of full coffers. Her prayer-book is made of purple parchment. Gold is melted into letters and the cover is clothed with gems and Christ dies starving at her doors. When she extends her hand to the needy, she blows a full blast on the trumpet. When she goes to mass, she hires the town-crier. I lately saw a noble Roman dame — no names, else you will think this a satire [we should n't have suspected it!] — on her way to St. Peter's. Her eunuch couriers were in advance, and she was actually passing out pennies to the beggars *with her own hand*, to create a finer impression of piety. One old woman, covered with rags and the ravages of time [another bit of Terence — which I cannot translate [19]], ran ahead to get another coin. When she had reached her turn again, she got a fisticuff instead of a penny, and was covered with blood for her criminal conduct. Aye, avarice is the root of all evils, and that is why the Apostle calls it the worship of idols. . . . Peter said, "Silver and gold have I not, but what I have, give I unto you. In the name of the Lord Jesus, arise and walk." But nowadays many say, — not verbally, but their actions speak louder than words, — "I have not faith and mercy, but such as I have, silver and gold — that I don't give to you either."

If Jerome will keep on in that vein, no one will question his complete humanism, or his mastery of satiric description. To come down the centuries for a moment, history repeats itself in Alexandre Dumas *fils*, who, in his preface to *Les Idées de Mme Aubray*, remarks of certain fashionable dames that they show themselves on the steps of churches with missals in their hands, to indicate their intimacy with God, much as certain coxcombs, after partaking of a modest *table d'hôte*, stand outside the door of the Maison d'Or with an ostentatious tooth-pick between their lips, to indicate that they have the habit of dining there and the wherewithal for doing so. St. Jerome would sign his *pinxit* to this picture. I have only begun with his vignettes of Roman Society. You will find other victims of his wit in the same letter.[20] There is the fashionable young priest who trots round to all the best receptions, attired as immaculately as a bridegroom. There is the gloomy ascetic who lectures at *conférences religieuses* in exclusive houses, and beguiles the poor little women there, *miserae mulieri-culae*, always sorrowing over their sins and never arriving at the knowledge of the truth. These hypocrites put on a sad face and protract their long fasts by stealthy meals at night — prototypes of Tartuffe, Mr. Stiggins, and Kiesewetter in Tolstoy's *Resurrection*. And their get-up! — girdles and mourning clothes, bare feet inured to the cold, hair as long as women's (this hit would be lost on a modern audience) and beards as long as goats. St. Jerome distrusted a long beard. In an epigram deftly borrowed by Erasmus, he remarked, "If there is any holiness in a beard, nobody is more holy than a goat."[21]

This was the society that Jerome set about to reform, and fortunately not all the women at Rome were of the kind described in his satire. A number of sainted names meet us as we turn over his letters, three in particular, who were the strongest supporters of his programme — Marcella, Melania, and Paula, with Paula's daughters, Eustochium and Blesilla. Says the blasphemous Gibbon, "The profane title of Mother-in-law of God tempted that illustrious widow to consecrate the virginity of her daughter Eustochium." [22] It is well that Gibbon could not have made this remark in the presence of Jerome; he would have got as good as he sent. To these friends and others, Jerome acted as a father confessor, a guide, philosopher and friend. He gave them instruction in monastic practice, or, if the actual monasticism was impossible for them, their application of its principles to better living in the world.

For three years Jerome lived in Rome, and assisted Marcella in founding the first convent there. In fact Marcella made over her palace on the Aventine for that purpose. Jerome was strongly supported by Pope Damasus, and at his suggestion began a revision of the Latin Scriptures. He was Secretary to the Pope, and he implies that he had a fair chance of becoming Pope himself. But conservatives did not fancy his tampering with Holy Writ, and he was also criticized by the party in the Church who were opposed to the new asceticism. They accused him of improper intimacy with Paula; that charge is absolutely false and was retracted by the calumniator. But when in 385 Blesilla died, they maintained, with more plausibility, that the excessive penances imposed by Jerome were the cause of her death. At any rate, the storm broke upon him and he left the city. In company with Paula, he fled from Babylon, as he calls Rome, to Palestine, and in the very cradle of Christianity, in the little town of Bethlehem, he established a monastery and a monastic school.

Before we accompany Jerome and Paula in their flight from Babylon, I will speak of one matter in which the humanist cries aloud in Jerome. It is his dislike of an excessive use of allegory. Of course, in the exegesis of the Scriptures he was committed to the allegorical method, which he had learned in the East and which, thanks to Hilary and Ambrose, was rapidly spreading in the West. It was the "higher criticism" of the day. But when you come to the Pagans, "Thus far and no farther," said Jerome. As we shall see a bit more in detail in our last lecture, Virgil's fourth eclogue was currently interpreted as a prophesy of Christ.[23] Let us hear what St. Jerome says on the subject, together with certain remarks on a practice, which we shall also notice later, of piecing together lines or parts of lines from Homer or Virgil into what was called a patchwork quilt or *cento*, in such a fashion as to show that Homer and Virgil were wise in the mysteries of the faith. In a famous letter to Paulinus on the study of the Bible,[24] Jerome speaks of the fatal facility with which everybody tries to expound it.

It is generally admitted [he remarks] that only a doctor should practise medicine and only a carpenter build a house. The art of searching the scriptures is the only one that everybody is sure that he possesses.

He rubs in his point by quoting Horace, who said the same thing of the similarly abused art of poetry:[25]

"Learned and unlearned we all can scribble verse."

The *Scriptures* [St. Jerome goes on] are common property for
the loquacious old woman, for the loony old man, for the long-
winded public-lecturer, for every Tom, Dick and Harry to
preëmpt and tear to pieces and teach before they learn them.
Some with knit brows and an array of big words, philosophize
about Sacred Letters *inter mulierculas* [they address women's
clubs on the latest results of disintegrating criticism]. Some
learn — good Lord deliver us — from women what they teach
to men [*men* attended meetings of the women's clubs and
took notes on *female* higher critics]. And as if that were not
enough, they acquire a certain facility, not to say audacity,
of terminology wherewith they can instruct others in what
they do not themselves understand. They can wrest from
Scripture any meaning that they wish to find there. As
though we were not familiar with Homer-centones and Virgil-
centones and had not learned to call Virgil a Christian without
Christ for singing

> Now comes the Virgin, Saturn's reign returns,
> And a new race drops down from lofty heaven.[26]

All that is childish stuff. It is like the performance of a
mountebank. It is bad enough to teach what you do not
know, but even worse (if I may be allowed to relieve my
feelings) not even to be aware that you do not know.

St. Jerome is in fine fettle here. He talks very much like
a humanist.

The monastery founded by Jerome and Paula at
Bethlehem was a coëducational institution, but rather
on the plan of Harvard and Radcliffe than of our State
universities. Jerome had charge of the monastery and
Paula of the convent. There was a common church, and
a school for boys who were looking forward to the monastic career. He also put an inn nearby, as he writes a
friend, so that if Joseph and Mary came again to Beth-

lehem, they would not be turned away. The institution
proved popular. The enrolment was as embarrassing
as that of some of our larger universities to-day. "We
are overwhelmed with the crowd of monks that flock
here from the whole world," are Jerome's words.[27] He
found it necessary to retreat to a special cave, where he
stored his books and papers and where he had a goodly
band of scribes at his beck and call. It was literally a
den, for it was inhabited not only by Jerome but by his
pet lion — at least you will always find a lion in works
of art devoted to St. Jerome. The good beast doubtless
attended the saint in the desert, but I am not so sure
that he followed his master to Bethlehem. In another
letter, Jerome writes, "Shut up in my little cell, far from
the madding crowd, I mourn my past offences." [28]
It must have been, however, a cheerful kind of lamentation, for he knew how to make of his cell a Paradise.[29]
Nothing, surely, would have induced him to return from
Bethlehem to Babylon.

Paula also writes in a charming way about the simplicity of their life. She composes a little pastoral about
it.[30]

In this little villa of Christ, everything is rustic, and apart
from the singing of Psalms, there is silence. The ploughman
driving the share sings an *alleluia*. The sweating reaper di-
verts himself with Psalms, and the vine-dresser clipping the
shoots with his curved pruning-knife [the phrasing here is
from Virgil] hums some snatch from David. These are the
songs in our district. These are the popular love-lays. This is
what shepherds whistle; this is what heartens the tillers of the
soil.

In the school connected with the monastery, Jerome himself taught grammar (that is, literature), using as textbooks the ancient authors. His horror of the Pagans had vanished. He had no more dreams about the iniquity of his Ciceronianism. He had had to defend himself for his relapse, for breaking his oath to read no more Greek and Latin Classics.[31] The enemy Rufinus had brought this charge, and Jerome's defence is not altogether satisfactory; its strongest point is a *tu quoque* argument. He had apparently kept his pledge for about fifteen years. President Pease of Amherst, a deep student of St. Jerome, examined the classical quotations or reminiscences in the letters written before the dream, those in the next fifteen years, and those later, assorting the correspondence after the dream into equal groups. He finds that in the period before the dream there is one classical allusion for every 1.6 pages, in that which covers the fifteen years one in 7.7 pages, and that in those that remain the proportions are one in 2.7, one in 5.1, and one in 4.7.[32] This, on the whole, is damaging evidence. Jerome did exercise a certain restraint in consequence of his dream, but after this period of reaction, he ended his days in what President Pease calls "true and ripe liberalism." Even if we consider those fifteen years in which he conscientiously sought to purge the ancients from his system, I think that, if a modern writer displayed in every eight pages of his work a Classical reminiscence as neat as those of St. Jerome, we should call him incorrigibly a humanist.

It is particularly in his pastoral retirement at Bethlehem, from 385 to his death in 419, that St. Jerome was able to carry out an extensive programme of scholarship, some parts of which he had begun before, that puts him in the front ranks of scholars and humanists of all time. I will mention first his three lives of saints. This might seem a normal and not particularly noteworthy thing for a Christian scholar to do, but in the case of St. Jerome these little works have a special significance. For all three of the saints whose careers he chronicled were hermits of the desert. Their lives become a brief for monasticism and a symbol of the satisfaction that St. Jerome took in escaping from the turmoil of Babylon to the calm of Bethlehem. One of the lives, that of St. Paul, the first hermit, he had written at Antioch (377–379) shortly after his own experience in the desert. He now adds, in reminiscence of those days and with a renewed enthusiasm for the great reform, the lives of St. Malchus (386–387) and St. Hilarion (389–392).[33]

Jerome is thus one of the first in a splendid line of tradition that runs down the Middle Ages and culminates in Jacopo da Voragine with his Golden Legend. Jerome's works have a close connection with the poetical legends current at the time, developed, as we shall see, by Pope Damasus,[34] and likewise with the Greek Romances, most of which were written by Pagan authors. Jerome's style in these narratives is purposely popular, and it almost seems as if he had purposely introduced some of the miraculous elements. The possession of two styles, an esoteric, or scientific, intended for the inner circle, and an exoteric, or popular, intended for mankind in general, was as old as Plato and Aristotle — and is a desirable acquirement for a scholar to-day.

The first of these works is the *Life of St. Paul the First Hermit*. This Paul lived during the persecution of Decius (249–251). He fled to the desert east of the Nile, near Thebes. Jerome describes the surroundings of his hut with some appreciation. Perhaps there is some connection between monasticism and the growth of a deeper feeling for nature. There is a chance for it. The hermit turns his back on man for a life in God; yet if some craving for earthly friendship remains, the hermit's friends are meadow, stream, and grove. Sulpicius Severus, the biographer of the blessed Martin of Tours, describes with sympathy the life of a recluse of Egypt who had made friends with his trim little garden.[35] Whatever St. Paul, the first hermit, thought about nature, he spent his days in utter simplicity. The palm tree furnished him both food and raiment, — dates for one and palm-leaves for the other. Another of his kind lived on barley bread and muddy water thirty years. Another, whose dwelling was an ancient cistern, sustained himself on five rush-stalks a day. This may seem impossible, Jerome adds, to those who do not believe that all things are possible to them that believe.

Now the holy man is warned in a dream to go in search of one better than himself, and accordingly sets out on his travels. On the way he meets a centaur, and then a satyr. Lucretius denied the existence of them both, and so would Jerome, seeing that in both cases, it was merely the Devil in disguise. At last St. Paul reaches a cave in which dwells the famous Antonius, first of the Greek anchorites. Their meeting is described with an affecting simplicity.[36] "Tell me pray," the aged Antonius says, "how fares it with the race of men? Do new roofs rise in the ancient towns? Are there still men left who are entrapped by the wiles of the Devil?" The two saints live together for a while, miraculously fed by ravens, till Paul, feeling death approaching, asks Antonius to bury him in the mantle of St. Athanasius. Antonius, in alarm, seeks help from a neighboring monastery. On his return, he sees Paul in a vision singing with the angelic choir and surrounded by the host of prophets and saints.

The *Life of St. Malchus* includes more adventures. The hermit is attacked by Saracens, compelled to marry a captive maid — who turns out to be a Christian and marries him only in name. The two escape together, cross rivers and deserts, and are overtaken by their master, when a lion opportunely disposes of the latter but spares them. They flee on the camels thus happily provided by their late master's retinue, and found a monastery of which Malchus becomes head of the men and the Christian maid that of the women, as in Jerrome's own institution at Bethlehem. The story is pointed with a moral; it is an exhortation to chaste living at any cost. *"Castis historiam castitatis exposui."* These legends, that is, are a moral appeal to the popular imagination, as Jerome's hortatory epistles are to the cultured. The connection of the plot with the Greek Romances and the Greek New Comedy is obvious enough. Two elements are especially prominent. First, there are "hairbreadth 'scapes in the imminent, deadly breach," like the adventures of Daphnis and Chloe with pirates. Then there is the inevitably happy ending, as in any one of Terence's plays.

The *Life of St. Hilarion* is longer, but has not even the adumbration of a plot discernible in the preceding tales. We simply have a string of miracles, chiefly miraculous cures, and of the penances of pious men. There are one or two sensational scenes, as where the devil appears to St. Hilarion in a fiery chariot,[37] and one or two interesting descriptions, such as the account of Hilarion's personal appearance, a matter, of course, to which the saint paid no attention. His only concession to the pomps and vanities of this wicked world was to have his hair cut every Easter.[38]

These *Vitae Sanctorum*, then, show that a great scholar like St. Jerome could condescend to write popular novels, or rather short stories, not that he coveted mention among the authors of the best-sellers of the

day, — though that distinction was forced upon him, —
but rather that he had anticipated St. Gregory's idea
of giving Christian readers something safe and Christian to read, and something as exciting as Pagans had
in the Greek Romances.[39] There was also, as I have in-
timated, the higher purpose of making the life of asceticism attractive.

Of St. Jerome's learned commentaries on the Bible
and his controversial writings, in which he proved a
stalwart champion against the various heresies that
attacked the Church in his day, I cannot speak in any
detail. Some of these discussions appear in his letters,
which for their manifold pictures of the times and their
pungent satire place Jerome among the foremost letter-
writers of all ages. For some heresies, he found elaborate
treatises necessary. The writing of formal treatises
against heresy has a far off sound in these days of ours,
when the title of heretic is accepted as a compliment,
and an eminent historian of the beginnings of Christianity can declare that a departure from orthodoxy is
always in the direction of truth;[40] but we can bring
these ancient battles within range of our vision by re-
flecting that they had an intense political significance.
They meant at the time what to-day a magazine article
means, written by a Republican to expose the calamitous views of Democrats, or by a Democrat to expose
the calamitous views of Republicans. And even to-day
the controversial writings of a Tertullian, an Augustine,

a Jerome, have a vivid and a burning interest for anybody who believes that Christianity brought new truth into the world, and who wishes to find out just how that truth works out in human thought and human society. One permanent characteristic of a humanist is, as I have noted, that, while his thought is much occupied with the traditions of the past, he endeavors to apply the lessons of the past to the problems of the present. And that is precisely what St. Jerome was doing in his attacks on the Luciferians, on Vigilantius, on Jovinian, and, in his latter days, on the heretical ideas in Origen.

Most interesting to a modern reader is his assault on Jovinian for the latter's somewhat too easy and, according to Jerome, Epicurean views on celibacy. Many even in Jerome's day thought that his reply had gone too far; but then, as now, his sarcasms must have been read with relish. They contain, I am sorry to say, a smart excoriation of poor woman, and I shall pay no attention to them whatsoever. Poor woman had come down to those times laden not only with the primal offence of Mother Eve, but with the abuse heaped on her by Semonides of Amorgos, by Juvenal in his sixth satire, and by many others, from whose writings Jerome collects a most discourteous array of epigrams. He quotes with especial favor what he calls that "golden little book" of Theophrastus, in which the philosopher broached the question, as *Punch* did once, whether the wise man should contemplate matrimony, and concludes, I hesitate to say, that "ye cannot serve — books and a wife." [41] I remember an occasion when precisely that advice was administered by an elder scholar to a younger — advice neither relished nor followed.

Jerome's interest in the past is shown by certain historical writings that I have mentioned, — his continuation of the *Chronicle* of Eusebius, and his *De Viris Illustribus*, a kind of "Dictionary of Christian Biography"; for the illustrious men whom he treats are all those of the Church. It is the work of a humanist rather than an ecclesiastic; for it includes heretics as well as orthodox writers. Whatever their mistakes, these authors, thought Jerome, had made their contribution to Christian thinking and merited the title of illustrious men.

The *De Viris Illustribus* is one of the products of his retirement in Bethlehem. The continuation of Eusebius was written at Constantinople, as we have seen, in 380–381. At the end of his preface he refers to his plan for a history of his own times, but adds that he was forced to abandon it. The writing of contemporary history is a notoriously difficult task. Horace likens it to the attempt to walk on ashes that are spread over a bed of fire; [42] you begin with a sense of firmness, but feel uncomfortable before you have advanced very far. Livy, in his history of all Rome, turns by preference to the brave days of old, where he is free from considerations which, as he says, "though they may not divert the purpose of the writer from the truth, may cause him some anxiety." [43] Jerome is bolder than the Pagans. "It is not," he declares, "that I am afraid to write freely and truly of the living, — for the fear of God banishes the fear of men, — but, because, while the barbarians still revel and riot in our land, all things are in turmoil." [44] He meant to wait till the world had quieted down.

Alas, that moment of quiet never came. What would not the historian give for Jerome's account of his own times! Think what he had lived through, from his undergraduate days in Rome, when the Apostate Julian was on the throne, down to the fall of the city in 410, and beyond. Of course, many contemporary events, along with his incomparable pictures of Roman Society, are outspread in the vivid pages of his letters; but we have missed an orderly account of the great movements of the day, with their appraisal by the keenest of observers. When we learn also from a statement in his *Life of St. Malchus* [45] that he planned, but never carried out, an account of Christianity from the earliest times, we may well regret that his numerous other occupations prevented us from knowing St. Jerome as one of the great historians.

One vast plan he was enabled to accomplish, his new translation of Holy Scripture, which to-day is the accepted or Vulgate text. Jerome began this monumental labor, we saw, under the patronage of Damasus, and he finished it in his retreat at Bethlehem. He had to pro-

ceed cautiously, for the old versions, despite their im-
perfections, were dear to old-fashioned Christians.
They did not like it — St. Augustine did not like it —
when Jerome made Jonah sit under ivy instead of a
gourd-vine.[46] While he was in Rome, therefore, he attempted merely a revision of the current text (or texts)
of the *Gospels* and the *Psalter* on the basis of the Greek.
This revision is represented by the so-called *Roman
Psalter*. In Bethlehem he studied the six-fold text, or
Hexapla, of the Old Testament that Origen had prepared — the Hebrew in one column, the translation
known as the Septuagint in another, and four other
translations in the remaining columns. This revision is
represented by the so-called *Gallican Psalter*. Finally,
he turned from these approaches to the original text,
and translated it afresh in the light of his voluminous
scholarship and profitable experimentation. The final
work as we have it to-day is a mixture of these different
methods, incompletely carried out in certain parts. For
all that, it is a κτῆμα ἐς ἀεί. [47]

The text of the Vulgate in use to-day is that sanctioned by Pope Clement VIII in 1592. It is accurate
enough for all practical and spiritual purposes; but the
Church is not blind to the scholarly demands of our
times, and owing to the initiative of Pope Leo XIII and
after him of Pope Pius X, a Pontifical Commission was
appointed to prepare a new edition of the text of the
Vulgate. A most thorough and scientific procedure has

been devised by the learned Benedictine order, to whom the work was entrusted, and has already borne fruit in a monumental edition of the book of *Genesis* by the noted scholar Dom Quentin.[48]

One of the tasks that Jerome assigned his monks was to copy manuscripts of works both sacred and profane. That is a humanistic undertaking. St. Jerome was also a born teacher. He had ideas on paedagogy that may seem very modern — to one who knows not the ancients. One of his letters is devoted to the subject of the proper education of a little girl.[49] It is written to the girl's mother, who perhaps had asked for it. It is a sample of the innumerable requests for advice and information that came to Jerome in his retirement. Here is his method for teaching the alphabet.

Have letters made for her, of box-wood or ivory, and let them be called by their names. Let her play with them and *let the play be part of her instruction*. [I pause to let these modern words sink in.] She must not only get the right order of the letters and memorize them in a song, but now and then mix the alphabet, last with middle and middle with first, so that she may tell them by sight as well as hearing. But when she begins with trembling hand to draw the pen through wax, either let her elder's hand guide her tender finger-joints, or let the letters be graven on the slate, that the marks she traces be confined within the edges of those furrows and not stray outside. Let her learn to join syllables to syllables by the inducement of a prize — something very acceptable to that tender age. She should have companions in her task of learning, whose accomplishments she may envy and whose praises may spur her sense of shame. Don't scold her if she is slow, but arouse her ambition by praise, so that she may delight at victory and smart at defeat. Above all, don't allow her to hate her studies, lest the bitterness of them, acquired in childhood, may last to her maturer years. The very names wherewith she gradually learns to put words together, should be purposely chosen — that is, those of the Prophets and the Apostles and the whole line of Patriarchs from Adam down, and those of Matthew and Luke, so that, while she is engaged in something else, she may be laying up a useful store in her memory. Choose a master of sufficient age and good conduct and sound learning. No really learned man will blush to do for a neighbor or girl of noble family what Aristotle did for the son of Philip; for despite the abundance of good elementary teachers he taught him his letters himself. We must not despise as little that without which the great cannot come to pass.

Oh how many morals could be drawn from this letter of St. Jerome's! How one could quote Byron on how Horace should not be taught, and add a bit from Pestalozzi and Angelo Patri and the latest circular of a model school founded on love, not fear! What consolation could be administered to "research" professors forced to give a Freshman course, or to candidates for the degree of Doctor of Philosophy engaged in the humble, slighted trade of tutors! I will do none of these things, but leave them to your imagination, remarking merely that St. Jerome has shown in this chance letter that humanism and humanitarianism are sometimes one.

St. Jerome, without doubt the greatest scholar among the Latin fathers, was the fountain of scholarship and of humanism for mediaeval men. They drew not only from his prefaces to the books of the Bible, but from his numerous commentaries and controversial works on the

heresies that vexed the Church. They saw in him a
keen theologian, that is, philosopher, with the humanist's
sharp tongue, who could demolish Jovinian with repartee and flay Pelagius with a verse of Horace.[50] That
letter of his to Paulinus on the study of the Bible [51] was
prefixed to every copy of Alcuin's version of the text,
and of these there were many copies; when a scribe
reached the remarks about conceited ignoramuses lec-
turing on the higher criticism of the Scriptures to
women's clubs, he exclaimed *Deo Gratias*, and wrote
cheerfully on. Ordinarily a scribe exclaimed *Deo Gratias*
when he finished a work, but St. Jerome gave him cause
for thanksgiving at the start. Mediaeval readers also
devoured his little romances on the lives of St. Paul, St.
Malchus, and St. Hilarion. They read his one poem, an
epitaph for Paula,[52] not very good poetry, but then,
Cicero wrote poetry, too — less successfully, because
he wrote more. Jerome's praise is sounded by writers
of most diverse tendencies in his own times, such as
Augustine, Sulpicius Severus and Cassian. Among his
admirers in the Middle Ages are Lupus Servatus, Hinc-
mar, Honorius of Autun, St. Bernard and that excellent
humanist John of Salisbury, who entitled him *doctor
doctorum* and *doctorum doctissimus*.[53] When the Renaissance dawned, humanists greeted him again as a Christian philosopher with a style. Let Erasmus speak for
them all. He mentions St. Jerome as the chief of theologians, yes, the only one who deserves the title.

Immortal God [he exclaims], [54] shall Scotus, Albertus and authors yet more uncouth than they bluster in all our schools while Jerome, the only champion, expositor and light of our religion who by deserts should alone be famed is alone passed by in silence?

Erasmus does not hesitate to compare his style with that of Cicero and adds, — I am afraid he is waxing extravagant, —

For a truth, unless my love of that most holy man deceive me, when I compare the style of St. Jerome with that of Cicero, I seem to miss something in the latter, aye, in the prince of eloquence himself.

We can match this praise with a passage from Cassiodorus,[55] one of our Founders, written in his *Divinae Lectiones*, in which the tenets of the New Education were proclaimed.

Clear, learned, interesting [he says of Jerome], he had a ready abundance of styles for any subject to which his genius turned. Now he allures the humble pleasantly, now he breaks the necks of the proud, now with appropriate tartness, repays derogators in their own coin, now preaches virginity, now defends chaste matrimony, now praises the glorious battles of the virtues, now chides clerics for lapses and monks for depravities, but for all that, whenever the occasion offers, he intersperses a delightful variety of examples from the Gentiles, making everything plain, putting it all in good style, preserving in diverse sorts of disputations an even tenor of eloquence.

This estimate of St. Jerome, which reckons with the diverse strands of his character, echoed through the Middle Ages in a work that everybody read; and I doubt not it was universally accepted. Although some mediaeval dreamers had visions like that of St. Jerome, such legends no more show what the dreamer thought than St. Jerome's vow shows how he treated Cicero. I can find in the mediaeval literature with which I am familiar no condemnation of St. Jerome for breaking his vow and relapsing into Ciceronianism.[56] Perhaps readers did not take the matter seriously then. In fact, the only people I can discover who did take the matter seriously are Rufinus and the careful scholars of our day. If Jerome could have dreamed his dream again in the days of Cassiodorus or of Charlemagne or of Hildebert of Lavardin, or of Dante, to say nothing of Erasmus, he would have heard from the throne a gentle voice of benediction saying, "Tu et Christianus es et Ciceronianus."

CHAPTER V

BOETHIUS, THE FIRST OF THE SCHOLASTICS

A CENTURY of barbarism had swept like a wave over Roman civilization, or dashed against its coasts, when there suddenly appeared the most thoroughgoing philosopher, and, with the exception of St. Augustine, the most original philosopher, that Rome had ever produced. Boethius must not be considered an altogether isolated phenomenon. He lived under an Ostrogothic king, whose capital was at Ravenna, or Verona, or Pavia; and yet Theodoric, like Odovaker before him, had brought law and order into Italy; he was far more true to the Roman ideal than various of his Roman predecessors had been. After his initial deed of treachery, the base murder of his rival, for which he had abundant sanction in the acts of various emperors before him, — in fact this sort of homicidal house-cleaning had become a species of Imperial good form, — Theodoric ruled wisely and well. He was a worthy precursor of Charlemagne, who admired him. Boethius, then, was not fighting single-handed. His philosophical endeavors were in keeping with the spirit of the age, that general movement toward peace and consolidation which set in after the confusions of the fifth century, and prevailed as long as Theodoric reigned. Theodoric was an Arian, but he had the support of the Catholic clergy in his contest with Odovaker; and, though we shall note that divergence on this theological issue had unpleasant political consequences, the beginning of Theodoric's reign saw all factions of the church and the state well united.

Once on a time, Boethius's *Consolation of Philosophy* was one of the hundred best books — one of those books that no educated man left unread. That was still the case in the eighteenth century, and had been so since the Middle Ages, in which period his influence was sovereign. As Morris puts it in the preface of his edition of Chaucer's translation of Boethius,[1] "No philosopher was so bone of the bone and flesh of the flesh of Middle-Age writers as Boethius. Take up what writer you will, and you find not only the sentiments, but the very words of the distinguished old Roman." This is true in general, and it is true in great and special cases, as is testified by the names of his royal translator King Alfred, Jean de Meung, Chaucer, and Dante. Boethius was a name with which everybody had to reckon. He is one of the Founders.

The mind of Boethius presents a problem. Was he Christian or Pagan? It is rather late, in the days of Boethius, for a Pagan to have a prominent political career. How many times must the historian record the "final triumph" of Christianity? In Boethius's last utterance, his *Consolation of Philosophy*, the name of Christ is not mentioned, and the Holy Bible is not cited.

At the same time, Boethius is apparently the author of certain theological tractates. Are these little works spurious? Or, as a Renaissance editor suggested,[2] is the *Consolation of Philosophy* spurious? And if both are genuine, how interpret the latter work? Did Boethius in his dungeon throw over the petty complexities of theology and lapse back to Plato and Aristotle, the masters of ancient thought?

Answers have been numerous and diverse. First of all, we should take account of the political situation, and in particular, of the code of laws promulgated by Theodoric.[3] This code is exceedingly severe. For instance, capital punishment was decreed for perjury and for the bribing of false witnesses in case the guilty party was of noble birth; if he was of low birth, the penalty was the confiscation of all his property. Here is the law against public informers, who had been a curse of the state ever since the days of Tiberius. "He who assumes the function of an informer as an ostensibly necessary act of public utility, . . . even so, in our opinion, ought to be thoroughly discountenanced and . . . in case his accusations cannot be corroborated he shall suffer death by burning."[4] This ferocious law gave cold consolation to Boethius, as we shall see. As for Pagans, "If anyone be detected in offering sacrifice according to the Pagan rite, or if anyone be found practising the arts of a soothsayer or diviner, he shall suffer capital punishment. Anyone who is an accomplice in magic arts shall suffer confiscation of all his property, and if of high birth, be sentenced to perpetual exile, or if of low birth, suffer capital punishment." [5] Not much inducement to be a Pagan in the days of Theodoric.

I have cited only one or two specimens, but they indicate the character of this remarkable piece of legislation. The only code more stringent that has come to my notice is one proclaimed by an undergraduate publication of Yale University not many years ago, which provided *inter alia* that cutting chapel should be punishable with death. I imagine that Theodoric before he got through was reminded of the wise Horace's maxim, "What profit vain laws without morals?" [6] To put through a Constitutional amendment you must have the sentiment of the country behind you. Yet Theodoric meant to have his code enforced. At the end of it there is a vigorous statement that the laws apply to high and low, Romans and barbarians alike; the nobility is warned that there will be no respecting of persons. It is also stated that judges who cannot enforce the law shall at once report to the Emperor; "for provisions in the interest of each section of the empire," it is declared, "should be maintained by the central power." [7]

Obviously Boethius, as man and office-holder, could not have been a professing Pagan in the days of Theodoric. But while outwardly conforming to the new faith, he might have mentally accepted something quite different, particularly after the orders of his royal master had landed him in jail. The standard historian of Greek philosophy, Zeller, can call "the noble Boethius the last representative of the ancient philosophy; for though he may have associated himself externally with the Christian Church, his real religion is philosophy." [8] Even a Roman Catholic theologian, who presumably accepts Boethius's Christianity, assigns him a lowly place in the history of thought, as one of those who labored "merely to preserve what the past had bequeathed and to transmit the legacy to times more favorable for the development of Christian speculation." [9] This is true so far as it goes: but it does not go very far.

The first thing that we note about Anicius Manlius Severinus Boethius is his noble lineage. The *Anicii* were an extremely important family in the fourth century and still earlier. The first Roman senator to be converted to the new faith was an *Anicius;* he is celebrated in Prudentius's poem against Symmachus. The *Manlii* take us back to the very earliest days of Rome, while the *Severini* are a branch of the *Severi*, who rose to imperial heights. From first to last, Boethius is an aristocrat, with a sense of *noblesse oblige*. He was born about 480 A.D., and must have attained distinction early in both scholarship and politics. Left an orphan at an early age, he became a protégé of certain eminent men, particularly of Symmachus, and he married the latter's daughter. The mention of *that* name takes us back to the fourth century and the leader of the Pagans.

Boethius's father-in-law was a lineal descendant of Quintus Aurelius Symmachus the opponent of Ambrose, and bore his very names. The family had renounced Paganism; in fact Symmachus and certain friends of his, members of the most exclusive circle of the nobility, were now pillars of orthodoxy and foes not only of Paganism but of the Arian heresy; the importance of this fact will become clearer as we proceed. It is a natural state of affairs; in one age as in the other, the nobles upheld the tradition, whatever that happened to be.

We think of Boethius as primarily a philosopher, snatching the moments of contemplation from a busy life devoted to the state; but his youth may have been as sentimental and poetic as that of any youth. We know that pastoral verse was among his early efforts, and he also probably wrote elegies; not elegies in a country churchyard — elegies outside his lady's window.[10] One feels a repressed emotion in Boethius. He has absorbed poetry, as Plato had done, only in a more sombre fashion; his prevailing mood is nearer to Dante's than to Plato's. He has not Plato's divine gift of comedy.

Boethius's political relations with Theodoric start at least as early as 506 — possibly 504, the date of Theodoric's entry into Rome. The monarch found his advice useful on the most varied subjects.[11] As mechanical expert, Boethius gave directions for the construction of a water-clock for Theodoric's brother-in-law Gundobad, king of the Burgundians. As musical expert, he selected a harper for the court of Clovis the Frank. As financial expert, he helped to convict the paymaster of the Guards of an attempt to cheat the men with light coin; some writers have inferred, with no real evidence at their disposal, that Boethius was in charge of the public mint. He had an eye out for financial affairs, at any rate, for on one occasion he prevented a cornering of the wheat market. In 510, he was elevated to the consulship. The year 522 was, in external pomp, the most distinguished of his life, for his two sons were the consuls, attaining that office, like him, at an extremely early age; it was natural that the panegyric on their inauguration should be pronounced by their illustrious father. In the following year, if not before, Boethius was created *magister officiorum*, a high position involving constant attendance upon the king. In the next to the last year of his life, Boethius received a quite unexpected honor, conviction for high treason. He was exiled to confinement in a dungeon at Pavia, and the next year, whether 524 or 525 is uncertain, he was put to death. The execution of his father-in-law, Symmachus, took place one year later. The exact place of the philosopher's confinement was the *ager Calventianus* (Calvenzano) between Milan and Pavia. Tradition has it that the Lombard King Luitprand transferred his bones, and those of St. Augustine, to the cathedral at Pavia. They can be seen there at the present time. I saw them on one eventful day at five o'clock in the afternoon, having visited the birth-place of Virgil at five o'clock in the morning.

Boethius's great plan was to translate both Plato and Aristotle for the benefit of the philosophically minded of his times, when the readers of the original Greek were getting fewer and fewer. Probably he had the same dismal feelings about the future that some Classical scholars have to-day. His fears were justified, for a period of about eight centuries came on, in which virtually nobody in the western world read the works of Greek literature in the original. But let us take heart. Perhaps eight centuries from now there will be another Renaissance of Greek.

Boethius's undertaking was a large one. Jowett had quite enough of an order with Plato alone. Boethius meant to translate all Plato and all Aristotle. Furthermore, his work was not to be a mere translation. In his day, and in all ages since, Plato and Aristotle have stood for opposite types of idealism, Plato for the transcendence of the ideal and Aristotle for its immanence. This is a rough and general statement, one which many would wish to refine, but if not quite true for Plato and Aristotle, it describes well enough what the Middle Ages regarded as Platonism and Aristotelianism. Now Boethius was one of those who were dissatisfied with the tendency to divide Platonists and Aristotelians. His ultimate purpose was to show that there is no essential difference between the two schools. His idea was not, as is sometimes set forth to-day, that Aristotle was a second-rate thinker who developed into ponderous systems what Plato preferred to leave as hints, patiently dogging his thoughts, a sort of metaphysical Boswell. Boethius would rather have accepted the memorable title that Dante conferred on Aristotle, "the master of those that know."

Boethius began his great plan with a comment on a work of Porphyry's, entitled *Introduction to the Categories of Aristotle.*[12] This is a natural starting-point, a consideration of the nature of reasoning, of the problem of cognition or "epistemology," and of the method of reasoning. The text used by Boethius was a translation made by Marius Victorinus, which eventually proved so unsatisfactory that he threw it away, prepared a new one of his own, and wrote a fresh commentary. He was working out his plan on a large and leisurely scale. There is a striking difference between the two commentaries. The former is put in the form of a Ciceronian dialogue. Boethius and a friend called Fabius meet at a villa out of town on the Aurelian road, and hold their very abstract conversation, on a winter's night. Never had a dialogue been given such a setting; it suggests that the passion of these friends for the eternal verities was such that they forgot that it was night and winter. But the second commentary drops this conventional device, which Boethius had found difficult to maintain, and gives straight science without palliatives. His scheme of translation is something new, and exceedingly scientific. He fears, he tells us, that Horace would not relish his method, which is to render the most trivial phrases and particles *ad verbum*;[13] thus there is something even for μὲν — δὲ (*quidem — vero*, or *quidem — autem*), while the Greek ὅτι is responsible for *dico — quoniam* in indirect discourse.

This carefulness on the part of Boethius led to the creation of a new vocabulary for philosophy, worked out step by step in the Middle Ages and appearing in something like a final form in St. Thomas Aquinas. It is a novel and elaborate diction, admirably suited for the need. Its history has never been adequately discussed, nor has Boethius's contribution to it received the attention that it deserves. The humanists of the Renaissance understood it, in their way. "Boethius was the first," remarks Georgius Valla, "to teach us to speak barbarian."[14] Strange to say, I think Cicero would have approved the whole business. For Cicero was also concerned in creating new philosophical terms for new ideas, and he too declared[15] that his method was to render those terms *ad verbum* in language that must have shocked the purists of his day and almost shocked St. Jerome. At least Jerome cites Cicero's authority for his own inventions in his rendering of the Hebrew Scriptures, and declares that the latter were far less numerous than the "monstrosities" that the master of eloquence had devised in writings of far less compass.[16] Time has condoned these novelties. Who to-day would think of the words *quality* and *specific* as barbarisms?

But nobody was audacious enough to say *qualitas* before Cicero or *specificus* before Boethius.[17]

By helping to create a new philosophical idiom, Boethius performed a valuable service to the development of thought in the Middle Ages. There is also a passage in his commentary on Porphyry that has often been cited as the starting-point for the most important discussion that agitated the earlier period of scholastic philosophy in the Middle Ages. Boethius, after Porphyry, is speaking of the nature of universals and asks whether *genera* and *species* have a real existence? Do they subsist? And if subsisting, are they corporeal or incorporeal? If they are incorporeal, are they separate from sensible objects? He asks these questions in such a way that we can at least see that he is not a materialist. He implies his belief in the actual existence of abstract ideas. But on the issue that would enable us to class him as either Platonist or Aristotelian, he suddenly becomes silent. "'T is a lofty topic," he declares, "and one that requires further investigation." [18] Of course, that was precisely the question with which philosophers in the early period of scholasticism started their disputations; the schools of realism and nominalism derive from the different answers given to it. Boethius's attitude of reserve — ἐποχή, or metaphysical neutrality — seemed rather cold-blooded to the fighting logicians of the twelfth century, and one of them, Godfrey of St. Victor, wrote a little poem about it.[19]

Assidet Boetius stupens de hac lite,
Audiens quid hic et hic asserat perite,
Et quid cui faveat non discernit rite,
Nec praesumit solvere litem definite.

(Sits Boethius quite stunned by this disputation,
Listening to this and that subtle explanation,
But to side with this or that shows no inclination,
Nor presumes to give the case sure adjudication.)

As a matter of fact, Boethius's commentary on Porphyry was not the place to go into the matter, for the writer's immediate concern was logic and not metaphysics. Nor is it doubtful, I believe, when one looks at all the works of Boethius, that he did definitely take sides on this issue.[20]

After the two expositions of Porphyry, Boethius changed, or enlarged, or perhaps really first formed, his great plan. We must not imagine that he had settled all the details before he started on his first work, any more than that Plato's philosophy sprang from his mind full-armed, like Athene from the head of Zeus. Boethius now turned aside, or apparently turned aside, to write a book on Arithmetic. It is, I say, only an apparent deviation. He had come to the conclusion, it would seem, that to present Greek philosophy to his countrymen effectively, he had better lay the foundations by treatises on the liberal arts. For the work on arithmetic did not stand alone; it was followed by one on geometry, of which only portions remain,[21] one on music, which we have almost complete, and probably one on astronomy. There was also a mechanical treatise after Archimedes, and something or other besides from Plato and Aristotle.[22]

Just how much else he accomplished, we do not know. His purpose, once more, was to lead up to philosophical studies, and he had a great predecessor in this very undertaking — St. Augustine, who likewise, as we shall see, wrote treatises on the liberal arts. Those of Boethius became firmly embedded in the curriculum. The *De Musica* was a text-book at Oxford way down into the eighteenth century. Modern critics are dubious as to its usefulness for the study of music to-day. One of them remarks [23] that "the very eminence of Boethius makes it a matter of regret that he ever wrote upon music," and an Oxford professor declares that Boethius is "no more useful to a modern musician than Newton's 'Principia' to a dancer." [24] We can only the more admire that stalwart Oxonian conservatism which prescribed "Boethius on Music" for so many centuries.

Those of my readers who are musicians may be interested to know what, according to Boethius, a real musician is. There are three classes of people, he explains at the end of his first book,[25] who have to do with music — performers, composers, and critics. Those of the first class, like harp-players, flute-players, and organists, must be excluded from the number of real musicians, since they are merely slaves. Their function is concerned with mere action, production, and is as sub-

ordinate and slavish as is the material body compared
to the mind. Even a good performer is nothing more
than a good slave. Then there is the second class, the
composers, who are impelled to music not by reason or
philosophy, but by a certain instinct, or inspiration.
The Muses are responsible for what they do, not they
themselves. They too, therefore, must be counted out.
There remains the third class, the critics. "They alone,"
he declares, "are the real musicians, since their function
consists entirely in reason and philosophy, in a knowledge of modes and rhythms, of the varieties of melodies
and their combinations, in short, of all the matters that
I shall treat in Volume II, as well as of the achievements
of the composers." [26] I once asked a friend of mine, a
musical critic of some note, what he thought of this
doctrine. He replied that he thought that Boethius was
considerably in advance of his time and of our own. I
did not venture to submit Boethius's ideas to a performer or a composer.

Boethius did more with the Aristotelian part of his
programme than with anything else; he finished his
translations of the *Organon*, the works on Logic. When
about halfway through this undertaking, he also busied
himself with Cicero, perhaps because Cicero, no less
than Aristotle, had written on the subject of *Topica;*
Boethius, at any rate, wrote a work *De Differentiis Topi-
carum*, in which he compared his two authorities. This
is the same leisurely method that we noted before. It is

a method not incompatible with the development of side-interests.

The final act of comparing and reconciling Plato and Aristotle, he never lived to accomplish. This is sometimes called a Neoplatonic undertaking, because certain Neoplatonists had felt that the breach between Plato and Aristotle could be healed. As I am concerned to prove that Boethius was not a Neoplatonist, I would point out that the idea is as old as Cicero. Cicero, no less than Plato and Aristotle, had a remarkable influence on Boethius, and doubtless helped him to his conclusion in this important affair. For with both Cicero and Boethius, it is Aristotle that is harmonized with Plato and not *vice versa*.[27]

It was in the last dozen years of his life that Boethius wrote on a vastly different topic, or what one might imagine a vastly different topic, namely, theology.[28] There are preserved under his name four brief but pithy letters, addressed, one to Symmachus and the rest to a mutual friend, John the Deacon, dealing with theological subjects of great contemporary importance. That to Symmachus is entitled "How that the Trinity is one God and not three Gods" (*Quomodo Trinitas unus Deus ac non tres dii*), and presents a specially vigorous criticism of the Arian heresy. No. II, addressed to John, continues this topic; it is entitled, "Whether Father, Son, and Holy Spirit may be substantially predicated of Divinity" (*Utrum Pater et Filius et Spiritus Sanctus de divinitate substantialiter praedicentur*). The last in the series, "A Treatise against Eutyches and Nestorius" (*Liber contra Eutychen et Nestorium*), takes up one of the great controversies of the age, the doctrine of the Person of Christ. Boethius upholds the orthodox view against the divergent heresies of Eutyches, who discarded the human element in our Lord's nature, and of Nestorius, who discarded the divine element. The little work, which was written most probably in 512, is one of the best contributions to the subject ever made. The definitions of *nature* and of *person* given by the author became classical and were constantly appealed to by the Schoolmen; "Nature," according to Boethius, is the specific difference that gives form to anything; "Person" is the individual substance of a rational nature.[29] One eminent Oxford authority regards the latter definition as "still, perhaps, take it all in all, the best that we have."[30] Among the mediaeval thinkers, I would call particular attention to John the Scot, who wrote a commentary on the theological *Opuscula* of Boethius, and had the latter's categories in mind in a way not yet explained when he composed his masterpiece on the *Division of Nature*.[31]

In short, the character of this treatise is fully as philosophical as theological. The author's report of the council that received the letters of the Eastern Bishops on the two heresies does not read like the work of an ecclesiastic. The ecclesiastics present talked most glibly, he declares, but nobody knew what the talk was about. Boethius himself preserved a haughty silence. He looked about him like Ferinata in Dante's *Inferno*, "as if he had Hell in great despite." He feared, he says, quoting Horace, "lest I should be rightly set down as insane if I held out for being sane among those madmen." [32] Methinks I hear the lashing of a humanistic tongue.

The philosopher is also evident in the title of the third letter — *Quomodo substantiae in eo quod sint bonae sint cum non sint substantialia bona* ("How Substantives can be good in virtue of their existence without being Absolute Goods"). If this piece had been separately transmitted as the work of the author of the *Consolation of Philosophy*, and the other theological tractates had been all lost, nobody would have thought of questioning the authorship. As it is, it is part and parcel of this little collection, the genuineness of which has the best possible attestation in the manuscripts. To anybody who has read through, or read in sufficient extracts, Boethius's works on logic, the theological tractates seem altogether of a piece. It is the same mind here as there, only exercising itself in a different field, with the result that Boethius has started a new method in theology, the application of Aristotelian logic to Christian problems.

This was a fatal step to take, according to Dr. Paul Elmer More,[33] who, in his admirable volumes to which I have referred so many times, is not altogether courteous to the scholastics, St. Anselm in particular, whose ontological argument for the existence of God he calls a nightmare of logic. He attributes the bad invention of scholasticism, not to Boethius, to whom he makes no reference at all, possibly including him in the general condemnation that he visits on the legalistic Romans, but to Boethius's eastern contemporary, Leontios of Byzantium. I would relieve the latter of the odium, for, so far as I can gather, Boethius published first.[34] And I would invite the attention of Dr. More, and others of his way of thinking, to the results obtained by Boethius in his treatise on Eutyches and Nestorius, results that I am confident Dr. More would accept. I would also suggest that a better guide to the scholastics will be found in two works, one on "Natural Theology" (1915), one on "God and Personality" (1918), by the Oxford scholar Clement C. J. Webb, well known as an editor of John of Salisbury, and also — this is something to say — as profound a student of Plato at first hand as Dr. More himself.

Of course Boethius was not the first of the Christian thinkers to resort to Greek philosophy. This resort had been made ever since Christians had begun seriously to connect their faith with the great systems of the past. "As certain also of your own poets have said" — the beginning was made by St. Paul. "As certain also of your own philosophers have said" — this was the next step to take; it was taken, not only by St. Clement of Alexandria among the Greeks and Minucius Felix among the Romans, but by the Gnostic heretics before them, and, earliest of all, it would seem, by whoever wrote the prologue of the Gospel according to St. John. In St. Augustine, we have a thinker who had gone through all the schools and had formed his powers of thought by training in the ancient method. In one way, Christian theology is no different in kind from any thought that had preceded it. It is just as free and just as human. It works with the same categories. But it reckons with a new historical fact, the person of our Lord, and on the basis of that fact proceeds to revolutionize previous conceptions of the nature of God and of man. There have been similar epochs in the natural sciences, created by the discovery of new facts, like that of radium in chemistry, and that of the moving and decentralized earth in astronomy. After such an event, the mind of man works on in its former way, adjusting the new condition to the old.

Now, in this sense, Boethius's procedure was nothing novel. St. Augustine had resorted to Plato and Aristotle quite as frequently as he. In his tractate on the nature of the Trinity, Boethius modestly states that he is but following in the steps of his great precursor, St. Augustine. What is new is the creation of a system, the reduction of the terms of thought to Aristotelian logic, and the application of them to theological problems. Thus the problem of the Holy Trinity must come under Aristotle's ten categories, and the meaning of person and nature must be settled in accordance with Aristotle's treatment of definition and division. A whole new science of theological procedure has been worked out. Axioms are established to control the processes of thought. At the beginning of the treatise on the substantiality of good things, Boethius lays down certain axioms, — he adds that he is proceeding like a geometrician, — which shall govern the course of his reasoning. In brief, so far as method is concerned, the relation of Boethius to St. Augustine is not unlike that of Aristotle to Plato.

Another feature of the method introduced by Boethius is its recognition of a body of revealed truth which exists by its own right and does not absolutely need the help of the philosopher. But he can help; he uses the free power of reason to substantiate, or rather to corroborate, the doctrine of the Church. He is aware that he may fall into error in this attempt, and is willing to suffer correction from those who are more intimate with the implications of the revealed truth. Thus, at the end of his discourse on the Holy Trinity addressed to John the Deacon, Boethius says, "If I am right and speak in accordance with the Faith, I pray you confirm me. But if you are in any point of another opinion, examine carefully what I have said, and if possible, reconcile faith and reason." [35] St. Thomas Aquinas could not have put it more clearly. The whole programme of scholasticism is already in Boethius. Everybody recognizes that he furnished the Schoolmen, in his translations of

Aristotle's logical works, with the chief *corpus* of philosophical material that prompted thought in the first half of the Middle Ages. He also, as we saw, broached a problem that led to the formation of important schools of mediaeval thought. He likewise invented a new philosophic vocabulary, a development ever on the increase in the Middle Ages. But, most important of all, he illustrated, in these brief tractates, the application of logical method, as well as the new vocabulary, to theological problems, on the understanding that *fides*, the ultimate truth, may be supported by the free effort of the human reason. To this conclusion we are forced by the acceptance of the *Opuscula Sacra* as the genuine productions of Boethius. Prantl, in his well-known book of the history of logic,[36] rightly caught the spirit of these works, and declared them the output of the incipient scholasticism of the ninth century. That was in the days when a scholar who valued his scientific reputation would not dream of attributing the *Opuscula Sacra* to Boethius. Now that we must attribute them to him, former accounts of the development of thought in the early Middle Ages must be extensively revised and the influence of Boethius be more carefully followed, not only in the works of John the Scot, but in various unpublished commentaries of the ninth century. The history of the great movement known as scholastic philosophy begins, not with the contemporaries of Abelard, but with Boethius. From one point of view,

Boethius is the last of the Romans; from another, he is the first of the scholastics.[37]

Among the theological tractates is one that I have not yet discussed, no. IV in the series, called by editors *De Fide Catholica*, but in the best manuscripts not called anything at all. The title *De Fide Catholica* defines its nature. It is a kind of expanded creed, with a glance at Old Testament history, the progress of the Church, and the most important heresies. These are the doctrines of Eutyches and Nestorius, of the Manichees, of Sabellius and of Arius, that is, the very issues that were exceedingly urgent in Boethius's day; the author calls all these false views the work of those who think "in carnal terms."[38] I once wrote a doctor's thesis to prove that Tractate no. IV was not the work of Boethius; but as even doctors' theses are sometimes not infallible, I have deemed it expedient to recant.[39] The style of the little work is different from that of the other tractates — but so is that of the *Consolation of Philosophy*. Boethius, like Aristotle and St. Jerome, as we saw, and like many scholars and scientists to-day, cultivated an *esoteric* or technical style, intended for the inner circle of specialists, and an *exoteric* or popular style, intended for the general public. Distinguishing between faith and reason, Boethius applied the principles of the latter to confirm the doctrines of the former. He accepted, therefore, certain articles of the faith. Well then, why should he not have stated them? The fourth tractate gives us such a statement. He drew it up, I should imagine, to clarify his thought and to provide a basis for further procedure. He did not intend to publish it, and had not given it a title. But it might have been found with his papers after his death, and, very sensibly, added to his works; for it is a clear and admirably ordered account, not without touches of poetic intensity, and a dramatic scope which in the compass of a few pages takes the reader from the creation of the world through human history to the last judgment. The work is a little masterpiece.

We have seen enough, I believe, to put Boethius in his historical setting and to determine his intellectual attitude. He is a Christian humanist and, indeed, one of the most satisfactory representatives of Christian humanism that we have examined thus far. In temperament he is more equable and urbane than Augustine or Jerome, though he can exercise a humanistic tongue, and he is far more profound than Lactantius. In his day, the stirring conflicts of the fourth century with Paganism were over, and the church was more at liberty to assimilate the best of the past. Boethius was not only a philosopher but a man of letters, as we might not have known so well had it not been for his imprisonment, which occasioned the *Consolation of Philosophy*. It is an ill wind that blows nobody good luck. In his philosophy, one may apply to him what Sidonius said of Claudian Mamertus: "He was a man of wisdom, prudence and learning; he was a philosopher all his days without prejudice to his faith." [40] The mind of Boethius, like that of St. Augustine, was impassioned for the philosophic quest, in which he engaged without let or ceasing. It was his chief solace in life — *summum vitae solamen*; I am quoting, not from the *Consolation of Philosophy*, but from one of the logical works, "On Hypothetical Syllogisms," written a dozen or more years before.[41]

Philosophy is also for Boethius, as for Lucretius and Cicero and Lactantius, a patriotic act. In the busy year of his consulate, 510, he remarks, as he writes his work on the *Categories*,

Although the cares of my consular office prevent me from devoting my entire attention to these studies, yet it seems to me a sort of public service to instruct my fellow-citizens in the products of reasoned investigation. Nor shall I deserve ill of my country in this attempt. In far-distant ages, other cities transferred to our state alone the lordship and sovereignty of the world; I am glad to assume the remaining task of educating our present society in the spirit of Greek philosophy. Wherefore this is verily a part of my consular duty, since it has always been a Roman habit to take whatever was beautiful or praiseworthy throughout the world and to add to its lustre by imitation. So then, to my task.[42]

One might imagine that the speaker is Cicero. Boethius virtually declares that he is continuing the programme of his illustrious predecessor in the consular office, as the latter had announced it at the beginning of the *Tusculan Disputations*.[43] Cicero had already introduced Greek philosophy into Rome, but much remained to do. Nor did Boethius live to achieve all, or half, of his impressive plan. He worked in a different way. His interests were more immediately philosophical; his method was more scientific. And yet in this passage, and in the style and in some of the substance of the *Consolation of Philosophy*, Boethius declares himself the successor of Cicero. We must add him to the list of Christian Ciceros of which we found the fourth century to be full. And we must conclude that Boethius, while the first of the scholastics, is also the last of the Romans. His worship of the eternal Rome is as devout as that of Cicero himself.

Such was his career, — and it is all of a piece, — up to the last year of his life. Then came the *peripeteia* of his fortune — his imprisonment in the dungeon at Calvenzano, and his death by execution. The reasons for his sudden downfall may never be accurately ascertained. He denied the charge of the informers that he was guilty of secret negotiations with the court of Byzantium.[44] He indicates that he was also accused of the malevolent practice of the black arts.[45] We may waive both indictments, the latter on the ground of common sense, the former from our belief in the integrity of Boethius. Why had Theodoric, then, come to regard him, after all his services to his monarch and the state, as a public enemy? I shall try to answer this question after we have taken a fleeting look at the *Consolation of Philosophy*.

The *Consolation of Philosophy* is prison-literature, and prison-literature often takes the form of a theodicy.

The solitary thinker, beginning with the sense of his own wrongs, — unless he is aware that his punishment is well deserved, — seeks justification somewhere. If the world does not give it, heaven will. The tyrant may win for a time, but the righteous knows that his own purpose is attuned to the everlasting purposes, which ultimately know no defeat. This is the way that proud spirits think the matter out; for them, the mind is its own place. It is not for them to weep and wail, to pine away or to end their lives in despair, but rather to justify the ways of God to men, and to know that they share in His victory. Besides Boethius, we may cite as examples Dracontius [46] and Bunyan and Sir Thomas More. There is something of this fine despite of the present moment even in Ovid — little, I fear, in those other eminent exiles, Cicero and Seneca. But the blind Milton belongs in the company; his latter life was in a cell, though not one built of iron bars. I have recently come across an instance in the literature of our own ancestors. Mrs. Mary Rowlandson, who in 1676 was dragged from her burning house by the Indians and kept in captivity for twelve weeks, wrote a narrative of her experiences bearing the title, "The Soveraignty and Goodness of God." [47]

This, then, is Boethius's starting-point. To whom should he look for help but to Philosophy, the guide and solace of his life from earliest youth? He thinks of her in personal terms. She is an allegorical symbol, and by the power of his imagination becomes something more. As Natura spoke to Lucretius, Patria to Cicero, and the divine Roma to Symmachus, Claudian, and, none the less commandingly, to Prudentius, so Philosophia visits the exile's dungeon, chases away the singing Muses from whom her favorite was seeking an ineffective consolation, and administers her own remedies.

Viewed simply as literature, this is a great work, "a golden volume," as Gibbon remarked, "not unworthy of the leisure of Tully or Plato." [48] First of all, its simple and Ciceronian style is well nigh a miracle in view of the tendency of deliberate rhetoric toward that distorted ornateness that we note in Sidonius and other writers of the times. Further, in its composition, it represents an exceedingly skilful combination of several literary types. It is dialogue, of the kind that Plato and Cicero had made popular in philosophical treatises. It is a talk between Boethius and Philosophy from beginning to end. Philosophy is at first the good physician; she hardly expects her patient to answer back — but before long he gathers strength and takes his share in the argument. The work is also an allegory, so far as the person of Philosophy is concerned, and suggestive also of the allegories found in certain apocalypses, like the Shepherd of Hermas and the Poimandres of Hermes Trismegistus. This is not a mere device; Boethius's passion for the dry light of reason makes it natural for him to speak in personal terms. Philosophy steps into the scene by her own good right, and plays her part convincingly to the end. The work also belongs, as the title indicates, to ancient consolation-literature, of which Boethius knew abundant examples in Cicero, Seneca, and the poets. But it is also a kind of introduction or incentive to Philosophy, a προτρεπτικὸς εἰς τὴν φιλοσοφίαν, like Aristotle's work by this title, and Cicero's *Hortensius*. As one reads on, however, the value of Philosophy needs no demonstration; nor do the nature and efficacy of her consolation. Both these elements are caught up in a higher purpose, which is, as I have explained, a theodicy of great power and scope — a προτρεπτικὸς εἰς τὸν θεόν. To assert the eternal justice, it becomes necessary to solve the mysteries of divine unity and goodness, of fate and human freedom. The writer is setting forth all that he can see of life and time and eternity.

Finally, the structure of the work suggests yet another literary variety; for to vary the presentation, to break the flow of dialogue, a number of little poems are interspersed, — thirty-nine in all, — which now sum up the argument of the preceding prose section, and now themselves carry it on. They vary in poetical quality. Some are exceedingly good, some are only moderate, and a few are insignificant — that being the only way, according to the poet Martial, in which one can write a book.[49] The metres of the poems are varied and skilfully wrought out. Boethius tries almost every metre going, and invents two or three new ones. This mixture of prose and verse at once classes the work as a *satura*, a literary form that has no equal for its Protean changes of contents throughout its lengthy history. Our English satire is only one moment in its career.

The circumstances in which the *Consolation of Philosophy* was written make the study of the writer's sources peculiarly interesting. We are given a clue, I believe, to the right way to examine the sources of any ancient author. Sometimes, after reading dissertations, let us say, on the plagiarisms of Virgil, one pictures the poet at a large desk on which ten or a dozen volumes of his more worthy predecessors are displayed, from whom he filches a line here, a half-line there, a quarter-line there, an epithet there, constructing in this way a painful mosaic or picture-puzzle. Virgil himself had answered this kind of criticism, if one would only hear him; when somebody charged him with stealing the verses of Homer, he replied that it was easier to steal the club of Hercules than a verse from Homer.[50] He implied that the process of making great and Classical poetry which, like a liturgy, pays homage to tradition, is other than an act of petty larceny, or if conceived in the spirit of petty larceny, it inevitably pays the penalty of detection. Now in the case of Boethius, — and likewise in that of the exiled Ovid, — the thieving author had no wares from which to pilfer. Boethius laments, in tones too sincere to allow us to suspect a literary device, that his library had not been shipped to his prison.[51] I will not deny that a few books might have come to him, but not so many as the patient investigators of his sources have tracked in the text of the *Consolation of Philosophy*.[52] For me the conclusion remains that this great work is not a thing of shreds and patches, of clippings and pilferings, of translatings and extractings, but springs from two main sources, *ingenium* and *memoria*. For the ancients had not lost the faculty of remembering. When a Virgil or a Boethius composed, he thought out a plan, wrote from the fulness of his own knowledge and his own inspiration, which depended in part on wide reading in the best of literature. His mind was mature and well stocked. He had something to say. He spoke as a prophet of the great tradition, but he added to its richness. He translated or half-quoted or borrowed a phrase to make his meaning clearer, to lend it distinction, or to summon the reader to inspect the past; and his product is more and not less original for this trait.

I am dwelling on this point, not only to save Boethius's reputation in general, but to refute a charge brought against him, I am sorry to say, by that great scholar Hermann Usener, whose golden little book, *Anecdoton Holderi*, is in other respects the best that has been done for Boethius in our times — or was until Klingner's recent work appeared.[53] Usener [54] pronounces unfavorably on the orginality of the *Consolation of Philosophy*, declaring it a tissue of two main sources of entirely different nature — one an Aristotelian passage, translated straight out of Aristotle's *Protreptikos*, the other a lengthy extract from a Neoplatonic work. These two sections were tacked together by Boethius, despite their incongruous nature,— and possibly Boethius was not original enough even to tack them together, but found them so united in some source, which he proceeded to translate. He then prefixed an introduction and interspersed throughout the work, as thus conglutinated, a number of sorry poems, which make a startling contrast to their context; for there one hears the voice of the ancients, but in them, that of a child of the sixth century.[55]

I cannot attempt here a full refutation of Usener's hypothesis, but I should like you to bear it in mind as I sketch the contents of the *Consolatio*; knowing how unoriginal it is thought to be, you may be better able to appreciate how original it is.[56]

The writer begins with a disconsolate poem, in elegiacs — for it is a real elegy, unlike those of his young manhood; he now has some cause for lamentation. The Muses are sitting sadly about his couch, keeping his sorrow alive by their sympathy. Of a sudden, My Lady Philosophy enters, drives the false comforters from the cell and clears the air of sentimentality. At her bidding, Boethius describes the miseries which have befallen him, and thereby starts the question with which the metaphysical plot of this treatise begins — the nature of fortune, that ultimate principle which permits a good man to suffer. Philosophy declares that her fosterling is a pretty sick man; he is sadly in need of her remedy. In answer to his reproaches for her desertion in the hour of his need, she reminds him that he is not the first to suffer for the truth. Socrates, whose heritage the Epicurean and Stoic pretenders so sorely mistreated, Anaxagoras and Zeno among Greeks, Canius, Seneca and Soranus among Romans, were martyrs for philosophy — why should Boethius shrink from such a fate? There follows a fine and thoroughly characteristic passage on the contempt of evil, a kind of translation into metaphysics of the Horatian despite of the *profanum vulgus*, a sentiment to which Boethius was no stranger.

Wherefore thou hast no cause to marvel, if in the sea of this life we be tossed with boisterous storms, whose chiefest purpose is to displease the wicked; of which though there be an huge army, yet it is to be despised, because it is not governed by any captain, but is carried up and down by fantastical error without any order at all. And if at any time they assail us with great force, our captain retireth her band into a castle, leaving them occupied in sacking unprofitable baggage. And from above we laugh them to scorn for seeking so greedily after most vile things, being safe from all their furious assault, and fortified with that defence against which aspiring folly cannot prevail.[57]

If this is the voice of a child of the sixth century, it is either a pretty good century or a precocious child. And possibly both. He is not too young a child to have learned of the inorganic character of evil, and he knows how to transfer this metaphysical notion into poetical imagery in a dignified style. He has also read deeply enough in the history of philosophy to have selected as his favorite period the best of all periods, when metaphysics was the prime interest and thought had not slumped into ethics. Plato and Aristotle form a kind of philosophical orthodoxy, of which the later schools had preserved only broken lights. As Boethius expresses it, the mob of Epicureans, Stoics, and the rest usurped the inheritance of Socrates and Plato and tore fragments from the robe of Philosophy, each imagining that he possessed the entire garment.[58] Here, as in other points to which I have called attention, Boethius is following the lead of Cicero. For Cicero is, in the best sense of the term, the first of the Neoplatonists.[59]

Boethius then proceeds to enumerate his services to the state and to dwell on the injustice of his degradation; it is a brief *apologia pro vita sua*. How can the good fall so low, he ponders, while wicked men flourish like the green bay-tree; there is a great contrast between the world of nature, which obeys a just and unalterable law, and the world of man, which tosses in the perpetual and irrational changes of Fortune. This arraignment of the universal order starts the whole problem, for which, however, Philosophy has a solution ready. Her method, first of all, is to arouse in her patient a better mind, a spirit capable of receiving the cure which she can impart. She speaks of a "gentler remedy" which she will first apply, and catches at his persisting belief in Providence, — whose ways, to be sure, seem very dark, — as the one last spark from which his former ardor may be revived. The closing poem of the book pictures the clouded mind, from which the light of reason should drive all the passions away.

The first book is the opening act in a metaphysical drama; it presents, in a pictorial form, and with a truer sense of the dramatic than Cicero shows in any of his philosophical dialogues, a speculative problem which the following books are to solve. The poems have something of the effect of the choruses in a Greek tragedy or the meditative passages in Lucretius. They give the reader an outlook, and a downward look from the height to which he has climbed by the steep path of the argument.

With the second book begins the "gentler remedy." It consists of an exposition of the essentially fickle nature of Fortune, whose only law is that of constant mutability. What was he to expect? Fortune's slave must follow Fortune's will; in fact, her very mutability is cause for hoping now. But this specious reasoning — which Philosophy herself had characterized as "Rhetoric's sweet persuasion" — fails to satisfy.[60] She adds thereto the suggestion that the memory of past success should be a solace, and that, if Boethius will but lump his experience, he will find in the total more good than bad. The philosopher replies sadly with a sentiment that Dante and many others have echoed, that the memory of happier things is of miseries most miserable.[61]

But Philosophy enumerates the blessings that remain, — his wife, his sons, and Symmachus, — and by this simple appeal to human affection draws from Boethius the admission that some anchors still hold despite the storm.

Thus far Philosophy has treated the gifts of Fortune as absolute entities, absolute goods or ills. Encouraged by the symptoms of convalescence in her patient, she now advances a point in the argument; examining the so-called goods in turn, she proves that felicity is merely relative. This is part of the "stronger remedy" — and just here, according to Usener, begins the passage that Boethius translates from Aristotle's *Protreptikos*. But the preceding part is far more than an introduction; it is an important part of the whole argument, and, in my opinion, altogether of a piece with what follows.

Philosophy now analyzes various of the goods in turn, — riches, aesthetic enjoyment, fame, — with the result that all these are relative, depending for their significance on the personality with which they are connected. Indeed, Fortune is kind only when her fickleness shows the true nature of temporal gifts, discloses false friends, and thus, negatively at least, points the way to abiding human friendship and to the universal principle of love, the only source of absolute good. The finest part of this discussion is a passage on the evanescence of fame.[62] Usener may well be right in believing that Aristotle had made similar remarks in his *Protreptikos*, but Cicero, whom Boethius quotes, is surely a direct model, and a reference to Ptolemy shows that Boethius did not confine himself to either Aristotle or Cicero. He sums up the idea in a sombre poem which various scholars who have forgotten their Classics think a harbinger of the mediaeval brooding over the transitory glories of earth.[63]

> Who knows where faithful Fabrice' bones are pressed,
> Where Brutus and strict Cato rest?
> A slender fame consigns their titles vain
> In some few letters to remain.
> Because their famous names in books we read,
> Come we by them to know the dead?
> You dying, then, remembered are by none,
> Nor any fame can make you known.
> But if you think that life outstrippeth death,
> Your names borne up with mortal breath,
> When length of time takes this away likewise,
> A second death shall you surprise.

This, true enough, is in the spirit of Villon's *Ballade des Dames du Temps Jadis*, but it is also in the spirit of Cicero and Juvenal, of Ovid and Ausonius, and of the author of the *Book of Kings:* "Where is the king of Hamath and the king of Arpad, and the king of the city of Sepharvain, of Hena, and Ivah?" [64] Melancholy meditation on the passing of the beautiful or the great is not confined to the Middle Ages.

The third book develops in positive form the reasoning which the second has negatively suggested. The opening sections, however, merely repeat the method previously employed. The various goods are again examined, with more detail, to be sure, than in the second book. They are first discussed in general, and then each is considered in turn — wealth, office, kingship, glory, nobility, carnal pleasures. The conclusion follows that the understanding of the false goods will lead us to the true. There certainly are traces of Aristotle apparent, but Epicurus is also mentioned and his doctrine of the *summum bonum* is briefly treated; Catullus is quoted; Decoratus serves as an illustration from Boethius's own times; the Roman praetorship is discussed; Nero, Seneca, Papinianus, and Antoninus are passed in review; and the argument is colored with personal touches, including a delicate compliment to the philosopher's wife and sons. In this section, therefore, while the writer is dependent on various thinkers of the past — here Aristotle notably — for some of his conceptions, he has combined diverse elements in an original fashion and fused the whole with his own personality.

The positive part of the "stronger remedy" appears in the latter portion of the book. The goods are subjected to a fresh analysis, this time to show their essential unity and their dependence on the ultimate principle of the good: *sufficientia, potentia, claritudo, reverentia, laetitia* have value and are worthy objects of human ambition, but only because they present different aspects of the *summum bonum*, the goal to which they lead. Man, therefore, should strive directly for this final idea of good, and not for the broken lights of it. But this source of all goods may be approached only by the way of prayer; so Philosophy prays to the Highest Good. The argument then turns to an analysis of the *summum bonum* and demonstrates its existence, its perfection, its unity, its inherence in God. Thus the idea of Good is identified with God, though the converse proposition, that God is nothing more than the idea of Goodness, does not follow; for the underlying conception of the divine nature is not idealism but personal theism — a step that neither Aristotle nor Plato (except for pictorial purposes in the mythological *Timaeus*) could quite take. But this God, though omnipotent, is incapable of one thing, evil, which is thereby pronounced non-existent. Dropping this utterance as a seed of further inquiry, Philosophy closes the book with a song on the "lucid source of good," illustrating her theme by a somewhat perverted application of the story of Orpheus and Eurydice that no lover, Browning, for instance, would approve.[65]

The treatment has been most impressive in these last chapters; the argument moves with a majestic sweep to the conclusion, which, like that of the first book, may fairly be called dramatic. In this entire passage, Plato is much more prominent than Aristotle. He is quoted several times, and the poetic prayer is a kind of summary of the *Timaeus*. But Boethius goes beyond both Plato and Aristotle, as I have pointed out, in his accep-

tance of a personal theism. He invokes the authority of
Plato for the need of asking divine aid before undertaking a great metaphysical quest, but while Plato calls
on θεούς τε καὶ θεάς,[66] Boethius prays to the very Being
that he is attempting to prove, assuming, it would seem,
that faith in deity must precede the endeavor to demonstrate its existence — *credo ut intellegam*. This proof,
therefore, to quote again from the treatise on the
Trinity, the philosopher does not discover, but corrob-
orates something that "stands by itself on the firm
foundation of Faith."[67]

Philosophy's stronger remedy has now been administered; she has shown her patient that the source of all
goods, and hence of the best fortune, is still at his disposal. There are some difficulties, however, still untouched — one in especial at which Philosophy has
hinted at the end of the third book. How can evil exist
in the presence of a Personal Good that is at once
benevolent and omnipotent? At the opening of the
fourth book, Boethius at once attacks this problem,
which has been his chief perplexity all along, and the
discussion of the nature of evil occupies the greater part
of this book. Philosophy demonstrates that the good
are always rewarded and the wicked always punished;
in fact, the latter virtually cease to exist. It is, finally,
the presence of mere brute chance, which intrudes after
moral evil has been comfortably explained, that leads
to larger issues, and, necessarily, to a new turning-point

in the argument. The new question is hydra-headed, Philosophy declares: the proper answer to it involves the discussion of five distinct problems — the simplicity of providence, the chain of fate, chance, divine cognition and predestination, and freedom of the will. With the words, "Leading off, as it were, from a new starting-point," [68] she approaches the first of these matters; precisely at this point, Usener sets the beginning of the Neoplatonic text. Surely the last part of the supposedly Aristotelian portion has been getting rather ethereal for Aristotle — and a bit too theological for Plato. Boethius is resorting to Plato and Aristotle as ever, — to the Stoics as well, — but he is thinking the thing out for himself in his own way.

"Leading off, as it were, from a new starting-point" — these words might indicate, as Usener thinks, that Boethius here takes up a fresh source; they might, however, simply mean that at this important turn in the reasoning a new method or line of thought is approached. Philosophy has been discoursing on human and physical evil; now, neglecting this aspect for the moment, she starts at the other end, at the divine simplicity where the thought of evil is out of question. Indeed, when we find Cicero using the same words at a similar division of the argument,[69] it becomes clear that Boethius is merely following his example.

Philosophy takes up the first two of the problems above mentioned, devoting to them the remainder of the fourth book. It is, after all, one problem, for the "simplicity of the divine providence" is but the inner aspect of which the "chain of fate" is the outer expression. Providence conceives, fate executes. Providence is simple, stable, eternal; fate is composed of multifold agencies, acts and shifts constantly, and is subject to time. Fate includes weather and the fortunes of men, which are thus indirectly of divine appointment. All, therefore, is done well, even by the apparently wicked, of whose moral temper only the all-seeing judge can be certain. Boethius reinforces his point by a witty quotation from Lucan,[70] who, so far as I am aware, was not often read by Neoplatonists. God gives to each, Philosophy continues, good and bad alike, exactly the medicine that his cure demands; perhaps the prison, she intimates, is exactly what Boethius needed. Nor is there any escape from the Divine dispensation. One may leave the order in which one is set, but only to fall into another order. Love rules all, and nothing can exist unless it return to this love that gave it being. Thus all fortune is good, and the sage should be as eager for his trial as the soldier is for battle. Every Hercules has his labors, but if he endures, heaven is his reward.

Throughout this discussion, Boethius is reckoning with certain ideas of the Neoplatonists. They, too, distinguished between providence and fate, but went much more minutely into the sorts and kinds of fate and of the different entities that led in a definite hierarchy from the one omnipotent essence, which was too holy and abstract even to name, down to that evil substance, matter. Boethius, however, is not afraid to name the supreme essence; he calls it God, he remarks, in the good old-fashioned way. But he does not bridge the gap between God and his world by any elaborate series of graded abstractions — mind, soul, nature, and the rest. Fate is directly under the control of Providence, which is of the very heart of divinity itself, not a principle depending on it at third or fourth remove. And the Neoplatonic agencies of fate, including angels and demons and the influences of the stars, are all lumped together as possible manifestations of the *fatalis series*, the order of fate. Any contemporary Christian theologian would not have put it otherwise. That is to say, the intimate association of fate with the providence of the Deity, as well as the wholesale levelling of the Neoplatonic hierarchy, is tantamount to an attack on a cardinal feature of that system. And so, more significant still, is the assumption of a personal Deity in place of the ineffably transcendent Being, or rather Superbeing, of the Neoplatonists.

At the beginning of the fifth book, we find Philosophy rather coquettishly changing the subject. The stronger remedy is now administered. Boethius has turned from the false goods to the true good, has seen that moral evil does not exist, and that even the shifts of fortune are part of the divinely appointed order of fate. What need of further argument? Still, though morally cured, the philosopher is not yet mentally illuminated as to the remaining questions bound up in the problem of fate, and insists now on the answers to these. With the discussion of chance, predestination, and freedom, the theodicy, and with it the full consolation, is brought to a close. I shall attempt to guide you no farther into Boethius's well-ordered thought.[71] If he has not quite solved the problem of freedom, we may pertinently ask who has? His solution, at any rate, is in accord with Christian theology in its insistence on the two opposing and logically contradictory principles of human freedom and divine omniscience.[72] Deity is personal and prayer is a vital act. "Wherefore fly vices, embrace virtues, possess your minds with worthy hopes, offer up humble prayers to your highest Prince. There is, if you will not dissemble, a great necessity of doing well imposed upon you, since you live in the sight of a Judge who beholdeth all things." [73]

These stately words, with which the *Consolation* ends, are anti-Pagan in general and anti-Neoplatonic in particular. I need not further labor either of these points. The Pagans are constantly used; both method and material come from Plato, Aristotle, and the "plebeian" philosophers. The thinker reasons solely with his own powers, without any revelation, save that of Philosophy, who is naught but the idealization of his own intellect. But the result fits in neatly with the revealed truth of

Christian theology. The latter is in the background of the thinker's consciousness. He is proving as much of *fides* as *ratio* will allow him. That explains why there is not a trace of anything specifically Christian or Biblical in the entire work; the assumption of any portion of faith in an endeavor of the unaided reason would defeat its very purpose. In similar fashion, though with a different goal in view, Minucius Felix — as we saw in our second lecture — carefully excluded Biblical quotations and the very name of Christ from his Christian apologetic. On the other hand, there must be nothing in such a *Consolation of Philosophy* that contravenes the principles of the faith. One or two points — particularly Boethius's theory of creation — call for comment, but, in brief, there is nothing in this work for which a good case might not have been made by any contemporary Christian theologian, who knew his Augustine.[74] Had Theodoric suddenly repented of his decision and the life of Boethius been spared, I can readily conceive that, after reconciling Plato and Aristotle, he might have gone on to harmonize the result with the doctrine of the Church, and thus have saved St. Thomas Aquinas his gigantic task, or, rather, have performed it in a different way.

But Theodoric did not repent. Boethius met his death. And not long after, so did Symmachus and John the Deacon, if he is the Johannes who had been elevated to the Papacy. The explanation of this *volte-face* on the

part of Theodoric, I believe, is that the circle of Boethius, in particular, and the Senate, in general, formed
the core of the Catholic conservatives who were bitterly
opposed to his Arianism. This issue also had its political
significance, for the Catholic conservatives were also the
old Roman conservatives, and whether or not they were
actually in communication with the Eastern Empire,
they were only biding their time. Theodoric saw it all
and struck suddenly, — and wisely for his own interests, — before the danger should come to a head. His
ostensible charge against the accused was treasonable
negotiation with the Eastern Empire; the actual reason
could hardly be stated.[75]

One of the mediaeval lives of Boethius states that he
was called St. Severinus by the provincials.[76] Those
provincials were wise persons. So was Abelard,[77] who
stated that the noble Roman senator had fallen with
Symmachus in that persecution in which Theodoric
raged against the Christians. So was Dante, who placed
the *anima santa* of the philosopher in the *Paradiso*, and
spoke of his coming from martyrdom and exile unto that
peace.[78] The learned Bollandists of the eighteenth century in their *Acta Sanctorum* call Boethius *catholicissi-
mus*, give him the title of saint, — St. Severinus Boethius, — and record his life with that of his friend Pope
John on May 27.[79] But no more recent publication,
authoritative or unauthoritative, on the saints of the
Church, so far as I know, ventures to include his name.[80]

I wish that someone influential with the Holy See would present a petition in favor of St. Severinus or St. Boethius, for, if I have stated the facts about him, the logic of the case seems inexorable. If he was put to death partly because of his defence of the Catholic faith against an Arian monarch, he suffered martyrdom; and if so important a person suffered martyrdom, he deserves canonization. Indeed, the honor might be given anyway to the the first of the scholastics; or — a point that may appeal to His present Holiness, once prefect of the Biblioteca Vaticana — a certain saintliness attends a scholar who lost so fine a library and who yet could transport so much of it, inside him, to his dungeon-cell.

CHAPTER VI

THE NEW POETRY

A NEW revelation, a new faith, a new philosophy — that means, or ought to mean, a new poetry and a new art. In the earliest stages of Christianity, there was not much place for art or *belles lettres*. Christian poetry was bound at first to subserve the needs of the Church. It was practical, just as the earliest Greek tragedy was practical, subserving the needs of a certain god. No poetry, and no religion, that is not also art will long survive. Neither will art for art's sake, art devoted to the beautiful and absolutely nothing else; for too often that means, not what it should by definition mean, but rather the proclamation of weird immoralities by an unbalanced and generally impecunious artist; it is art for the artist's sake.

The earliest form of poetry devoted to the needs of the Church is a poetry of defence, apologetic, following in the wake of the prose apologies, like those of Tertullian and Minucius Felix. We find a curious specimen in the third century, the *Carmen Apologeticvm* of Commodian, a converted Jew born at Gaza in Palestine, whose most interesting characteristic is his illiteracy — or his unmetricality. His little knowledge of the Virgilian hexameter was a dangerous thing for art; his verse is fearfully and wonderfully made. But it is an extraordinarily significant landmark in the course of Latin versification from Classical times down into the Middle Ages.

If Commodian marks the depths to which apologetic can sink, Prudentius shows how high it can rise.[1] Pray let not the modern reader imagine that a forbidding term like "apologetic" precludes the possibility of good verse. Let him rather read the *Contra Symmachum*, of which I gave an idea in the opening lecture; he will find there a new sort of epic, on a high theme, a battle of mighty forces, not in the legendary past but in the present, with the human race as prize.

The same two poets represent the worst and the best in another form of verse to which an equally unattractive name, didactic, is given. Commodian's poem,[2] called *Instructiones*, is divided into acrostic paragraphs. The Pagan gods have each his paragraph, signed acrostically with his name. This is not a bad mnemonic device; learn a paragraph and you will have a god. Who can forget what Saturn is like after the following? I translate the rude original into even ruder lines, preserving the acrostics.

> Senile Saturnus, if senile, how god?
> A god that eats his sons strikes me as odd.
> Tortured with terror — for no god was he —
> Under his belt he stowed his progeny.
> Raised on Olympus, king of earthly line,
> No god, the coxcomb *thought* himself divine.
> Unwary dotard, he gulped down a stone.
> So scaped the next god, who as Jove is known.[3]

I might add a specimen of Commodian's verse:

Terrori/bus ac/tus // sed qui/a deus / non erat / ille —

every foot but the last two (which are prose rather than verse) contains some metrical howler that would horrify a Sub-Freshman, or that ought to horrify a Sub-Freshman. The poem ends with a description of the Millennium. In the final couplet, the author remarks that the curious may detect his name in his very verses. If the curious will take the successive initial letters, beginning with the last verse and going backwards, he will spell out the legend COMMODIANUS MENDICUS CHRISTI, — Commodian, the Beggar of Christ. We may allow this humble title to cover the multitude of Commodian's doctrinal and poetical sins.

A much greater in didactic poetry than Commodian — in fact a worthy descendant of the royal poets of antiquity — is again Prudentius. I shall have to discuss his works separately according to the classes of poetry that I am describing (*disiciam membra poetae*), though he deserves better treatment than this; for his poetical achievements give him a place among the Founders. Just now I will say merely that he was born in 348 and died about 410 (the date of the sack of Rome), and that he came from Spain.

Prudentius has left two specimens of didactic poetry, the Greek titles of which, *Apotheosis* and *Hamartigenia*, will lure few readers to examine their contents. The subject of the first has often been called an argu-

ment on the Holy Trinity. Part of the problem of
the Trinity is involved, but only part. The poem is primarily concerned with the person of Christ and through
Him with all mankind. The poet has a vision of a Lord,
both human and divine, who is the leader of his race.
For frail humanity, despite its sin, shares with the God-
Man both its present lot and his apotheosis. *This* is the
subject of Prudentius's poem, the apotheosis, or deifica-
tion, — *divinatio*, as the subtitle defines it, — not only
of Christ himself, but of man.

This work must have produced a profound impression
on the contemporaries of Prudentius. To repeat the
phrase that a French critic whom I mentioned applied
to the *De Officiis Ministrorum* of St. Ambrose, it was a
poetical, as that was an intellectual *coup d'état*.[4] For the
first time, Christians had an imaginative presentation in
excellent verse of the inmost mysteries of their faith.
This is what "didactic" poetry becomes when treated
by Prudentius. The author of the *Apotheosis* must have
known his Virgil as intimately as Virgil knew his Homer
and his Lucretius. I am not speaking of direct appro-
priations, which have all been duly collected and which
do not bulk large,[5] but of the general flavor of Prudentius's verse. He has not the magic touch of Virgil, but
he has mastered the art of the Virgilian hexameter with
more delicacy than those martial and resonant singers,
Juvenal, Lucan, and Claudian. Without the strength
and the sublimity of Lucretius, he has evened off the

crudities of Lucretius's splendidly archaic verse. Manilius had achieved a similar polish, but has nothing of
Prudentius's originality of expression or intensity of
feeling.

Now that we understand the real subject of the *Apotheosis*, it is easier to see that the *Hamartigenia* is a com-
panion-piece. The sub-title, *De Origine Peccatorum*,
explains its theme. Roughly speaking, — the comparison must not be pressed, — the former is a "Paradise
Regained" and the latter a "Paradise Lost." To illustrate his method and the spirit of his argument, I select
the poetic treatment of the problem of evil. Here he pays
particular attention to the views of the heretic Marcion.
Marcion was one of the higher critics of the Scriptures.
He was a metaphysical Puritan, who could not attribute
to God the creation of evil. The presence of evil he
would not deny, and therefore he found it the work of a
rival God, a power of darkness and malignity. As matter is a form of evil, it is this black Deity, the Demiurge,
who created the world. The Old Testament gives the
account of his performances, and therefore the Old
Testament, with considerable portions of the New, is
not a part of the real Christian revelation, and should
be excised from the Scriptures of the Church. Prudentius likens Marcion to Cain, in that he assassinates the
substance of God, dividing it into good and evil.[6]

Now, though Prudentius parts company with Marcion in this matter, he is quite as insistent as he, or

Plato, that the essence of Deity harbors no evil. How, then, does evil creep into the world? God has assuredly created the world and with it man. It is Lucifer first, and then man who, by the free act of his will, has chosen the evil course, and thereby opened the floodgates to all the maladies to which nature and the soul of man have since been heir. For in endowing man with freedom, God has created the possibility of evil, leaving to man the question of its necessity. We Christians, says Prudentius, are well acquainted with Marcion's evil God; he paints the ogre, though in phrases from Virgil, with the lurid and unmistakable features of the Devil.[7] Marcion, he implies, is repeating in universal terms what the primitive Pagans did in a more diversified and picturesque fashion when they erected separate shrines to Fever and Scurvy and the host of minor imps of darkness. The problem of physical evil has no terrors for Prudentius. He recounts, in perhaps the strongest passage of the poem, the gradual transformation and degeneration of nature ensuing on the evil choice of the perverted angel and of perverted man.[8] Both Virgil and Lucretius, who furnish various details of this description, would sympathize with the reasoning that underlies it. It starts with the principle that

Nature takes pattern from the sins of man.[9]

The spring is not muddy till the soil pollutes it. The steel is not responsible that is directed by the murderer's blow. The lion is not guilty of the human blood that flows in amphitheatres. Translate these instances into modern terms, and though scientific invention has multiplied the examples, the principle remains the same. Gasoline is not an evil because a young Automedon drives his car over a human being. Prudentius sweeps through history to recount the evils that have come in the course of human progress in the arts. He rises to a Lucretian intensity in his denunciation of human cruelty and greed.

> Ah me, what suffering has shameless war
> Brought on mankind! What iron savag'ry
> Has crushed the vanquished with the victor's heel! [10]

We rebel, and ask how a benevolent God can permit it all. But God *is* benevolent; none but a benevolent God could give to man the boon of resurrection. And he has also given man the boon of freedom. There, once more, is the answer. Without freedom, the prize of attainment is impossible. With it, the way is open for the very course of sin and suffering that man has made his own. Freedom is the cause of the good and the evil in human society in this present life, and freedom is ours to choose our lot in the life to come. The poem closes with the picture of these different lots, an eternity of blessedness or an eternity of hell. Between them is a temporary state, assigned to souls too stained with sin to enter at once into the everlasting joys to which they are ultimately destined; the doctrine of Purgatory, toward which Plato and Cicero and Virgil had led the way, was becoming Catholic in Prudentius's time. The poet, conscious of his infirmities, prays for himself one of the more comfortable corners in the Inferno, where he will not see the visage of the Evil One and where

> The tempered heat exudes a vapor mild,
> And where Hell's furnace breathes a gentler blast.[11]

This unfortunate petition has excited the ridicule of critics. An epigrammatic historian of Latin literature rather blasphemously suggests that Prudentius was attached, or had been attached, to the Roman hot bath.[12] What the poet would have said if he had spoken simply would be, "Lord have mercy on my sins." The unhappy imagery with which Prudentius expressed this meaning has at least an historic significance; it is a precursor of the dusty wind and the milder heat of the Limbo in Dante's *Inferno*.

I would not make too much of this lapse on the part of our poet, for it does not represent the spirit of his work. As in the *Apotheosis*, he has done a remarkable thing. He has supplied Christian readers with a new Lucretius, a *Lucretius Christianus*. Taking the two poems together, we find that their theological titles cover a variety of topics familiar to the reader of Lucretius — the nature of the soul, the question of immortality, the creation of the world, the freedom of the will, the origin of evil, the descent of man, and the corruption of nature. Those who read Lucretius for all that he burned to say, and not merely for the purple patches of sublime poetry which makers of anthologies instinctively seize, will find these two poems by Prudentius of much interest, both for their own argument and for their relation to Lucretius's philosophy. Prudentius anticipates the mellifluous Cardinal Polignac in composing an *Anti-Lucretius*, in a fashion more effective because less obvious.

Of the new Christian Romance, the legend of saints, later to be gathered into a Golden Legend, I gave some account in speaking of St. Jerome.[13] The matter of such legends passed into verse, and thus a third variety of Christian poetry was created. Pope Damasus, the friend of St. Jerome, had a gift for composing epitaphs in neat, or at least brief, verse; in fact his productions constitute a little chapter in the history of Christian epigraphy.[14]

It is easy to see that, if you allow an epitaph to grow, — to grow too large for a tombstone, — it is no longer an inscription but a poetical narrative or biography. If long enough, and if the hero is heroic enough, we have an epic. If the hero is a saint, his life includes some touch of the miraculous; the result is a poetical legend. There is a little poem attributed dubiously to Damasus, which commemorates the martyrdom of St. Agatha.[15] It is a doggerel affair, with end-rhymes. For the first quality it might be assigned to Damasus; for the second it probably cannot be. It is a useful bit for our purpose, as it well illustrates the transition from the epitaph to the legend.

For the best poetical legends, we go to Prudentius, as we go to him for the best of almost any kind of Christian poetry in the fourth century. His work, as usual, bears a Greek title, *Peristephanon* — "The Martyrs' Crowns." It contains fourteen poems on the lives and deaths of famous martyrs, most of them from Spain, some from Rome, some whose sepulchres Prudentius visited in a journey from Spain to Rome, and among African martyrs, the blessed Cyprian, revered by Prudentius as by all who knew and all who lived after him. In a way, then, this little work is an exalted and poetical Baedeker, as helpful for ancient pilgrims to those holy tombs as, let us say, *Hare's Walks about Rome* is to modern pilgrims who care not only for places but for their poetical associations. It so happens, also, that one of the poems (No. 8) is also a good specimen of a transitional piece, as it is only 18 lines long. Another (No. 11) immediately suggests Damasus. Prudentius describes a visit that he paid to the Catacombs, which Damasus had restored with considerable splendor. The poet, with a few swift strokes, paints a scene that calls to the remembrance the awe and the darkness and the musty odors of the underground street of tombs. He notes the inscriptions on some of the tombs:

> Yet some are mute, and on their marble face
> Tell but the number of the dead within.[16]

The tomb for which the poet was looking was that of St. Hippolytus. In another visit to the Catacombs, he sought out the burial-place of St. Agnes, which Damasus had inscribed with an epitaph, preserved to-day. It is exceedingly interesting to compare this rude first essay with what Prudentius makes of the legend (No. 14). Poems like these fill the American exile with longing to start a new pilgrimage to the Catacombs, and St. Clement and St. John Lateran, and the Galleria Lapidaria in the Vatican, and even some of the more Pagan attractions of the Eternal City.

One noticeable feature of the *Peristephanon* is its wealth of metres — trochaic septenarius, iambic dimeter and trimeter, dactylic tetrameter catalectic, hendecasyllabic, sapphic, glyconic, the cleven syllable Alcaic, the elegiac distich, and various strophaic combinations of the more difficult metres of Horace. The poet handles them all with ease and at times with grace.

I am here reminded of a remark by Anatole France in his tragic work *L'Île des Pingouins* — tragic, because it marks the eclipse of the urbane wit that shone so pleasantly in *Le Crime de Sylvestre Bonnart* and *Le Livre de Mon Ami*. In the Christian heaven, he says, the only poets are Commodian, Fortunatus, and Prudentius, "who were born all three in those tenebrous times when prosody and grammar were known no more." [17] I am inclined to believe that, if a stiff examination in ancient metres — with or without an original composition or two — were imposed on Prudentius and M. Anatole

France, a comparison of the papers would induce in the latter a mighty respect for the former.

We thus have a *new* Prudentius here; he is a Christian Horace as well as a Christian Virgil and Lucretius. Moreover, we discover two moods in his poetry, two styles displayed. One is what we should expect from the author of the *Apotheosis* and the *Hamartigenia* — a Classical treatment of the legend in a complicated metre. The other style is utterly simple. Prudentius brushes aside all gorgeousness and lets the story of a sainted life and a martyr's death shine in its own light. At the end of the poem on St. Lawrence, he calls himself a rustic poet, and so he is, in deep sincerity, at the moment. But that is only one mood in Prudentius, whom the great Bentley well called the Horace and the Virgil of the Christians. In illustrating so clearly the two opposite styles, Prudentius provided models for them both in Mediaeval Latin literature, where the two courses, high and low, run on in both prose and verse.

To illustrate, a charmingly simple piece (No. 3) is in honor of the Spanish martyr, St. Eulalia, a plucky little girl, who, bent upon martyrdom, stole out of the house one night, tramped the wild country under the escort of a band of angels all unseen, and going straight to the judgment-seat of the Praetor, reviled the gods before his face. The Praetor has to condemn such a blasphemer to death, but he begs her to be sensible; he is ready to pardon, if she will but touch with her fingertips a bit of sacred Pagan salt and incense. For reply, the fierce little girl — *torva puellula* — spits right in the Praetor's eyes, knocks the idols over, and stamps on the sacred salt. Dear, dear, she will have it, then. The executioners stab her and put her body on the fire. A sweet odor ascends as the fire burns, and her soul mounts to heaven in the form of a white dove. The fire burns low, and snow falls from heaven to cover her mortal remains with its white mantle — *pallioli vice linteoli.*

Apart from its beauty, which, as I have indicated, is of a fresh and delicate sort that, helped by the liquid diminutives, reminds us of Catullus, the poem is of considerable historical importance. One of the earliest monuments of the French vernacular is a sequence of the tenth century in honor of St. Eulalia, the matter of which is, at least indirectly, connected with Prudentius.[18]

I must not spend too much time on the *Peristephanon,* but I cannot fail to mention one piece which suggests the Baedeker again, and is also of a somewhat frightful interest to those who profess the teacher's and the stenographer's art. It is on the martyrdom of St. Cassian No. (9). Prudentius, on his way to Rome, stopped at Imola, between Ravenna and Bologna, and entered a church to pray. As he was at his devotions, his eyes fell on a curious picture, the subject of which he did not understand. The Verger, who seems to have been expectantly on hand, kindly explained it. St. Cassian had been a teacher of stenography,

> Skilled to confine whole words in little signs,
> And quickly take dictation down with dots.

The distich is an admirable prophecy of the clicking of the typewriter long before its invention. I think you can hear the typewriter in that second verse — not in my translation, but in the original:

> verba notis brevibus comprendere cuncta peritus
> raptimque punctis dicta praepetibus sequi.

Cassian was not a gentle teacher; he spoke up if anything went wrong — and consequently he was not a favorite.

> For teachers ever are a bitter pill
> To college youth, nor any serious course
> Is ever sweet to infants.[19]

Such were the conditions in Cassian's school, when a persecution was decreed and Cassian was on the list of the condemned. The executioner, knowing his reputation with his pupils, hit on a novel and awful mode of torture, which, some scholars maintain, was devised by that Arch-fiend, the Apostate Julian. Cassian's pupils were invited to take him captive, bind him, and, armed with their styluses and slates, to pay off their old scores. This they proceeded to do with intense enthusiasm. They smashed their slates over his head and jabbed their pens into him, asking him if those dots were n't all right, and please to criticize anybody who did not make his mark in the right place. It was *sartor resartus* — or, shall we say, *notarius notatus*. It was a rather inglorious sort of martyrdom, in which the pen was as mighty as the sword, but uncomfortable enough, certainly, to merit the reward of the palm. The same fate later befell the learned philosopher John the Scot, according to tradition.

From the legend, we pass to another invention in Christian poetry. The reader of Milton's *Paradise Lost* and *Paradise Regained* is sometimes surprised, or even shocked, at the extraordinary coloring that Milton gives to the narratives of the Old Testament and the New. His Jehovah and his Christ are not altogether those of the Bible. Milton's God is also something of an Olympian, presiding over a court of lesser divinities strongly resembling the other members of the Pantheon. All manner of Classical allusions and traits of style are woven into Milton's narratives; the most striking that I remember is the account of the temptation of our Lord, when Satan offers him, among other attractive dishes, those delicacies condemned by the ancient satirists and appreciated by the ancient *gourmets* — oysters from the Lucrine bay.[20] How could a Puritan venture to treat a sacred subject in a fashion so scandalously Pagan? Milton is not altogether a Puritan, and he was not solely responsible for the Classical colorings of his Biblical epics. He is the inheritor of a tradition which started in the occidental world as early as the fourth century, flourished in the Middle Ages and the Renaissance, and is not over yet. It is the practice of adapting Biblical subjects to Greek and Roman literary forms.

If we look for the ultimate origin of this hybrid art, we must go back, as for most things, to Greece, in particular to the Hellenistic Age and the Jewish dispersion in Alexandria. We cannot pause to pay the inventors their due tribute, but pass at once to the first of the Latin Biblical poets, virtually the founder of this literary form, so far as the Middle Ages were concerned — Juvencus.

Gaius Vettius Aquilinus Juvencus published about 330 A.D., in the reign of Constantine, an heroic version of the four Gospels — *Evangeliorum Libri IV*.[21] Like Prudentius, he is of Spanish origin. The poem is divided into four books because there are four Gospels, but this has nothing to do with the contents of the poem, which naturally does not tell the story of the Gospel four times. The author apparently takes the Gospel of St. Matthew as his basis and weaves in episodes from the other Gospels which St. Matthew did not record.

What strikes a believer's ear at once as reprehensible, if not ludicrous, is the arraying of the simple phrases of the Gospel in ultra-rhetorical finery. God becomes "The High-Thunderer" and "The Lofty-Thronéd Parent." [22] The phrase "When the morning was come" is enough in the Gospels to inform the reader that it is the next day.[23] In Juvencus,

> The fire-tressed sun shook from his rosy mane
> New light to earth. [24]

However, the Virgilian extravagances in his poem are really not numerous. The general impression, after you have accepted the conditions under which the experiment is tried, is pleasing. Juvencus does translate, as Jerome said of him, *ad verbum*. The narrative flows off smoothly. It is easy to read, and you find yourself reading on. Disgust gives place to amusement and amusement to admiration. The mood to cultivate is not a critical desire to see how tawdry the poet has made the Gospel story — you will have permanent dissatisfaction if you approach it in that way. Instead, imagine that this is a problem set to a Virgil, a minor Virgil, who is given the New Testament and asked to render it into verse. You will at once agree that on the whole Juvencus has succeeded well, and, in certain passages, very well. The man who could write a poem like this, knew his Virgil to his finger-tips. There are touches of Ovid and Statius, but Virgil is his great master.[25] He understands Virgilian niceties and delicacies. He can translate atmosphere as well as words. Take the Sermon on the Mount; it is a little stroke of genius to render *beatus* by *felix*. Only a mind steeped in Pagan poetry could have done that. I will cite but one verse from Juvencus, selected some years ago by one of my pupils, I think aptly, as the poet's best verse, which describes the dance of Salome,[26] —

alternos laterum celerans sinuamine motus, —

a verse with something of the sibilant liquefaction of the silks in which our Herrick's Julia goes. Juvencus was commended by St. Jerome and Pope Gelasius and was a favorite school-book in the Middle Ages.

Furthermore, Juvencus's example proved contagious. He had opened a broad field for experimentation, into which poets rushed in troops. Juvencus had covered only the Gospels. What a chance to become a second, and perhaps a superior, Christian Virgil with an epic on some theme from the Old Testament or the Apocrypha or the history of the Church! Cyprianus Gallicus staked out his claim in the *Pentateuch*.[27] He covered the five books of Moses, and swept on to *Joshua*, *Judges*, and as far into the Old Testament as he could get. Somebody else, whose name has passed into oblivion, wrote one poem on *Sodom* and another on *Jonah*. The first needed the inspiration of Ovid as well as of Virgil, as the story included the unfortunate metamorphosis of Lot's wife.

I may also mention here a woman-poet, Falconia Proba, a writer of the fourth century; her poem is a specimen of the womanly art of quilting, for she wrote a *Cento*, a patchwork of verses or parts of verses all from Virgil.[28] Many such affairs were produced in the Christian centuries, and hers is one of the best. It is not a high form of art: St. Jerome, you remember, lavishes his sarcasm upon it,[29] and I will devote to it a mere parenthesis. Such as it is, Proba was the founder, so far as the Middle Ages are concerned. She deserves a modest place in that galaxy of which Sappho, Sulpicia, and Mrs. Browning are more conspicuous examples.

It is difficult to give you in a translation an idea of the cleverness with which this good woman accomplishes the seemingly impossible undertaking. I will venture a mock-Miltonic rendering of Proba's account of the temptation of Eve in a patch-work of verses from Virgil. The translation is well-nigh literal and will at least show that our poetess can contrive an even and unified narrative.[30]

Now dawned th' unhappy day. Up from the field
Of roses, see! th' insidious Enemy steals,
The snake, of slippery spirals sevenfold,
And hatred on his face, wrath in his soul,
Hangs from the branches of a leafy tree,
Breathing out viper-breath in loathsome hisses,
Brooding on envy, spite, and treacherous war,
Detestable to God himself. The beast
Bristled his scales and to the utmost pitch
Of crime he stirred himself and thus he spake.
"Tell me," quoth he, "oh Virgin, dwell we not
In shady groves by banks of pleasant streams?
What cowardice has come into thy soul?
Under each tree the ripened apples lie;
Here are sweet potions in the liquid springs,
And yet 't is sin to touch these natural bounties.
This only failed us for our utter bliss.
What hinders us to know the hidden truths?
Naught but vain superstition! The half
Is ours, and we are robbed of half.
Why should he mock us with eternal life?
Dare but to heed me! Break the accursèd law!
Thou'rt the man's wife, and thine the privilege
To melt his purpose with caressing pleas.
I am your leader. Heed me! We will build
Soft, sylvan couches round th' inviting feast."
He said, and they, swift-heeding, spread a store
Of fruit forbidden. The once sacred board
Then was polluted by their profane touch.

Unhappy Eve, fulfilling her own doom,
Eyed the strange leaves and apples not her own,
Cause of our ill, she touched her lips to them,
And, fury-driven, daring greater sin,
Ah me, she offered of the alien fruit
Unto her consort — and her charms prevailed.
Forthwith a strange light flashed before their eyes.
They shrunk in terror at th' uncanny sight
And taking covert under umbrageous boughs
Made leafy plaids — and knew that all was lost.
But the Creator, watching all, foresaw
The Archfiend's crime; and well he also knew
What a mad woman ventures when she will.
Straightway the mighty Lord of earth and heaven
Called in loud tones, "Hence, get ye hence, profane."
When him they saw advance with awful strides,
Wrath on his face, they turned in fear and fled
To distant woods and secret caverns dim,
Shamed of their deed and of the light of day,
And shamed to raise their faces to the sky.

One may laugh at such a performance, but also agree
with the verdict of St. Isidore, that "we do not like the
idea, but cannot help admiring the author's ingenuity." [31] For it is with an almost diabolical ingenuity —
perhaps we should say inspiration rather than diabolical
ingenuity, for by St. Isidore's time the little work had
been numbered among the Apocryphal Scriptures —
that this Christian undertaking is performed; Proba
must have known her Virgil through and through. Stop
and think! How long would it take anyone of us to get
the like from Virgil? Or, how many of the verses or
half-verses can we spot as we read? We can spot them
all in Schenkl's edition, and when we recognize the in-

congruous matter out of which the mosaic is made, the effect is enlivening in the extreme. I really suspect that a quiet smile played about the face of the saintly compiler as she put these bits together, and that a little problem sometimes arose in her mind as to the propriety of getting heavenly results out of very earthy material. Still, she got them.

And the poem was very popular in the ages to come. A long line of *centones* may be followed into the Middle Ages and the Renaissance, and I have even read one in the *Harvard Lampoon.*[32]

The effect of the cento on the writing of Biblical Epics is also obvious; it acted as a spur. Read Juvencus's account of the storm on the Lake of Galilee, or the Crucifixion, which I would recommend as specimens of his better poetry,[33] and then turn to Proba for what we might call the original models. Your respect for Juvencus's acquaintance with Virgil's art will increase, and you will perceive that later Biblical poets must have frequently consulted such models as Proba's metamorphosis of Virgil.

Herewith we end our parenthesis and return to the Biblical Epic. This loitering with parentheses cuts down our text, and yet I must at least mention Dracontius, who wrote in Africa at the end of the fifth century after the invasion of the Vandals.[34] Most of his work was done in the reign of Gunthamund, an exceedingly barbarous monarch, who threw the poet into prison, where he first wrote a *Satisfactio*, or apology, with a plea for forgiveness, and then turned to a higher theme — *De Laudibus Dei*. The work is in essence a theodicy, an attempt to "justify the ways of God to men," a natural form, as we have seen in the case of Boethius,[35] for prison literature to take.

To prove the justice of the Deity, Dracontius begins at the beginning, with an account of creation. This takes up the first, and by far the best, of the three books of the poem, and is the part related to our present theme. Dracontius's strength lies in his descriptions, some of which are highly poetic. I will pause for only one, the account of the first fall of night. This is the first nightfall in history, and to the primal pair, seemed the destruction of the universe.[36]

> As slow the sun set, they in awe looked on,
> Thinking its light was never to return.
> Their hearts were solaced as th' effulgent moon
> Broke through the shadows and a radiant host
> Of stars they counted in the cloudless sky.
> But when the Day-star, rising from the deep,
> Shook his bright mane and called the new-born light
> Flushed with the sun, to ride above the stars,
> They warmed their souls with yesterday's delight;
> Knowing the daily change, they calmed their dread
> And cheered night's shadows with the hope of dawn.

It is strange that Dracontius, so far as I know, is the only poet of the story of creation who has described the feelings of our first parents when the blackness of the first night came on. Milton has not done it, nor any of the modern Biblical poets, so far as I can discover, though there is something similar in a sonnet of Blanco White's, much admired by Coleridge.

The strength of Dracontius is his imagination and his choice of unhackneyed phrases. His verse is occasionally rough, and he is not good at construction; at least the *De Laudibus Dei* becomes rambling and tiresome in the last two books. In this respect, we have a favorable contrast in Avitus.

Alcimus Ecdicius Avitus, Bishop of Vienne, who was born about 450 and died about 525, wrote in his youth a poem that in point of construction, is the best of all the Biblical epics.[37] It is entitled "The Deeds of Spiritual History" (*De Spiritalis Historiae Gestis*), and the first book is headed "The Origin of the World" (*De Origine Mundi*). The part of *Genesis* that interests Avitus is the creation of man. He feels that he is writing *epic*, the deeds of a hero, or heroic deeds, and does not spend much time, like Dracontius, on the budding eyes of fishes. Avitus replaces picturesqueness by the larger sweep of the argument, heightened by allegory and mysticism. He is at his worst where Dracontius is at his best, and *vice versa*. His Eve is almost worthy of the tragic stage. She is of the race of Tullia and Clytemnestra. She balances desire and fear in an Ovidian *suasoria* at the moment of her temptation, and is the victim of the furies when she offers a share of the forbidden fruit to Adam. After the Fall, the two have acquired the knowledge of good and evil — that is to say, the craze for forming hypotheses about what they do not know. Satan also is no longer the simple serpent of *Genesis*, he is an indeterminate, vast power of evil, manifesting himself in diverse ways; and for the moment, as he declares, he is the real ruler of mankind.

> For God, who formed you, has no greater right
> Over your souls than I. What he has formed
> That can he keep. What I have taught is mine, —
> The major portion. For ye surely owe
> Much to your Maker, to your Teacher — more.[38]

Render unto Satan the things that are Satan's. Avitus has faintly foreshadowed Milton's Satan, called by some the hero of *Paradise Lost*.

The concluding books (IV, "The Flood," and V, "The Crossing of the Red Sea,") might seem at first to have strayed entirely from the author's original intention. But we have only to read a little in them to see that there is no break in the unity of the poem. For Avitus is thinking of the allegorical meaning of these bits of Old Testament history, whereby he can sweep through the course of human sin down to the redemption of the race in Christ. The poem thus includes a Paradise Lost and a Paradise Regained. The Psalm *In exitu Israel de Aegypto* has an allegorical flavor both in the service of the Church, and at the beginning of Dante's *Purgatorio*.[39] Dante explained the four-fold meaning in his letter to Can Grande, as we saw before,[40] and when he inserts it in his psalm, he is thinking no less of the liturgy than of the Bible. It is

Easter Day when after the blackness of Hell the poet and
his guide see the sapphire lights above the sea. In the
service for Holy Saturday, the day before Easter, twelve
Prophecies from the Old Testament form a part, each
containing a suggestion of the Resurrection. The fourth
Prophecy is from the fourteenth chapter of *Exodus*, which
tells of the crossing of the Red Sea, and from the fifteenth chapter, which contains the Song of Moses. The
preface to the first Prophecy, accompanied by the light-
ing of the lamps, begins with the words, *O vere beata nox
quae expoliavit Aegyptios.* Thus to a trained allegorical
mind, or indeed to anybody who knew the service of the
Church, there is no lack of connection in the closing
books of Avitus's epic. The allegory is managed deli-
cately. The name of Christ appears only often enough
to suggest that the treatment *is* allegorical. At the end
of the poem, the narrative of Moses becomes a prophecy
of Christ, whose coming deeds the "pious seer set forth
in his five volumes," and

> Whose clarion measures my poor scrannel pipe
> Repeats as best it can. And now my little bark
> I bring to anchor on his harboring shore."

We cannot take leave of the Biblical Epic without a
mention of Prudentius. All the sections of our present
topic lead up to him. According to Gennadius, who at
the end of the fifth century continued the *De Viris
Illustribus* of St. Jerome, Prudentius composed a work
called *Hexaemeron*.[42] If a poem, it would be an epic on

the first six days of creation, of great interest to compare with the commentaries of St. Ambrose and St.
Basil, and with the poems of Tasso and Du Bartas, as
well as that of Dracontius. But no such poem exists to-
day. In case Prudentius wrote one, he was not satisfied
with that alone. He wanted, as ever, to do something
new. He composed a new epic of a high order, as we have
seen in the *Contra Symmachum*.[43] He also composed the
first allegorical epic in Christendom, the *Psychomachia*,
an allegory of the battles of the virtues and the vices
for the soul. These are lively abstractions, and owing
to the necessities of Latin Grammar they are all female
— Amazons (*Virtus, Superbia, Pudicitia, Luxuria*); the
good Amazons he calls *virgines*, the bad, *viragines*. Men
are there, for Luxuria, as she scatters flowers coquettishly from her chariot, works havoc among them.

Saucia mirantum capiebat corda virorum.[44]

The feminine abstractions, therefore, must be all officers, and the men merely privates, enlisted under the
banner of the superior sex. Prudentius intersperses
touches of satire in his way, with many a flavoring from
the ancients, and conducts the high narrative in noble
Virgilian verse. His poem was a pattern of poetic allegory for many generations to come.

I have said nothing as yet about what is admittedly
the most original contribution made by the Church to
poetry — the Christian hymn.[45] The hymn was part of
the liturgy of the Church from very early times, and back

of it lies the liturgic use of the Hebrew psalms, the sweetest and tenderest and deepest religious lyrics in all literature. The synagogue then passed on the hymn to the church; and it also found favor with certain heretical bodies, particularly the Gnostics. But it was not till the fourth century that the history of the Latin hymn begins. It was then that St. Hilary and St. Ambrose, taking a hint from Eastern practice, applied it to controversial and doctrinal purposes in the West. St. Ambrose's hymns, while admirably adapted to their immediate end, are incidentally lyrics of crystalline simplicity and sincerity; with allusion to the story of the bees that played about the lips of the infant Ambrose, the poet Arator, a century or more later, called these hymns Hyblaean;[46] no epithet could be more just. Except for the regular iambic dimeter, there are few suggestions in St. Ambrose of Classical models. Trained by the old poets in the art of metre, he gives the new message in the most direct way. There may be unconscious flavors, for Ambrose was well read in the authors, and other Pagans besides Horace had written hymns. There are lyric moments in Virgil, and passages in Ovid, even, that sing in the manner of a hymn.

The hymns of St. Ambrose are perfect after their kind, and summon the imitator to despair. But Prudentius entered the lists, and it was not his nature to do the same thing twice.[47] He calls his little collection by a Greek title, as usual, *Cathemerinon*, meaning "Hymns

Day by Day"; broader than its title, the book includes hymns not only for the canonical hours of the day, but for solemn festivals of the year and for the last rites of man's life. We see at once from their length that they never were intended for use in the liturgy. At least, a modern clergyman gave out Hymn No. 7, which has two hundred and twenty verses, he would mitigate the announcement by adding, "the first two and the last two stanzas." We next notice the metres. Some are of the simple sorts, and some are exceedingly ornate. For the funeral march in the hymn for the dead (No. 10), Prudentius has anapaests. One hymn is daringly done in anacreontics; it is the hymn before sleep (No. 6), whereas anacreontics suggest a festivity that lasts all night. In short, this is the same Prudentius that we have learned in the *Peristephanon*; he is master of two kinds of art, the elaborate and the simple.

We can best appreciate the nature of Prudentius's hymns by comparing them with those of St. Ambrose. St. Ambrose wrote a hymn — *Aeterne rerum conditor* — for lauds, the daily service at cock-crow; and so did Prudentius (No. 1). The former is one of the familiar hymns of the Breviary, and possesses the virtues that I have already described. Prudentius begins in an Ambrosian way, but soon passes into something allegorical. Chanticleer becomes a symbol of Christ, the poet says, just as our sleep is but an image of death. Now Ambrose, who in his prose works, as we saw, frequently indulged in allegory, also has a touch of it here; but it is merely an incidental coloring; he is writing with a service in mind. Prudentius, apparently with the whole morning before him, is giving us a learned exposition — the kind of material that would go into one of the good bishop's sermons. In proof of the divine power of the cock, Prudentius continues, "'T is said that it can put wandering demons to flight." "'*T is said*" — now nobody should say, "'*T is said*" in a hymn. It is good for epic; it is good for the lighter sorts of narrative. In a hymn, we give thanks and offer prayers and take things for granted. Nor in a hymn do we give reasons and inferences, as Prudentius proceeds to do, inserting particles like *nam, namque, inde est quod*, and *nempe*. Then he introduces the mention of St. Peter, as Ambrose does, only again in a different way, with the flavor of an *exemplum* in a sermon or in certain kinds of ancient and mediaeval poetry, but not that of a hymn. It was at cock-crow, Prudentius proceeds, that Christ returned from the harrowing of hell, which he subjected to his own law. So we should subdue the hell of our vices, which make up the night of our souls, and we should sweep from our vision those false dreams that so easily beset us — the dreams of gold and pleasure and power and honor and prosperity, those phantoms that blind us to reality. With Christ's help, we can quickly bid them be gone. "Do thou, O Christ, dispel our sleep. Break thou the bonds of night, absolve our ancient sin, and pour new light into our hearts."

> Tu Christe somnum dissice,
> Tu rumpe noctis vincula,
> Tu solve peccatum vetus
> Novumque lumen ingere.

Here, of a sudden, at the end of the poem, we have the simplicity of an Ambrosian hymn. It might all have had this character, had its author so chosen. But it is not so much a hymn as a poem of reflection, — in which description, narrative, and allegorical exposition are all germane, — written for a moment of the day when a hymn would be appropriate. The poet allegorizes the moment, he shows its moral significance, he calls up a typical example, and finally, he lets us hear the echo of the hymn itself, as if it stole in from the chapel near-by. It is almost as if the poet preferred to keep to his couch and ponder on the sacred meaning of the moment, instead of arising and taking part in the service.

A very beautiful hymn, which shows the same method, is that for candlelight (No. 5). The poet begins with an invocation to the Father of Lights, and prays for the light of Christ to illumine the faithful. He thanks Him not only for the luminaries in the sky, but for the light that man himself can make with a spark from a flint. He sees the lamps lit one by one, and muses on the meaning of the marvel. Surely fire is of heavenly origin; it comes from God. That we see from the story of Moses and the burning bush. This sets him to thinking of all the glorious deeds that Moses wrought for the children of Israel. He describes the escape from Egypt, the wandering in the wilderness, and the entry into the Promised Land. The story is full of allegory, and portends the deeds of Christ, and the unwonted light that shone in hell when He descended there before His resurrection. That is why we light our candles at Easter, so many of them that the ceiling looks like the starry firmament. Light is a worthy offering to thee, O God, for it is the most precious of thy gifts to us. The time has come in this poem for Prudentius to break into his own hymn; it is the lyric moment, to which he has been leading up: "Thou art the true light for our eyes, a light for our senses, a mirror within, a mirror without. Accept the light that I thy servant offer, dipped in the ointment of the oil of peace."

> Tu lux vera oculis, lux quoque sensibus,
> Intus tu speculum, tu speculum foris,
> Lumen quod famulans offero, suscipe
> Tinctum pacifici chrismatis unguine.

This light that the poet offers is his own life, fragrant with the ointment of his consecration to the faith.

We do not read far in these novel hymns before feeling that somehow they are not so new. Though the substance is Christian, there is something indefinably Pagan about them. All of a sudden, the Muse is invoked; she is exhorted to spurn her wonted ivy and weave mystic garlands of simple verse.[48] Or take the opening strophe of the "hymn at Candlelight": "O Maker of the glowing light, good Leader, who dost divide the times with certain shifts, the sun is overwhelmed, rude Chaos storms. Restore thy light, O Christ, to thy faithful."

> Inventor rutili, *dux bone*, luminis,
> Qui certis vicibus tempora dividis,
> Merso sole chaos ingruit horridum,
> *Lucem redde tuis* Christe fidelibus.

The first and the last line repeat Horace's appeal to the absent Augustus — *lucem redde tuae, dux bone, patriae*.[49] This is not a comparison of our Lord to Augustus, but it hovers dangerously near that possibility. It shows the lengths to which Prudentius is willing to go in his Pagan flavors. So in the account of the harrowing of hell, we find that the river Styx is still flowing below, and that our Lord returns from "Acheruntian pools." [50] Moreover, these hymns are *in their entire framework* Pagan. They suggest Pindar, who will begin a hymn with an invocation, tell a myth to illustrate a point or honor the god, and pass on into the general and the ideal. I am not sure that Prudentius knew Pindar, but we can find in Horace, who did, plenty of examples of briefer compass but identical character.

Prudentius, then, is not writing hymns for the liturgy of the Church, but is filling the framework of Pindaric and Horatian hymns with Christian feeling and belief, and Christian story. He is showing that the new faith has a wealth of material just as poetic as the facts and fables of ancient tradition. Yet his purpose is not to supersede Pagan culture, but to include it. The culture which Prudentius embodied in his hymns, and which he passed on to the coming generations, could not dispense with the ancient authors who had contributed to its making.

In this finely Pagan performance, there are, we saw, exquisite bits of the simplest and sweetest sort, worthy of a place beside those Hyblaean hymns of St. Ambrose. The Church recognized this, and culled them out for its use. Some are in the Roman breviary, and one is in the Mozarabic liturgy of Spain. Surely lines like the following could not lie buried in a Pindaric hymn when they might adorn the feast of the Holy Innocents: "Hail, flower of the martyrs, whom on the very threshold of light the persecutor of Christ swept away, as a whirlwind scatters roses at their bloom."

> Salvete, flores martyrum,
> Quos lucis ipso in limine
> Christi insecutor sustulit,
> Ceu turbo nascentes rosas.[51]

However, these centonic hymns of the Breviary are only partially successful. The excerpter never knows when to stop; his excerpt ends in incompleteness or anticlimax. That is because Prudentius did not intend this use to be made of such passages; he meant them for contributing effects. He had few successors in his rare art, so far as I have observed. One of the most conspicuous, and one of the best, is Theodulph of Orleans, who wrote his "All Glory, Laud and Honor," not so much as a hymn for Palm Sunday as a description of the celebration of that festival, containing, in Prudentius's way, echoes of a splendid hymn.[52]

To appreciate a Latin hymn with all its flavors, we must take it not merely for itself, but as a part of something larger. First of all, it is wedded to music, which makes its own appeal. Then, it is caught up into the larger atmosphere of some religious office — Vespers or Compline or the supreme sacrifice of the Mass. Finally, this service is celebrated in a church, which, however humble, decently puts the altar in the place of reverence and adorns it with candles, type of a shining faith. We must know the whole to appreciate the part. As we read *Veni redemptor gentium*, or *Gloria, laus et honor*, or *Pange lingua gloriosi corporis mysterium*, we must not translate, or — *absit omen* — read the pious doggerel of somebody else's translation, but listen to the Latin words, hear the deep voice of the organ, glance upwards, in imagination, at the Gothic vaulting of Amiens or Chartres, see the light sifting in through the flaming windows and the purer flame of the candles shining on the altar where the holy sacrifice is made. And, above all, we must consider these beauties, not as the moving force that brings the worshippers to church, — who then would be idolators indeed, — but as the offering of their richest treasures made thankfully for the revelation of the truth. This is the whole body of the hymn, which loses flesh and blood if you tear it away. If we can merely read hymns, let us not read them in anybody's chronological collection of hymns, but in connection with the offices of the Church, as for instance, in the admirable volume of Dom Britt.[53] Read them so, and imagine the rest.

This is inadequate praise to bestow on the Latin hymn. I have said less than I should have, not merely because the limits of this lecture allow us no more, but because everybody knows the merits of the Latin hymn, and because the art of hymnology did not reach its full fruition till the Middle Ages. Yet dashes of mediaeval mysticism, and more than dashes of mediaeval sweetness, appear in the hymns of St. Ambrose, while Prudentius's invention, highly original and poetic, appears not to have been understood. He laid a foundation, but few built thereon.

Nor have I mentioned all the Christian Latin poets in this summary discourse. Some will miss the names of Claudian and Ausonius.[54] They both were Christians, nominally, and Ausonius, though gay of heart, was, I believe, sincerely attached to the new faith. But their poetry, though containing much of interest and of charm, is almost altogether run into the ancient moulds. In that of Ausonius there is, I should say, about 17 3/10 per cent of Christian sentiment; in Claudian, about 3/10 of 1 per cent. They therefore may be dismissed in a treatment of the new poetry that embodied the new faith. In a treatment of Christian humanism, they are both of exceeding importance.

I have failed also to comment on the fondness of the French symbolists for this new poetry — of Huysmanns, or of Rémy de Gourmont, with his decadent's library in *Le Latin Mystique*, or of Baudelaire, the father of that family, who scorned the classicalities of the ancient poets and with an intensity worthy of Gregory the Great, revelled in the barbarisms and solecisms of the later Latin—those "negligences forced by a passion that forgets itself and mocks at rules." [55] I am not repeating his own Latin hymn, *Francescae Meae Laudes*, which, true to type if curious metricalities are a test, suggests a prayer to the Blessed Virgin, but is addressed to a favorite "*modiste, erudite et devote*." [56] I fear that these Bohemians mistook the decadence of Latin grammar for their own variety of decadence, and that their tribute to the mysticism of Christian Latin poetry, though welcome from so unexpected a source, is more quaint than convincing.

My great neglect has been to pay too meagre a homage to Prudentius, even though you may think that I have mentioned him too often. I am aware that almost everybody who writes about him is quick to condemn his lapses from good taste. He has his defects, but I am more concerned with his extraordinary merits, which have hardly been given the credit they deserve. I will leave you to piece together the *disiecti membra poetae*, to survey his works as a whole, and thus best to relish that new poetry which the Christian faith contributed to the Western world and founded for the Middle Ages.

CHAPTER VII

THE NEW EDUCATION

THE present age takes a lively interest in education. Hardly a period in history can show so many educational methods, so minute an investigation of the idea of education itself. We wonder sometimes at the reverential care with which the ancient Roman summoned so many divinities to guard his growing boy — Edulia and Potina to teach him to eat and drink, Cuba to put him in his crib and take him out, Ossipaga to strengthen his bones, Statanus to set him on his feet, Abeona and Adeona, that sedulous pair, of whom the one guided his first tottering steps away from his mother, and the other brought him back, Fabulinus, who first opened his lips in speech — surely the Roman needed no reminder that heaven lies about us in our infancy.[1] Our less imaginative age has done what it could; it has translated these kindly gods into educational theories and child-psychology, whereby, to quote a headline of the day before yesterday, "Scientists Note Baby's Every Act."

I advocate a return to the ancients — not to their polytheism, but to their theory of education, which, formed at Athens in the fifth century B.C., developed more and more definitely, assumed a fixed shape in the fourth century A.D., and became one of the most important instruments for the transmission of Classical culture to the Middle Ages. It was the basis of all humanistic culture from the Renaissance to the latter half of the nineteenth century, when the "Elective System" struck it, and struck it hard.

First, a word on the apparatus or machinery of education, the libraries and the schools. Public libraries were a Hellenistic invention, as the great library at Alexandria testifies.[2] So was the Museum, a kind of Carnegie Institute, wherein learned scholars, well paid and well fed, pursued their investigations — a "bird-coop of the Muses," as a contemporary scoffer called it.[3] At Rome, the first public library was established by Asinius Pollio in 39 B.C., on the proceeds of his Dalmatian campaign. This was eclipsed by the famous Palatine Library, opened by Augustus in 28 B.C., as a part of the temple of Apollo on the Palatine. It possessed several thousand volumes and had both a Greek and a Latin division. Within these were subdivisions; the authors were classified according to subject — poetry, philosophy, history, oratory. Much instruction centred about the libraries. Teachers would give lectures in the colonades (*porticus*) connected with temples or with libraries, and also in the withdrawing-rooms of the baths. For the bath as well as the library was an intellectual resort; cleanliness was next to culture. The third and the fourth centuries are the most flourishing periods for the development of the library in the Roman world.[4] At the end of the fourth century, there are said to have been twenty-eight public libraries at Rome. However, their prosperity was short-lived. The Pagan collections were closed, and as the historian Ammianus Marcellinus remarks, became so many tombs,[5] Church libraries, we may infer from St. Jerome,[6] took their place, but both sorts suffered from the ravages of the barbarians, and by the end of the sixth century had sunk to a pitiable estate.[7]

The fourth century was also the great century for schools. Since the times of Hadrian the state had supported the schools, and spent larger and larger sums on their maintenance. The decrees of the Emperors from Constantine on, relating to schools, were gathered together in the Theodosian Code in the second quarter of the fifth century, and contain much valuable information.[8] Constantine enacted that a comfortable salary should be paid to professors, apart from the voluntary honoraria that parents might contribute. A rhetorician received a higher salary than a grammarian. Greek and Latin teachers were on an equal footing in Rome, but at Treves a professor of Greek "if a worthy one can be found" was not paid quite so well as his Latin confrère.[9] I have no information on the point, but presumably a professor was paid more than a trainer of gladiators. Furthermore, schoolmasters were hedged in with a certain divinity. If a slave did them injury, he was punished with flogging; if his master had connived at the

act, he was condemned to pay a goodly fine. They were
exempted from arrest and from public duties, including
military service. The Emperor Julian, apostate though
he was, did not lack an insight into the problem of a
professor's household, for he specially enjoined [10] that
the wives of professors and of doctors should not suffer
unnecessary vexation, and in particular that their lords
and masters should not have to entertain military men
as guests. Before this discreet provision, many a poor
professor's larder and his cellar must have been ran-
sacked *in toto* by visiting colonels. The same Julian
wisely proclaimed [11] that the first requisite in a teacher
was character, quality; a secondary requisite was eloquence. He advised none to jump too lightly into the
career of a teacher, and required in each case a certifi-
cate from the candidate's town, to be supplemented
later with the higher honor of the Imperial approval.

Under the Empire, institutions of learning in the west
had steadily increased in dignity. Hadrian had established a university or "Athenaeum" at Rome, and from
that time, especially in the fourth century, similar estab-
lishments sprang up all over the Roman world.[12] Students from other lands could come to Rome for their
"graduate work," and young Romans no longer found
it necessary, as in the days of Cicero and Horace, to go
abroad to finish their education. Various decrees relate
to the floating population of students in Rome and Constantinople.[13] The new-comer had to present a certifi-

cate from the proper authorities in his home town and matriculate in due form. He had to specify the studies that he wished specially to pursue. There were no dormitories for him to lodge in, yet he was under strict supervision, with particular attention to questionable "clubs," frequent attendance at the theatre, and participation in nocturnal feasts.[14] If he disported himself in a fashion beneath the dignity of a student of the liberal arts, he was publicly flogged, embarked on a boat, and returned to his domicile. A well-behaved student ordinarily was allowed to stay for four or five years, and then, unless there were good cause, was obliged to return to his native place and report to the authorities there. He generally started his academic career at the age of sixteen.[15] Those two years that are somewhere lost in our secondary-school training were apparently well accounted for in ancient Rome. The fourth century was one of the great creative periods in the history of education, ranking with the twelfth, the fifteenth, and the nineteenth. It was a period of Foundations for the intellectual ideals that dominated the Middle Ages.

What, now, was the regular course of study, the prescribed curriculum in the ancient university?[16] The elective system flourished, only that you elected your teacher, not your programme, which remained the same. By the end of the fourth century the necessary subjects were included in the *trivium* and the *quadrivium*. Those who are helped by mnemonic devices may learn the couplet contrived by Nicolas de Orbellis, a French Franciscan, about the middle of the fifteenth century.

Gram loquitur, *Dia* vera docet, *Rhet* verba colorat,
Mus canit, *Ar* numerat, *Ge* ponderat, *Ast* colit astra.

This brief poem was exceedingly valuable for young gentlemen who had forgotten what subjects they were studying. The first three on the list, grammar, rhetoric, and dialectic, make up the *trivium*; the last four, arithmetic, geometry, astronomy, and music, are the *quadrivium*. These seven subjects were known as the *artes liberales*, or *artes* for short — not *any* arts, but *artes liberales*, the arts appropriate for the training of a gentleman, *homo liber*. The term survives in our scholastic titles A.B. and A.M., *Artium Baccalaureus* and *Artium Magister*, though heaven knows what those titles mean now! I sympathize with the recent utterance of my colleague Irving Babbitt that "rather than blur certain distinctions, it would have been better, one might suppose, to use up all the letters of the alphabet devising new degrees to meet the real or supposed educational needs of the modern man." [17] I fear we have gone too far on the other course, but if we can return, I vote for the most comfortable-sounding degree that I have ever heard of, — it is given by an American institution, — the degree of B.E.D., *Bachelor of Elementary Didactics*.[18]

Now, though the final classification of the arts was not perfected till the fourth century A.D., the essentials of the ancient system were proclaimed by Plato. He explains in the *Republic* [19] that studies will tend to draw the soul from the region of the Becoming to that of the Being. Gymnastic and music make a beginning, but only a beginning. Arithmetic gets one farther on the road. For "even the dull," he declares, "if they have had an arithmetical training, gain in quickness." [20] I quote this to show how far Plato lags behind contemporary paedagogy, which, if I am rightly informed, would banish the idea of "mental discipline." Geometry is also recommended by Plato; likewise astronomy, and a more serious study of music. All these are but the prelude to dialectic. [21] Please notice these words. Also note what Plato omits. There is apparently no place for rhetoric and none for grammar, or rather, *grammatica*, which included literature. But Plato was a consummate rhetorician, in the best sense of the word, and he takes it for granted, I should say, that young men had fed on the best literature. I am not sure that we should take in utter seriousness all parts of Plato's statement here. He sets aside ten whole years, from the ages of twenty to thirty, in which the correlation of the sciences should be taught, and not till then does he advise the pursuit of dialectic. Then follow fifteen years, in which the aspiring philosopher holds high offices of state. At the age of fifty, if all goes well, he spends most of his existence in the contemplation of the Good. [22] Allowing a certain discount for exaggeration, we may safely say that Plato would not advise young gentlemen to begin the study of philosophy in their Freshman year, that is to say, on an empty stomach.

The subject of the proper curriculum was much pondered in the Alexandrian age. Τέχναι meant then — and with Plato, too — what *artes* did in all the centuries to come — the subjects of the liberal programme.[23] We turn to Cicero for a summary of what had developed since Plato.[24] He speaks of the "arts that are called liberal and gentlemanly — geometry, music, the study of literature, prose and poetry [we are glad to note this addition to Plato], and the natural sciences [here would come not only astronomy, but any natural science of importance], those that pertain to human character and customs [ethics, sociology, economics], and those that pertain to public affairs [history and government]." This is a more humanistic programme, or rather a more humanistic statement, than Plato's and is broad enough to comprise most subjects taught in colleges to-day. We may take it for granted that arithmetic, which is not named, formed a part of the plan, since it is essential for the other mathematical sciences. Grammar is not mentioned, but is of course included in the "study of literature." And note that when Cicero, or any ancient, spoke of *grammatica* he did not mean merely grammar. Cicero defines this art as including a study of the poets, a knowledge of history, an interpretation of words, and the art of pronunciation; the ancient grammarian taught not only grammar in our sense, but literature, history (as in the Harvard programme of History and Literature), and the art of reading aloud, elocution.[25] We also see that both rhetoric and a more intensive study of philosophy than that indicated here are essential in Cicero's programme; to him as to Plato philosophy is the queen of the sciences.[26]

A contemporary of Cicero's, the learned Marcus Terentius Varro, defined the liberal arts in a more technical way and, in fact, wrote the first treatise in Latin about them.[27] The arts have become nine, and are, according to Varro, *grammar, rhetoric, dialectic, arithmetic, geometry, astronomy, music* (that is the *trivium* and the *quadrivium*), and also *medicine* and *architecture*. I am convinced that there must have been Alexandrian works on the arts quite as definite as Varro's, and I admire all the more the informal treatment of them given by Cicero. Cicero must have been familiar with the sort of material that was accessible to Varro, but he wished to broach the subject in his own way. Cicero received about the best and broadest education that has ever fallen to the lot of man. It is on his statements and on his experience, as well as on the later formulations, that true programmes of humanism have always been based.

Neglecting various partial statements of intervening writers, we may pass to the fourth century, which I have characterized as one of the creative epochs in the history of education. Among the Greek fathers, St. Basil is a splendid specimen of a well-educated man. St. Gregory of Nazianzus lets us know the subjects that St. Basil had studied.[28]

Who was to be compared with him in rhetoric? [he asks]. Who excelled him in philology [= grammar] and in the understanding and practice of the Greek tongue? Who gathered more narratives, understood better the forms of metre, or laid down the laws of poetry more exactly? Who went deeper into the mysteries of philosophy, both that high philosophy which holds its face upward toward the sky (*theoretica*) and that which is more concerned with the daily actions of life (*practica*), as well as that third kind which deals with demonstrations, oppositions and arguments and is called dialectic? Of astronomy and geometry and the properties of numbers [arithmetic] he obtained such an insight that even with the best he could hold his own, and with medicine, both theoretical and practical, he made himself thoroughly familiar.

This looks like the programme of Varro, minus architecture and plus a wider and more searching study of philosophy.

Augustine, who surely was deeply versed in Varro, planned a complete set of textbooks on the arts, in the interval between his conversion and his baptism. He finished the *Grammatica*, but lost that book later; an abridged treatise on that art is ascribed to him. He also finished the *Musica*; this is a very competent affair, and includes a most thorough study of the metres, with specimens of his own poetry, of which I am inclined to believe that St. Augustine, like Plato and Boethius, had written a considerable amount in his youth. The *Musica* was written after his baptism; conversion did not mean for him the abandonment of culture. He also began *De Dialectica, De Rhetorica, De Geometrica, De Arithmetica, De Philosophia,* but lost even the parts begun. Apparently he had not planned to include astronomy.[29] In his *De Doctrina Christiana* he explicitly recognizes the value of the arts as a precursor of the higher studies of divinity; he recommends that the learner begin the difficult programme early, and pursue it vigorously and steadily.[30] Now this is precisely the plan of Plato and Cicero, a curriculum of two parts, an introduction and a fulfilment. For Plato and Cicero the crown of such a course is philosophy. So is it with St. Augustine, save that it is Christian philosophy, that is, theology. It is a pity that he had to abandon his plan of writing introductions to the various arts. In his *Retractationes,* St. Augustine discusses the question of the arts, and concludes that he had praised them too highly in one of his early works, since "many saintly men know them not, and some who know them are not saintly men." [31] Nevertheless, he makes no changes in the programme of Christian education as he had announced it in his *De Doctrina Christiana.*[32]

We now turn to Africa, where, probably in the early fifth century, Martianus Capella wrote a work with the curious title of *De Nuptiis Mercurii et Philologiae.*[33] Mercury, who has had considerable experience in matrimonial affairs as the messenger of the Gods, decides to take him a wife, and after unsuccessful negotiations

with certain allegorical young ladies, of whom Psyche
is one, is introduced by Virtue to Apollo, who introduces
him to Miss Philology. She is very much of a college
graduate, and just the girl to take Mr. Mercury in
hand. He at once feels the tender passion, and after a
proper amount of hesitation she consents to name the
day. Jupiter, after some deliberation, gives his consent;
Miss Philology, attended by her mother, Phronesis,
mounts to the Milky Way, and the ceremony is held in
the Palace of Jupiter. All the best people are there, and
all the best abstractions, including the Muses, the four
Cardinal Virtues, Philosophy, and the three Graces, and
Immortality. At the proper moment Apollo introduces
the bridegroom's gift to the bride in the shape of seven
servants. What bride to-day would not welcome such a
present from her beloved? But how disappointed she
would be at finding that the seven servants are the
seven liberal arts in disguise, and that each, as introduced, gives a comprehensive account of herself in one
volume.

The picturesque setting devised by Martianus Capella for his textbook is doubtless intended as a decoy
for the reader. The modern reader is glad when the
long and rather tawdry introduction is over and the
liberal arts are allowed to speak. But the pious fraud
was successful. The work was extraordinarily popular
in the schools of the early Middle Ages; Irish scholars
were particularly fond of it, and John the Scot devoted

a commentary to it.[34] It held its own beside the more scientific treatises of Boethius, and the serviceable *compendia* of Cassiodorus, of which more anon.

On this programme of the *trivium* and *quadrivium*, education throve, with natural modifications, through the Middle Ages. It was continued, with an increased devotion to the ancient Classics, by the Italian humanists of the Renaissance. It is the programme presented in an exceptionally serious chapter in Rabelais's gigantesque romance.[35] It is the foundation of the system of the Jesuits.[36] It is the essence of Oxford Greats, and of the former curriculum of Harvard College.

I would here call the reader's attention to a page of the Harvard Catalogue for 1830–1831.[37] My copy is unbound, but even when bound, this volume of thirty-one small pages would still be portable. It sets forth the course of instruction for Freshmen, Sophomores, Junior Sophisters, and Senior Sophisters. The programme is founded on the literatures of Greece and Rome, and many of the authors are listed. But there are also mathematics through calculus, general history and ancient history, with "Greek antiquities," Grotius, *De Veritate Religionis Christianae*, English grammar, rhetoric and composition, with themes, forensics, and oratory, modern languages, logic, philosophy and theology, natural philosophy, including mechanics, chemistry, electricity and magnetism, with "experimental lectures" — all this by the end of the Junior year.

The great feature of the Senior year is that no Classical literature is prescribed; the ancient authors have been transcended for the higher learning — natural philosophy, including astronomy, optics, mineralogy, and the philosophy of natural history, also intellectual and moral philosophy, and theology both natural and revealed. Modern languages are still pursued, themes and forensics are still required. Finally, we note political economy, anatomy, and Rawle "On the Constitution of the United States."

This is a humanistic programme, reaching to the upper heights of thought and concentrated on the present time. It were ridiculous to suppose that all of these subjects were pursued as thoroughly as they are in colleges to-day. It were also ridiculous to suppose that we could probably reintroduce such a programme in all its parts. Yet I venture to think that the lads of 1830 had their minds touched at more points, and with more points, than our undergraduates to-day. The elective system in college education seemed inevitable, particularly after President Eliot's prophetic address in 1884.[38] But the democratic principle of admitting all subjects as of equal educational value, this universal extension of the citizenship in the domain of intellectual inquiry, resulted for the lazy in the search for what was not hard, and for the industrious in the search for what they could do best. The danger is not great to the former class, the poor in spirit whom we always have with us; they will always employ their wits, which are often considerable, in performing the minimum of their teacher's expectations. The danger is to the serious students, who, no less than their leisurely brethren, pursue the path of least resistance; for them the lure is proficiency in some special subject, or their future career in life. It is not reprehensible early to lay plans for a career; quite the contrary. Specialization is not an evil, but a necessity for one who would advance in his profession and benefit mankind. But not to question the usefulness, or rather the indispensability, of vocational schools and schools for graduate research, the four years of college life should be consecrated to the attainment of a liberal or aristocratic education. Yes, I have ventured to say it, aristocratic, for it is a synonym for liberal, in the original meaning of the latter term. Aristocratic it is, for it aims at the best; it ennobles; it puts the stamp of a civilized gentlemen on those who possess it; or, in case we do not all turn out Lord Chesterfields, it at least makes our uncouth spirits finer than they would have been. It is a vocational programme, for one whose vocation is the art of life. It is a utilitarian programme, for it is of inestimable utility whatever one's trade. Without it, we are nothing but tradesmen, whether our trade is cobbling, chemistry, Latin, or Greek. In many of our colleges the elective system is modified by the requirement of some major subject or field of concentration, combined with a more or less systematic provision for excursions in outlying fields. This is a great reform, but it is a halfway house. It is a modified specialization and may be pursued in a spirit that misses the idea of a liberal education. The times are ripe, as President Lowell pointed out in a recent address,[39] for many experiments in education, among which training in the liberal arts deserves a place. There is a fine field for some adventurous and humanistic soul, at once reactionary and progressive, who would construct, despite the astounding wealth of new matter presented by the natural sciences and the social sciences, a clean-cut system, not coinciding with the programme of 1830, but based on the same principles, with Philosophy, perhaps in the form of Science, perhaps in some other form, restored to her throne.

But the reader may wonder whether I have forgotten the subject of my discourse. I can only plead that its title is the "New Education." However, I have stretched its scope egregiously. Let us hasten back to the time when the new education was monasticism.

Monasticism, as we saw, was introduced into the western world in the fourth century.[40] The first original anchorite seems to have been St. Paul, in the third century, and contemporary with him St. Anthony, whose ideas were furthered by St. Athanasius. St. Jerome was mainly instrumental in popularizing monasticism in the West, and he has left three important documents in those lives of St. Paul, St. Malchus, and St. Hilarion, as well as the descriptions of his own monastic practice and the founding of the monastery-convent at Bethelehem. We saw that he had firmly imbedded the study of the liberal arts as a part of monastic training; this was in the last period of his life, when the Christian and the Ciceronian parts of his nature had been comfortably harmonized. Indeed, St. Jerome is the founder, before Cassiodorus, of the more liberal monasticism in which the ancient studies had a place.

But St. Jerome's programme was not the only one. An entirely different, and far less pleasing, sort of monasticism was advocated by *Iohannes Cassianus*, who flourished in the last quarter of the fourth century. We do not know his birthplace or his station in life, but he was probably of a distinguished family, and Christian from his youth. He studied under Jerome in the East, and then, in 390, wanting something a bit more strenuous, he made a tour of the regions of Egypt occupied by Anchorites and Cenobites. After a stay of ten years, he left for Constantinople, where he studied under the great Christian scholar and orator, St. John Chrysostom. Finally, in 415, he went to Marseilles, established a double cloister like that of St. Jerome, and there spent the remainder of his days.

Cassian not only established his monastery, but wrote two treatises that set forth his principles in a scientific and comprehensive style. The first of these is called *De Institutis Coenobiorum et de octo principalium vitiorum remediis Libri XII.* "The Organization of Coenobitic Monasteries and the Cure of the Eight Cardinal Vices," in 12 volumes.[41] You can see from the very title that this is a standard work. Books I–IV discuss the organization of monastic life, its rules of discipline; all sorts of details are here considered — dress, food, proper psalms, hourly employment of the monks. Books V–XII discuss the eight vices and their cure. These books are of value for the student of ethics, of mediaeval poetry, and of Dante. Somewhat later, in the Middle Ages, the scheme of vices and virtues was fixed at seven, the number followed by Dante in his *Purgatorio*.

The first five vices according to Cassian are, in the inverse order of seriousness, gluttony (*gastrimargia*); incontinence (*forniculio*); avarice (*philargyria*); anger (*ira*); despondence, pessimism (*tristitia*).

The sixth vice is an interesting one, which we no longer have — I mean to say we no longer have the name of it, as the Middle Ages had. It is ἀκηδία, which Cassian defines as *taedium sive anxietas cordis*, listlessness, spiritual sloth or ennui.[42] The Greek word, which Cicero had applied to Atticus long before,[43] was taken over into Latin as *acedia*, which later became *accidia* and naturally, though incorrectly, suggested something acid. This brought the vice pretty near to *tristitia*; St. Thomas associates the two,[44] and Chaucer defines bitterness as the mother of *accidie*.[45] This sin would visit a monk in his desert retreat, appearing often at the noon-day haze, when the noon-day devil, *meridianus daemon*, was taking his strolls. It is a pity that we have the word no longer, the last appearance of which was about 1520, according to Murray; perhaps the term "Harvard indifference" (in the wrong sense of that generally misused term) approaches as near as anything. St. Thomas à Kempis, in the *Imitatio Christi*, remarks that a man's besetting sin will be more vigorously punished in the next world than the others to which he is addicted. The gluttonous will be tortured with thirst and hunger, and the *acediosi* will be stirred to action by the application of red hot pokers.[46]

The seventh vice is vanity, conceit, κενοδοξία, and the eighth and worst is pride. This scheme is virtually the same as that of Dante. The exaltation of *superbia* to the sovereignty of the vices starts as early as the days of the Jewish dispersion in Alexandria. For we read in *Ecclesiasticus*: "initium omnis peccati est superbia." [47] I think it can also be shown that the vice most often hit in the beast-fables of the humble Phaedrus, is *superbia*. It was likewise the vice that caused frequent disaster to heroes in Greek tragedy. To-day, in the Gospel according to Nietzsche, it is one of the cardinal virtues.

This is Cassian's classification of the vices. What of his educational programme? It was distinctly narrower than that of St. Jerome. He remarks [48] on the practice of reading sacred authors at table, that it was a Cappalocian, not an Egyptian practice, and that it was designed not so much to give the monks spiritual enlightenment as to keep them from talking and quarrelling. We also learn much of Cassian's educational plan from the types of piety that he presents for our admiration. There are certain Egyptian monks, careful of both tongues and eyes, who peep out from under the edge of their cowls enough to see the table and the food, but not enough to see how much anybody else is eating.[49] Then there is brother Machetes, a paragon of propriety, who during any religious conference never was known to go to sleep, but the moment any scandal or frivolous tale was told, he would drop off immediately; he had acquired this facility as a result of a long course of daily prayers.[50] There is also a pious Abbot, who, though he knew only a few words of Greek, was deeply versed in the Scriptures. When asked about the necessary preparation for an intelligent reading of the Holy Writ, he replied that the heart enlightened by devotions and other moral regimen could understand, without studying the books of the commentators.[51]

For a brilliant exposition of the weaker side of monasticism, I would commend Gibbon's chapter to your attention.[52] He turns on St. Jerome as acid a satire as Jerome had turned on the Rome of his day. This is one of the few places where I think we may really charge Gibbon with a *suppressio veri;* his material is drawn mainly from Cassian and the worst parts of Jerome. In a word, he does just what a good satirist ought to do, but not a good historian. Monasticism, we must admit, may encourage the individual to centre his attention overmuch on himself, his spiritual condition, and his relation to his Maker. Moreover, the monastic is concerned rather with his moral than with his intellectual welfare. The movement is a great Puritan protest against the iniquities and frivolities of a Pagan and a Paganized Christian society. At first, it hardly had a place for the cultivation of the liberal arts. But we should not call monasticism altogether selfish or unsocial, because self-centred; for the monk wished not merely to flee the world, but to give an example to society of a life of simplicity and godly living which one attained by self-denial. Monasticism is also the first attempt in the history of Christianity (of which there have been many since) to peel off the accretions and to return to the primitive faith. It is also one of the earliest practical endeavors for communism, again a return to the original Christian communism, and perhaps the only kind of communism possible in our imperfect world — communism in spots. This is the starting-point, which under Jerome was broadened to include the pursuit of the liberal arts. There were then two types of monasticism represented in the fourth century, that of Cassian and that of Jerome. We shall see how they fared in the decades to come.

In the year 529 A.D., St. Benedict established a monastery at Monte Cassino. It is related that he found a temple of Apollo there, and that he tore it down; in the words of the poet, his pupil Marcus, he converted the "stronghold of Hell and Death" into a "stronghold of life." [53] This is a typical act, for Christians of another sort would have made over the temple, like the builders of Santa Maria sopra Minerva. Benedict's character seems not to have been much affected by learning or art. St. Gregory, in his biography of the Saint, refers to him as one who was "sagely ignorant and wisely uneducated." [54] How literally shall we take these words? At the end of the seventeenth century, the great Benedictine, Mabillon, the father of the science of palaeography and an extraordinarily learned man in various fields, believed, as others have believed, that the régime established by St. Benedict had a place for the liberal arts. [55] We have learned not to believe a Christian writer, necessarily, when he calls himself "rustic"; and so it may be when one of them is called rustic by an admirer; this may be a kind of compliment intended to cover a multitude of learned accomplishments. We turn to St. Benedict's *Rule* for information, and find that an amount of sacred reading is prescribed. [56] But there seems to be no provision for the cultivation of the liberal arts that in St. Jerome's programme led up to the sacred studies. The secular schools were operating at the time, and young Benedict at least began his education in one of them; [57]

perhaps you may call his monastery a kind of Graduate
School or Theological Seminary, which is not hostile to
secular learning, but presupposes it — please note here
that I say "perhaps."

Next to Boethius, Cassiodorus was the most important figure at the court of Theodoric. He was born at
Squillace in the Bruttii, of a well-to-do and noble family,
about 480, and died, at the ripe old age of over 90, about
575. His life falls into two sharply defined periods. In
the first of these, he was a statesman, secretary to Theodoric, and influential in administrative affairs; he was
consul in 514, and later, like Boethius, *magister officiorum*. In this period he wrote his *Variae*, or *Miscella-
nies*. This is a collection of state papers and letters on
political and other topics. It is admirably translated by
Hodgkin, and is an all-important index to the political
and intellectual conditions of the times.[58] To quote but
one example, Cassiodorus records a fine utterance of
Theodoric's which shows the tolerance of the Gothic
monarch — at least in one of his dealings with the Jews.
"We cannot prescribe religion," Theodoric declared,
"for no one can be forced to believe against his will." [59]
One might imagine that such a sentiment could not have
occurred to anybody before the time when voluntary
chapel was introduced at Harvard College.

In the second half of his life, which began in 540,
Cassiodorus turned his back on the world completely.
He founded a monastery on a new plan and lived in re-

tirement there till his death. He was about sixty years old at the time, and he had thirty-five more years to live.

Cassiodorus had always been interested in education. In 535–36, he had planned with Pope Agapetus to found a Christian university at Rome,[60] on the model of the ancient universities to which I have briefly referred; the liberal arts were to be taught as a precursor to sacred learning, — theology and the interpretation of the Scriptures, — just as formerly they had led up to philosophy. It was high time. The ancient ideal of education had become bankrupt. Philosophy had been virtually driven from her throne by Rhetoric.[61] The goal of liberal studies was no longer the purging and exaltation of the mind in the life of reason, but the flashy success of the sophistic art. One must know the intellectual background of the times to see that Boethius, no less than Cassiodorus, was a deliverer and a restorer, in his vision of a Philosophy that relegated the false charms of Rhetoric to their rightful place.[62] If the university planned by Cassiodorus and Agapetus had been established, it would have closely resembled Harvard College in the old days, or any humanistic institution of learning. However, Agapetus died in 536. The times were troublous, and Cassiodorus gave up his plan. Instead, four years later, he founded his monastery.

This change of purpose on the part of Cassiodorus gives us the very moment when the old went out and the new came in. And it was right for the new to come.

The essential elements in this historical problem — the reasons for the success of monasticism — are three: the necessity of preserving the ancient civilization; the necessity of counteracting the new and, at first, destructive forces of barbarism; and the necessity of propagating the Christian faith, which began with an emphasis on moral training. Just as in the early centuries of Christianity, this moral element constituted the heart of the new movement, only later — in the fourth century — absorbing Pagan culture as well, so now the Church, when confronted with a new force which also threatened the old civilization, insisted first and foremost on its own essential message; it was Christian life that the barbarians needed first, and the liberal arts later. The great institution for setting forth an example of Christian life was the monastery; Cassiodorus turned perforce to that and not to the university, when his plans were matured.

For all that, though accepting the essential purpose of monasticism, Cassiodorus did not forget the ancient ideal. In fact, as I have just set forth, he restored it. Returning to St. Jerome's plan, he fused the two in a new system of education. We may credit Jerome with the inception, and Cassiodorus with the establishment of this system. Cassiodorus sets forth his ideas in a work entitled *A Manual of Instruction in Divine and Human Readings*. It is a better title than the *Divine Institutions* of Lactantius, since it makes explicit the union of the two cultures, Christian and Pagan, which, though clear enough in Lactantius's text, is not recognized in its title. Reading, we see, is the basis of Cassiodorus's curriculum. Divine reading holds the foremost place; the goal of monastic education is the knowledge of theology, Holy Scripture, and Church history, but for the proper understanding of these matters the study of the *artes liberales* must precede. In treating the latter, he first gives a sketch of the seven arts, briefer and less technical than in either Martianus Capella or Boethius, and then appends a list of the most important treatises on the different subjects. In brief, the work is a kind of syllabus of universal knowledge, the *omne scibile*, with a bibliography.

Cassiodorus was naturally anxious to preserve the educational apparatus necessary for carrying out his scheme. A monastic library was indispensable, and therefore the copying of books became a part of the monk's duty. He heaps encomia on the *antiquarius*, or scribe, by whose "fingers divine treasures are scattered abroad." "Oh, blessed the perseverance," he exclaims, "laudable the industry which preaches to men with the hand, starts tongues with the fingers, gives an unspoken salvation to mortals and against the iniquitous deceits of the Devil fights with pen and ink. For Satan receives as many wounds as the scribe copies words of the Lord." [63] In this way, the pen becomes as mighty as the sword. The scribe could feel that, despite his sedentary occupation, he was a combatant in the *ecclesia militans*.

Now Cassiodorus is speaking here of copies of the Bible; but this plan made necessary the transcribing of the heathen authors as well. In one of his chapters on dialectic he turns for illustrations to Cicero, Virgil, and Terence.[64] The monastic preceptor would therefore study such models, and need editions of them. To this broadly laid plan of Cassiodorus we owe, in large part, the preservation of such works as we have of Classical Latin literature to-day.

Not all the monks were to be copyists. Cassiodorus made allowances for the weaker brethren. With a witty quotation from Virgil's *Georgics*,[65] he provided for those "about whose heart the chill blood clots" (or, as we should say, "about whose brain a thick fog rests"); he permitted them, like the poet, "to love woods and streams inglorious." This did not mean a life of inactivity. The humbler brethren were not to repose on the banks of slipping streams and catch impulses from the vernal woods, but they worked the farm. Further, Cassiodorus cites for their benefit a small bibliography on agriculture — Columella, Gargilius Martialis, and the rest. In fine, they were taking a kind of college course, in a lowly or snap subject, with extensive laboratory practice; it is a primitive School of Agriculture.

In general, this sacred retreat established by Cassiodorus was by no means the cheerless prison that the term monastery popularly connotes. It included various attractions that the Roman satirists had condemned as luxuries, such as elaborate baths — as those should note who think that cleanliness was not next to godliness in the ancient monastery! However, these baths seem primarily for the needs of the sick. There were also fine gardens, and fish-ponds.[66] From the latter extravagance, the institution derived its name of *Vivarium*, or the "Fish-Pond." The site was near Cassiodorus's birth-place, as we have noted, down on the east coast of the Bruttii. Cassiodorus comments on the beauty of the site, with an enthusiasm that suggests Pliny's comfortable satisfaction in the charms of his villas; he declares his intention to make the place so attractive that, instead of having his monks drift off elsewhere, others would be drawn perforce to it. A delightful way to visit Cassiodorus's retreat without leaving your armchair, is to turn the pages of George Gissing's *By the Ionian Sea*.

As we might expect, Cassiodorus did not forego his literary activity during the years of his retirement. He wrote a work on spelling, *De Orthographia*, as a help to his scribes. He wrote a *Commentary on the Psalms*, and other commentaries, to show how liberal learning might be applied to a sacred subject. He wrote a treatise on the soul, *De Anima*, which indicates his interest in philosophy. He also assigned various useful tasks of scholarship to his monks, such as the translation into Latin of the *Antiquities* of Josephus, which made a convenient manual of Pre-Christian Hebrew history; as a manual of the history of the Christian church, he arranged for a translation of the so-called *Historia Tripartita*, by Theodoretus, Sozomenus, and Socrates — a work much cited in the Middle Ages. Thus Cassiodorus, in a different way, was as useful as Boethius in providing the Middle Ages with an intellectual equipment.

The point to be emphasized above all is that a monastic developed under such a system as that of Cassiodorus is far from being a narrow sort of man. In his work *On the Soul*, Cassidorus paints two types of character. The first description he calls "How to tell a bad man." [67] This is how.

His face is clouded with evil, whatsoever his bodily grace. He is sad, even when making merry; later, when repentance comes, deserted by the impulse of pleasure, he forthwith returns to sadness. His eyes move restlessly; as a second thought comes, he is unsteady, roving, shifty, a prey to anxiety, disturbed by suspicions; he is much influenced by other's judgments about himself, since in his folly he has lost all judgment of his own.

Now we may turn to the other picture — "How to tell a good man."

His face is ever joyous, and reposeful, strong though it be thin, seemly though pale, happy despite constant tears, reverend with its long beard. [Cassiodorus does not share St. Jerome's animosity towards beards.] The good man, further, is neat without adornment. Thus does the just mind turn the opposite qualities into beauty. His eyes shine with joy and an honorable courtesy. His speech is true, penetrating good hearts, desiring to commend to all the love of God with which he is filled. His very voice is moderate, not weak from constant silence, or strained by boisterous clamour.[68]

This last remark looks like an application of Aristotle's principle of the golden mean, which here runs between loquacity and dumbness, and is quite the reverse of Cassian's dictum that a monk should be seen and not heard, and that not very much of him should be seen — just the two eyes of him, peeping from under his cowl.

In the midst of Gibbon's satire on monasticism, there is one sentence which, if he were writing history and not satire, would deserve amplification.[69] He has just remarked that "The monastic studies have tended, for the most part, to darken, rather than to dispel, the cloud of superstition." He then adds: "Yet the curiosity or zeal of some learned solitaries has cultivated the ecclesiastical, and even the profane, sciences; and posterity must gratefully acknowledge, that the monuments of Greek and Roman literature have been preserved and multiplied by their indefatigable pens." "Cassiodorus" he adds in a footnote, "has allowed an ample scope for the studies of the monks; and we shall not be scandalized, if their pens sometimes wandered from Chrysostom and Augustin to Homer and Virgil." This last is deliberate misstatement conveyed by an innuendo. Gibbon insinuates that the copying of the Classics was a kind of transgression, into which the monks were tempted now and then. On the contrary, it was a regular part of their task; for the study of the Pagan authors was ingrained in the scheme of monastic discipline as established by Cassiodorus.

A French scholar, in an important book on the history of Classical education, is similarly belittling in his account of Cassiodorus.[70] He has to admit that the study of the ancients was essential to his plan, but he insists that the monks, though edified, were never entertained by what they read. They laboured to understand, but "*une fois arrivé là,*" once they got there, they took care to allow no ounce of pleasure to corrupt their edification, "*se bien garder d'y prendre plaisir.*" I think I have shown by his quotation from Virgil that Cassiodorus took the same sort of enjoyment in reading him that any lover of literature would take to-day. Roger's treatment of the whole subject is what the Germans would call "step-motherly." A juster estimate of Cassiodorus is given by another French scholar, with whom a noted German agrees, who calls him "The hero and restorer of science in the sixth century."[71]

The last name that I shall mention in connection with the establishment of monasticism is that of Pope Gregory the Great, to whom I paid some attention — insufficient attention — in the first lecture in this course. And here I will merely say that, while we cannot help admiring the tremendous energy, ability, and persuasive force of this great man, it is plain that in him we have force and not culture, a clear vision of immediate needs and long plans for the future, but little reverence for the past. Gregory may not have burned the Palatine library, as John of Salisbury relates,[72] but really he did not need to burn it. His programme, if universally accepted, would automatically close the doors of the collectors of ancient books and leave their treasures to moulder on their shelves. Gregory was building for the present, but the present was but a moment in our life. His ultimate outlook is on eternity.[73] The literature which a Christian should read, and which Gregory accordingly composes, is full of visions and miracles; he has no time for comic mirth or Horatian urbanities. Gregory acts and organizes in the present, but he organizes the present as a precinct of the world to come.

In thus turning his back on the past, Gregory represents a different attitude from that of Cassiodorus. The two are members of opposing schools. The Christian humanism which was firmly established in the society of Ausonius, of Sidonius, and of Boethius has found a new rival. And a larger conflict is on than that between Gregory and Cassiodorus. It is that old quarrel of which Plato speaks, between philosophy and poetry.[74] The quarrel takes different forms in different ages. For poetry, we sometimes say "humanism," and for philosophy, "science," or, if we have a low form of philosophy, "practicality," or "modernism." Sometimes it is hard to affix these labels. It is hard to label Plato who, though he may seem to a humanist to fly the wrong colors, somehow is ever on the right side. It is hard, when you know all of him, to label Cicero, who is nothing if not a humanist, yet a humanist who has no quarrel with philosophy, and who can view our little life with sombre and mediaeval eyes *sub specie aeternitatis*. But between Cassiodorus and Gregory, both to be numbered among our Founders, the issue is clear. The former would include the culture of the past in his plans for a liberal monasticism; the latter would throw the past away. We have returned to *our* ancient question, the attitude of the Christian Church toward Pagan culture; it assumes a new aspect and gives promise of a new quarrel, as the Middle Ages come on. There will be ups and downs, the reactions of various temperaments and various moods in individual minds. There will be different effects from different men and moments of the period of Foundation. There will be a powerful effect from the master-mind of Gregory. But the ultimate victory will be that of the party of Lactantius and Cassiodorus, advocates of a Christian humanism in which the old education is vitally embedded in the new.

CHAPTER VIII

ST. AUGUSTINE AND DANTE

THERE is a Spanish proverb, Mr. Santayana once remarked, which says that every good house contains a wine-cellar and every good sermon a quotation from St. Augustine. I cannot give any other source for this proverb, but since Mr. Santayana said it, a Spanish proverb it is. The second part of it, at all events, would win unanimous approval in the Middle Ages, when none of the Fathers of the Western Church occupied a higher pinnacle of fame than St. Augustine. In the Renaissance, St. Jerome, the humanist, somewhat pushed ahead, — very much so in the opinion of Erasmus, — but St. Augustine was by no means shoved aside.[1] Filelfo presents a discriminating estimate of the two.[2] St. Jerome he finds the greater scholar and master of style, St. Augustine incomparably the greater thinker, not only for his original contributions to theology and philosophy but for his knowledge of mathematics and natural science. Filelfo concludes that, if you could only roll those two intellects into one, nothing greater could be expected of humanity; the force of nature could no farther go.

Dante, with all the Middle Ages, paid homage to St. Augustine. He does not quote him often, but in most of the places in which he does, his homage is of exceeding significance. One of the passages occurs in the *Convivio*, where he is discussing the question of when it is proper to talk about one's self. He selects St. Augustine's *Confessions* as an appropriate example, for the motive of that work, he finds, was to instruct. Humanity will be instructed by seeing the progress of such a life from bad to good, and from good to better, and from better to best.[3] Dante perhaps is considering the history of that great soul as we can read it in the *Confessions*; or he may have had in mind that ladder of the vices of which Augustine speaks in one of his sermons: [4] *de vitiis nostris scalam nobis facimus, si vitia ipsa calcamus*, translated by Longfellow in his "Ladder of St. Augustine,"

> Saint Augustine! Well hast thou said,
>   That of our vices we can frame
> A ladder, if we will but tread
>   Beneath our feet each deed of shame.

Tennyson rendered this into better poetry in *In Memoriam:*

> I hold it truth with him that sings
>   To one clear harp of divers tones,
>   That men may rise on stepping-stones
> Of their dead selves to better things.

I am aware that, when Tennyson was asked whom he meant by these verses, he replied that it was probably Goethe.[5] But poets never like to be asked whom they meant. Ask them whom they meant, and they will forget or equivocate. There is no doubt at any rate whom Dante meant in the *Convivio*.

It is fortunate that a writer of such genius as St. Augustine has left us probably better means of ascertaining his real opinions than any other historical character of equal fame. Horace has turned himself inside out as thoroughly, to the lasting benefit of humanity, to whom, however, he makes a different gift — not a profound searching of the mysteries of heaven and earth, but the most satisfactory art of human living ever yet devised. Augustine has left in the *Confessions* an unexampled record, not only of his outer, but of his inner life; some deductions must perhaps be made, but these do not affect the value of the whole. We see how the development of Augustine's intellectual views corresponded with the external events in his career; how the great turning-points in his progress from a Carthaginian roisterer to a Christian saint were largely the result of his studies in heathen philosophy. Moreover, we have a criterion of the genuineness of the writings ascribed to Augustine and his own estimate of their value. For in that splendid work of his, written almost at the end of his life, *The Retractations*, St. Augustine gives a complete chronological catalogue of his works, with an account of the circumstances under which each was composed, and an enumeration of the passages which his maturer judgment would lead him to emend or excise — a list of *errata* submitted to the Divine Reader, who would scan the whole book of his life.

I am not going to fill this lecture, as I might, with a mere enumeration of the works of St. Augustine, nor am I going to rehearse the familiar facts in his career. Instead, I will leave you to the reading, or the re-reading of his *Confessions*, one of those numerous works which no liberally educated person can afford to miss.[6] This act of profound introspection, this offering of one's past, with all its lights and shades, to God, is as novel as it is subtle. It might well engage the attention of our keen searcher of souls, Mr. Gamaliel Bradford, who, to the best of my knowledge, has not yet included in his studies this monument of autopsychography.[7] The motive that inspires a work like the *Confessions* is open to criticism; it is a question whether a wholesome mind is anxious to write minutely about itself. Dante, as we have seen, finds a *grandissima utilitade* in a self-examination like that of Augustine, because it illustrates a progress, and constitutes a manual of instruction. Critics who have called the *Confessions* morbid and self-conscious, like those of Rousseau, cannot have read the work, or read with understanding. The emotions that Augustine describes are subjective; his treatment of them is, strange to say, objective. One can point to a number of writers whose interests might seem self-conscious, but who in virtue of their inspiration, their brusque disregard of the impropriety of their endeavor, transcend self-consciousness. In literary creation, might makes right. Thus Horace acquits himself through his sense of humor,

Juvenal through his bitterness of soul, Keats through his love of the beautiful, St. Augustine through his sombre imagination and his mystic passion.

We may better approach the mind of St. Augustine and understand its kinship to the mind of Dante, if we consider for a moment a highly interesting little group of works, written between Augustine's conversion and his baptism, or, in some cases, immediately after his baptism in 387. Our studies thus far have revealed a number of writers to whom the title of Christian Cicero is not inappropriate. Minucius Felix, Cyprian, Arnobius, Lactantius, and Ambrose, in different ways and in different degrees, are followers of Marcus Tully. There is no doubt about Jerome, for the voice from on high pronounced him a Ciceronian. A profound interpreter of the Middle Ages, Ludwig Traube, has applied the names *Aetas Vergiliana*, *Aetas Horatiana*, and *Aetas Ovidiana*, to certain mediaeval periods.[8] It is just as true that the most conspicuous influence on the style and thought of the Latin Apologetes and the fathers of the fourth century, as I have already hinted, comes from Cicero. Let us call it, then, the *Aetas Ciceroniana*.

You will think at once of other interests of the age besides Cicero, but can you think of any ancient writer whose influence was quite on a par with his? You will also wonder whether Augustine has part in a Ciceronian age, whether, if he was in it, he was of it. It is something to wonder about, but it is none the less true that, though

Augustine may more aptly be called a Christian Plato, there is a notably Ciceronian period in his career. Cicero's *Hortensius* was the book that intellectually awakened him, and he must have studied Cicero intensely while he was a teacher of rhetoric.

But I am thinking, besides, of the period of his conversion and baptism. It was then that he wrote certain dialogues, the record of actual conversations, taken down by a stenographer, doubtless somewhat embellished in their published form, that recall the days of Tusculum and prophesy the academies of the Renaissance, and the schools of Guarino and Vittorino.[9] The meetings were held at the villa of Verecundus. Mother Monica had joined her son, who welcomed her presence at the debates. The beloved Alypius was there, and also two pupils, Trygetius and Licentius. Pagan and Christian authors contributed alike to this pleasant form of culture. In the morning the little academy would interpret a book of Virgil. In the afternoon they engaged in a debate in which Plato was cited quite as often as St. Matthew. Now they would sing a Psalm, and now compose a poem on Pyramus and Thisbe. The style of the dialogues is Ciceronian, with periods and metrical *clausulae* — evidently the kind of prose that Augustine had been writing all along, and very different from that of the *Confessions*. The spirit of these dialogues is also in marked contrast with that of the later works. They are light and easy in tone. There is jest and banter, and a comfortable sense of philosophic leisure.[10] The poets are not infrequently quoted, particularly Virgil and Terence, along with a verse of the beloved Ambrose.[11]

In Dante's *Inferno*, before one descends into the gloom of the nether hell, there is a pleasant greensward, within the Castle of Wisdom, on which are strolling, in apparent comfort, the old Pagan poets and philosophers.[12] I would not press the comparison, to the point of calling the later works of Augustine infernal, but it is pleasant to look back from certain serious and sombre moods to the cheerful humanism of his Ciceronian days.

The titles of two of these works at once suggest Cicero — *Contra Academicos* and *De Beata Vita*. There is also the *Soliloquium*, really not a soliloquy, but a dialogue between Augustine and his Reason, a device that reappears, in a more elaborate and picturesque form, in the *Consolation of Philosophy* of Boethius. The subject of the *Soliloquium*, is the problem of cognition, the possibility of knowing, the nature of the real and the false. The *De Ordine* starts off with a discussion of providence; but as Augustine saw that his hearers were getting beyond their depths, he discoursed on a simpler sense of the word "order," — the sense of orderly conduct, — and thus passed to a consideration of the seven arts that formed the basis of a liberal education. Indeed Augustine began at this time, as we have already seen, a set of text-books on the seven arts.[13] I will merely mention once more his *De Musica*, which includes a minute treatment of metre. I doubt not that he had written reams of verses in his youth. Finally, there should doubtless be assigned to this period a dialogue on the Soul, — *De Quantitate Animae*, — a work which Dante mentions and which I believe may have exercised a profound influence on his imagination. We will return to it in a moment.

Meanwhile, we may note, Augustine's text-books are a kind of farewell to his old career as rhetorician. The dialogues, similarly, are a farewell to Cicero. For though in style and method they are a tribute to him, although he is frequently praised, he is just as frequently criticized; Augustine has transcended him, along with one who was even more potently his master, Plato.

When St. Bernard, in the heights of the Empyrean, sets forth to Dante the mysteries that only so exalted a spirit can utter at that height, he points out Augustine, sitting with Francis and Benedict only a little lower than the blessed John.[14] He is not of the company of St. Thomas Aquinas and the other giants of the intellect, whom he has passed below in the heaven of the Sun.[15] Philosophy, the encyclopaedia of the *omne scibile*, has its reward, but it moves on a lower plane. Augustine is exalted with the most sublime of mystics who have penetrated into the very essence of Deity. He is raised to that good eminence, I believe, not only because of the higher flights of his thought that Dante had followed in others of his works, but because of the argument of that Ciceronian dialogue *De Quantitate Animae*. Dante makes reference to this work in his letter to Can Grande, that precious document for the understanding of the *Paradiso*, of the poet's mind, and of the amazingly intricate rhetorical doctrine through which he made his way to the crystal clarity of his poetry.

In commenting, in this letter, on the opening verses of the first canto of the *Paradiso*,[16] where he declares that he cannot describe all that he saw, inasmuch as his mind plunged deeply into its own desire, or God, cannot recall it, he cites the vision that St. Paul records and the story of the Transfiguration, and then requests readers who do not understand to turn to Richard of St. Victor *De Contemplatione*, Bernard *De Consideratione*, and Augustine *De Quantitate Animae*, "and," he adds, "they will cease from their cavilling."[17] The passage in Augustine's work that Dante has in mind occurs towards the end of the treatise.[18] I infer that he had read it all. Since the work is not often emphasized in accounts of St. Augustine or of Dante, I will briefly describe its contents.[19]

It is a curious subject, the *Quantity of the Soul*. Augustine begins by denying that the soul has length, breadth, or thickness, using mathematical arguments and diagrams which I cannot understand, and enlivening his discussion with quotations from Horace which I can. He shows eventually that what he means by *quantitas* is rather *quanta est*. What is the greatness or the power of the soul — *quantam habet vim?*

He distinguishes seven aspects of the Soul, or rather seven steps, *gradus*, by which it climbs to its perfection. Its first condition is that of mere *animatio*, its physical life, which it shares in common with trees and other growing things. Its second is *sensus*, or feeling, all the five senses, which animals also possess, but plants do not. He rebukes what he calls the rustic and sacrilegious error of supposing that a vine is pained when the grapes are plucked from it.[20] Perhaps he had heard some tender-hearted rustic sigh, "Poor vine," as he loaded his baskets. But Augustine is not a sentimentalist. In the third grade we have reason, peculiar to man and not to beast. The classification, thus far, is exactly that of Aristotle in his treatise on the Soul. If Augustine did not take this much directly from Aristotle, he would have found the gist of it in Cicero.[21] Surely the account of the manifestations of the third state of the Soul, reason, or art, as Augustine calls it, has a strangely familiar ring. We see it, he says, in memory, in art, in agriculture, in the building of cities, in the invention of the alphabet and of language, in man's interest in posterity, in the organization of society, in military and civic government, in institutions both sacred and profane, in philosophic thought, in streams of eloquence and varied modes of music, in the thousand and one forms of mimicry devised for sport and jest, in exact measurements, in trained calculations, in the ability to infer both past and future from the present.[22] The reader of Cicero's *Tusculans* [23] will recognize here the workings of those divine powers of the soul, memory and inventiveness, that guarantee its immortality. Augustine has supplemented the illustrations and adapted them to a new scheme.

For he now forges ahead from the point where Aristotle had stopped. This third stage of the Soul, its reason or art, is attained by both learned and unlearned, by both good and bad men. Divine inventiveness may be put to a diabolical end. The fourth state is attained when the soul becomes good, when it learns that the goods of the body are not its own, when more and more it abstracts itself from what defiles, when it devotes itself to the welfare of human society and the application of the Golden Rule, when it follows authority and the precepts of the wise and believes that God is speaking to it through them. This task of purgation is often accompanied by an intense fear of death, lest the soul be found stained with sin when death arrives. In this section of the argument, as before, Ciceronian, and Platonic, matter may be observed, adjusted to Augustine's new purpose.

When the soul becomes fixed in virtue, it has ascended the fifth stair. It has surmounted its fears and solicitudes. It proceeds with a mighty and incredible confidence toward God, that is, to the contemplation of truth, to the secret place of the high reward of its struggling.

Thus morally purged, the Soul is ready for its sixth condition, the beatific vision of the things that really and supremely are. For it is one thing to purify the eye of the Soul that its vision of truth be not vain and distorted, but another to guard and establish its health, keeping its look serene and straight toward that which should be seen. For those who would do this before they are cleansed and healed, are so beaten by that light of the truth that they think not only that there is no good therein but that great evil is there — they objectify the beam in their own eyes.

Now, when the soul is finally cleansed, it mounts the seventh step, which is no longer a step, but an abiding-place of delight and the enjoyment of the highest and true good. And such pleasure is there in contemplating the truth, such purity, sincerity, and unquestioning assurance, that the thinker will believe that he has never known anything before, when he seemed to himself to know. For the less the soul is impeded in clinging wholly to the whole truth, the more will that once-dreaded death, namely the utter flight and escape from the body, be coveted as the best of boons.[24] "And even as we do now," — I here am translating directly, — "when we are freed from cares so that we long to examine and behold a thing, so shall we do then more freely and lose ourselves in contemplation and perception. For there is ingrained in our souls an insatiable desire to behold the truth, and when we arrive on the shores of that realm, the greater our longing to know heavenly things, the easier will be our knowledge of them."

I have translated directly, but have treated my readers unfairly, for I have appended to Augustine a sentence from the *Tusculan Disputations*.[25] Forgive the trickery if it makes clearer the truth that Augustine's argument is, in its essence, contained in Cicero's work. Cicero, too, is among the mystics, so far as the poor Pagan could be, and his mysticism comes from Plato. Augustine has apportioned the matter differently, and made the soul climb seven steps. He names them in order, from lowest to highest, Vitality, Sensation, Art, Virtue, Tranquillity, Approach, Contemplation.[26] In its progress, the location of the soul and the centre of its attention may be described in seven phrases as "of the body," "through the body," "about the body," "toward itself," "in itself," "toward God," "in God." [27] It will be noted that the soul in its journey passes through three realms. In the first three stages, it is in the realm of body or matter, taking successively higher attitudes toward matter. In the next two it deals with itself, or soul. In the last two, it first approaches God and then abides in Him. In each of these conditions, Augustine declares that the soul has its distinct and proper beauty, so that it successively acts and thinks beautifully of another, beautifully through another, beautifully about another, beautifully toward a beautiful, beautifully in a beautiful, beautifully toward beauty, beautifully in beauty.[28] What aesthete could be more intense? This aesthetic contemplation, this dwelling on beauty, may doubtless surprise some who expect nothing but legalistic formalism and Roman hard-headedness from the man who damned infants and crushed the human will; yet climb with St. Augustine step by step, and you will attain a region where beauty is truth, truth beauty. Of course, he would lift his brows rather high if a young poet informed him that this is all we know on earth and all we need to know.[29]

It is Neoplatonism, doubtless, that is mainly responsible for this new ladder of St. Augustine and that shapes his imagination in forms strange to Cicero and Plato. But the essence is the same, the sharp distinction of matter and mind, the recognition of a fundamental and cosmic dualism — to use a term once shunned by true philosophers, but now, thanks to Dr. More, rolled sweetly under the tongue.[30] We are apt to dwell on the absurd aspects of Neoplatonism, its love of big words and subtle distinctions, its extreme courtesy to the Ultimate Entity at the heart of things, a courtesy so humble that, after stripping off one attribute after the other, it finds Being too belittling a predicate to apply and thus leaves the great Something, or the great Not-any-thing, out in the cold with the non-existent. But

f we forget the metaphysical jargon of Neoplatonism
.nd reduce it to the moral and psychological facts upon
vhich it rests, we find something simple and sane. As-
uming, that is, that the Platonic sort of mysticism is
imple and sane, Neoplatonism is nothing but this mysti-
ism with ladders. Plato, as I observed in the lecture on
it. Ambrose, arrives at mystic heights only after toiling
ıp the path of reason.[31] When once there, he may soar
urther than any Neoplatonic eye can follow. But the
Neoplatonists lengthened the journey by marking its
tages; they craved in their morsel of ecstasy a linkéd
netaphysical sweetness long drawn out. The construc-
ion of metaphysical ladders may not be in itself more
nystical than the ladder that a carpenter builds of
vood; the scheme lends itself to a wooden formalism if
:reated by a wooden mind. But the mind of a poet, of
ın Ambrose or an Augustine, helped both by Neopla-
onism and by the new vision of allegory, finds the gate
)f heaven by the stones that served as Jacob's pillow,
ınd sees the Angels of God ascending and descending on
the ladder of his dream.

The history of such imagery, in its main outlines,
nust hover before our minds as we read the *Divine
Comedy* of Dante. For Dante's world is built on ladders,
ladders down, ladders up, ladders far up till one climbs
no more. In planning his journey of the soul, Dante
thought of many other such journeys, many visions
dreamed in the Middle Ages or in antiquity. For in-

stance, in the resonant and liturgical Latin of Cicero's *Dream of Scipio*, he found ready for his purpose a journey to celestial heights, the same scheme of the nine spheres that he adopted, and sombre reflections on the life that is death and the death that is life.[32] The spiritual ascent of the soul, till it loses itself in the contemplation of the divine mystery, he would find implied in St. Augustine's *Confessions*, and elaborately set forth in his dialogue on the *Quantity of the Soul*. He had read many things else, of course, before the ascending heavens of a new *Paradiso* took form in his creative mind.[33] But Plato, Cicero, St. Augustine, Dante — these are links in one chain. We naturally impute more mysticism to Virgil than to Cicero; and yet, in the scheme of Dante's poem, Virgil can show the way only through Hell and Purgatory. Marcus Tully has risen to a state even more exalted than the consulship of 63 B.C. Dante finds him in the Limbo, with the noble company who inhabit the Palace of Wisdom;[34] and yet his spirit, unnamed, to be sure, is one of the guides, the lesser guides, in Paradise.

But there is another mystic approach from St. Augustine to Dante, where Virgil leads the way. We may find it in Augustine's greatest, or at least most elaborate work, the *City of God*. On this he toiled for about thirteen years — 413–426. In contrast to the *Confessions*, it is a thoroughly objective book, a constructive historical treatise, not the record of a soul. The general plan is clear and systematic; there are digressions, but the digressions are part of the plan.

The primary purpose of the first ten books is to prove
to the Pagans that the destruction of the Roman Empire by the barbarians was due, not to the advent of the
Christian religion, but to the corruptions of Paganism
itself. The charge that the new faith had called down
the anger of the gods on the world was, as we have seen,
a necessary subject for refutation in many of the early
Christian apologies.[35] Here it challenged refutation
anew since the Pagans' prophecy seemed fulfilled by the
event that they had apprehended, the fall of the city
itself, before the hosts of Alaric. The times have forced
Augustine into the ranks of the defenders; they draw
from him a work which is a kind of apotheosis of the
whole course of apologetics. It sweeps over the history
of the Roman state, of ancient religion and of ancient
philosophy. Plato holds for Augustine, as for Cicero and
Boethius, the sovereign place.[36] Aye, Augustine exclaims,[37] he would have made a far better god for the
Pagans than those that they worshipped. And Plato
most nearly approaches the Christian ideal. He does
not attain it, and Augustine shows why.[38] Here at last
is the answer to Platonism, and to its contemporary
form, Neoplatonism, that we had missed in Lactantius
and the other apologetes. Augustine's criticism of
polytheism is more valuable than that of any other
apologete, even Lactantius, for it gives more illustrations of Pagan rites and beliefs, drawn particularly from
a work, now lost, of Varro. Like Minucius Felix and

Lactantius, Augustine would not condemn Pagan re
ligion wholesale, as something wicked and unprofitabl
but examine it for harbingers of Christianity. He woul
show that natural religion was widespread, and tha
monotheism underlay the Pagan superstitions and wa
virtually accepted by many of the enlightened.

Augustine's feeling about the ancient culture, if I ma
run on with this topic for a moment, is at once like, an
unlike, that of Jerome. The external events in the
careers are similar. Though Jerome was nominally
Christian from the start, spiritually both he and Augu
tine came into Christianity from Paganism. They bot
show an inevitable reaction against Paganism after the
conversion, but in a different way. With Jerome, whos
agile temperament plunged readily into extremes, th
reaction both took a more violent form and more quickl
cleared away. With Augustine, it was slower in comin
and more lasting in effect. His life developed evenl
from beginning to end, *di non buono in buono, di buono i
migliore, di migliore in ottimo*. After his conversion, h
was not dreaming of his damnation for Cicero's sak
but conducting Tusculan disputations. Yet, little b
little, he grew into another estate. While Jerome, in h
retirement at Bethlehem, was lamenting the degenerac
of his style in his separation from Tully and Maro,
Augustine was making his confessions to God in a Chri
tian language of simplicity and humility. The tendenc
to open himself to the immediate inspiration, to giv

imself to the needs of the present, and to put away
1e past, increased with his years. It has been remarked
1at Augustine was more the philosopher at the begin-
ing of his career, and more the theologian at the end.
1 one sense, that is fairly self-evident. But if it means
1at Augustine had slackened the wings of his imagina-
on or checked his ventures into the unknown, it is not
·ue. It is true, I believe, that Pagan culture seemed
ss vital to him. That we could gather from the _Con-
·ssions_. In the _De Doctrina Christiana_, one of his later
·orks (397–426), a work most important for estimating
is attitude toward Pagan culture, he subscribes to the
rogramme at which Jerome had arrived; he regards the
.udy of the Classics as a necessary step in the attain-
1ent of the higher and distinctively Christian learning.
ut when, in the _Retractations_, he examines that early
iceronian dialogue, _De Ordine_, he states, as we have
:en,[40] that he had there ascribed too much to the liberal
·rts, since they were no criterion of sanctity. Sanctity,
1en, not culture, is his ultimate standard.

Sanctity, however, for St. Augustine, was no barren
bstraction. He was prophet and thinker both. Rarely
as there been a mind so impassioned for the dry light
f reason, and at the same time so profoundly stirred by
:ligious emotion. Norden well calls him the greatest
·oet of the ancient church, even though he wrote as
·ttle in verse as Plato did.[41] He had not — or rather he
·radually cast aside — the belletristic interests that

Jerome cherished to the end. But he had a profounde
sympathy with what is real in ancient thought and senti
ment. One of his utterances in the *De Doctrina Chris
tiana* proclaims a splendid programme of Christia
humanism, at least so far as philosophy is concerned
"He that is a good and true Christian," he declares
"will understand that his Lord has spoken in whatso
ever words he finds the truth." [42]

But let us now return to the *City of God*. The secon
half of the treatise, Books 11–22, rises beyond the spher
of apologetics; Augustine manages the transition to th
constructive part of his theme with skill. Having prove
that Christianity was not the cause of the fall of Rome
he contrasts the perishing Roman state with an immor
tal state, God's state, within which Rome is include
for God's purposes, but in which it is merely a moment
vanishing when its time has come. This contrast be
tween the human and perishable city and that which i
not builded with hands, runs through the remainin
books of the treatise. It has been called the first philos
ophy of history,[43] but Augustine's work had precursor
in the treatise of Lactantius *On the Death of the Perse
cutors*, in Prudentius's poem *Contra Symmachum* and i
Cicero's *De Republica*; for the *fatum Romanum* make
an excellent background for a view of the world *su
specie aeternitatis*. And it all goes back to Plato, a
most things do. For Plato not only built a heavenl
city, — ἐν οὐρανῷ ἴσως παράδειγμα,[44] — but he sketched th

course of human events as an adumbration of a divine order.[45]

History of this sort is not for the scientifically minded gatherer of facts. It belongs in the domain of poetry, where Plato and Augustine belong, alike and unlike in their poetical contemplation of life. Augustine replaces Plato's sprightliness and grace with a Roman sobriety — *gravitas*; his imagination is as powerful, and his zest for following the truth to its lair as keen. For us, who luckily have their works preserved, Plato and Augustine are better types of the laughing and the weeping philosopher than those nearly inaccessible masters, Democritus and Heraclitus. I am speaking of the general mood, not of the ultimate vision. For ultimately Augustine is not a weeping philosopher. His temperament, in some of its aspects, suggests that of Lucretius. Both of them are pessimists, if you like, in certain moods. Their minds and their utterances are permeated with a deep sense of the sadness and the badness of life. They are strong men who know their world; their pessimism is most refreshing in contrast to the cheap cheerfulness of some of our modern evolutionary optimists. But the cosmic outlook for both Lucretius and Augustine is one of hope and satisfaction. Lucretius looks forward with jubilation to the smashing of the universe, and the fulfilling of his theory, in a new chaos of atoms, and Augustine watches with a tranquil delight the slow dissolution of the earthly Rome, and the absorption and transmutation of its errors and its sins by the eternally appointed order of God.

Besides Plato, a sovereign influence on the imagination of Augustine as he dreamed of his *City of God*, is Virgil. For Virgil's epic shows glimpses of a heavenly city; it is no simple story of heroic fights. Allegory is present in Virgil's earlier poetry, particularly in the *Eclogues*, always illusive, shimmering through the pastoral setting; we may not identify any of the shepherds with any of Virgil's contemporaries or with the poet himself; we find some *impasse* if we try. Similarly in the *Aeneid*, the discovery that Dido is really Cleopatra, or Turnus really Antony, brings nothing but confusion to the discoverer. We may see a touch of Cleopatra here or of Antony there, or looking back to Homer, of Nausicaa or Achilles or Hector. These are the colors on the brush of the artist, who is not making a photograph of anybody. Nevertheless, in the *Eclogues* and the *Georgics* and, above all, in the *Aeneid*, through the veil of the narrative we see the Roman State and its mission, "to spare the conquered and fight down the proud" —

> parcere subiectis et debellare superbos.

There is a prophecy in the *fatum Romanum* of the ultimate reign of justice and of peace.[46]

Virgil came to Augustine's hands laden with the interpretation of a long line of commentators, who more and more give evidence of the spirit of allegory, which as we saw, had been firmly embedded in Christian exegesis of the Scriptures by Augustine's time. The Christians' allegorical defence of ethically difficult parts of the Old Testament was met by the Pagans with a new search into the real and inner meanings of Homer, particularly on the part of the Neoplatonists. Porphyry discovers in the cave of the Nymphs described in the *Odyssey* enough Neoplatonic abstractions to make the nymphs flee in alarm to some other covert.[47] It may possibly be, as an eminent German scholar has surmised, that the converted philosopher Marius Victorinus, whose conversion was a triumph for the Christian camp, had written a similarly profound commentary on Virgil.[48] If so, Augustine would hardly have failed to know it.

That Virgil in his fourth *Eclogue* had prophesied the coming of the Messiah, Augustine believed, with most thinkers of his day and of the Middle Ages.[49] This interpretation, curious in our eyes, yet true in a way to the tender mysticism of the poet, had been officially proclaimed by no less an authority than the Emperor Constantine, in an oration, possibly composed by Lactantius, that he gave before a church assembly.[50] St. Jerome, the humanist, ridiculed the idea; as we saw,[51] he compared such a method to the writing of *centones* and called them both mere juggler's tricks. But Augustine believes profoundly that various heathen prophecies had spoken of Christ; he adds [52] that he could not so believe had not "the noblest of the Roman poets" prefixed to his description of the new Golden Age the verses:

> Now comes the last age of the Sibyl's song,
> Now comes the Virgin, Saturn's reign returns,
> And a new race drops down from lofty heaven.

Augustine does not hesitate to take from the fourth *Eclogue* illustrations of his doctrine of sin and grace, once in a letter written in the year before his death in 430.[53] In a passage in the *City of God*,[54] he states that Virgil in his prophecy is not speaking in his own person but repeating the words of the Sibyl. Perhaps he felt that the fourth *Eclogue* was a prophecy of Christ but that Virgil was not a Christian prophet, merely speaking better than he knew. At all events, the poetry of Virgil was not, for Augustine, pinned down to actualities. It was pregnant with the vision of a new empire, of a Christian Rome.

This becomes evident — and its significance for Dante will soon appear — as we read through the *City of God*. In reviewing the story of the earthly Rome, Augustine not only draws on the ancient historians, Livy and Sallust particularly, but he has Virgil in mind at every turn. In one or two philosophical matters, particularly the transmigration of souls, the peculiar sort of purgation to which they are submitted, and, more important than these affairs, the essentially evil nature of the body, he cannot accept the poet's *dictum*; but there is nothing harsh or defiant in such criticisms.[55] Throughout, Augustine treats Virgil with the utmost respect — *poeta nobilissimus* he calls him, more than once.[56] It is the Virgil whom he loved in his school-days, when he wept over the death of Dido — *exstinctam ferroque extrema secutam*.[57] One cannot forget that early training, he declares with a witty quotation from Horace, any more than the empty wine-cask loses a fragrant reminiscence of its former days.

> You may break, you may shatter the boy if you will,
> But the scent of old Virgil will cling to him still.[58]

Augustine feels a kindred nature in Virgil; deep calls unto deep.

In the argument of the *City of God*, as I read it, Virgil plays a not unimportant part. He is cited often, particularly, of course, in the first part of the work, though quotations occur at the very end. With the few exceptions to which I have referred, the Pagan is always on the right side of the debate, and once he is quoted in the same breath with the Gospels.[59] Augustine repeats in his preface the poet's admonition to his nation:

> To spare the conquered and fight down the proud.

That is precisely, according to Augustine, what Rome, mastered by the lust to conquer, had never done;[60] it had never been true to the ideals that Virgil sets up for it. It is in this spirit that Augustine draws constantly from the poet's works, the *Aeneid* above all, for illustrations of the short-comings of Rome. Virgil, he implies, is not far removed from true theology, the belief in the one true God,[61] and his vision of a universal and perpetual peace is the very goal toward which the City of God aspires.[62]

Nor is Augustine himself insensible to the appeal of the earthly city, the golden and eternal Rome, *urbs aurea, urbs aeterna*, adored not only by Horace and Virgil, but by Lactantius and Prudentius, glorified by Claudian before its downfall at the hands of Alaric and his Goths, glorified after that disaster by the Pagan Rutilius Namatianus as a goddess still triumphant, strengthened by her wounds.[63] Augustine cannot be false to a patriotism so deep. He has not forgotten the verse of the old poet:

> In the might of its men and its ancient worth the Roman state stands firm.[64]

He inquires what were those ancient virtues, and summons Virgil, as ever, for the answer.[65] The City of God is established, after all, not only in the heavens, but upon this earth; the rule of the Christian emperors but carries on a great tradition; [66] and when Augustine points his Pagan readers to the worship of the true Deity, he dares to use Virgil's prophecy of the greatness of the earthly Rome and to attribute to God the words that in the poem are spoken by Jupiter: "For there thou shalt see no hearth of Vesta, no Capitoline stone, but the one true God

> Who sets no goals nor times
> But grants an empire without end."[67]

Thus the *fatum Romanum* has been transformed into something rich and strange. The Roman Empire has become that Holy Roman Empire which Augustine helped to create for the Middle Ages. No wonder that Charlemagne, who with his poets had created a new *aetas Vergiliana*, should have been specially fond of Augustine's *City of God*.[68] The *City of God* is, in one of its aspects, a kind of *Aeneis sacra*, with an exalted Papacy in full view. "Alas," says Cotton Mather of Augustine in that very great work, the *Magnalia Christi*, "alas, how much of Babylon is there in his best book, *De Civitate Dei*." [69]

Perhaps you will now see the bearing on Dante of this long intermezzo. Between St. Augustine's time and his own, both the conceptions of the Holy Roman Empire and the allegorical reading of Virgil had grown apace. Fulgentius, some fifty years after the death of Augustine, provided the Middle Ages with a terrific exhibition of what a penetrating intellect could derive from Virgil, in his *Expositio Vergilianae Continentiae Secundum Philosophos Morales*—"The Contents of Virgil"[70] I will tell you merely what part of the first line of the *Aeneid* contains — "Arms and the man I sing, who first . . ." *Arma*, "arms," signifies physical valor; *virum*, "the man," intellectual wisdom; and *primus*, "the prince," all that is ornamental, or beautiful, or pleasurable — beauty evidently being for Fulgentius, as for Mr. Santayana, objectified pleasure. The words therefore sum up the progress of human life. While the literalist hears nothing but "Arms and the man I sing," the enlightened mind of the moral philosopher catches the overtones; "I sing of the advance of physical to intellectual virtue and thus to true happiness."

I will leave you to calculate how long it would take to read the *Aeneid* at this rate, and how supernally wise you would be at the end. Fulgentius's Virgil presents the moral history of a human being, the characters of the story all figuring qualities, good or bad, which help or hinder the soul in its advance to better things; the *Aeneid* is exalted, or reduced, to a 'Battle of the Soul,' a *Psychomachia*.

Now Fulgentius was widely read in the Middle Ages from the beginning; he too, unhappily, is one of the Founders. In the twelfth century, one of the Bernards, probably Bernard Sylvester of Tours, wrote a new allegorization of the *Aeneid*, — which some enterprising student ought to study and publish in full,[71] — and Dante, as he worked out the plan of his *Commedia*, with Virgil very much in view, would know the mediaeval, and the ancient, tradition which had turned the *Aeneid* into an epic of the soul. Of his own poem Dante said in the letter to Can Grande, *subiectum est homo* — "the subject is man." [72] It would be profitable, I believe, to examine anew the relation of the *Divine Comedy* to Fulgentius and the mediaeval allegorizations of the *Aeneid*, and likewise to think over Augustine as a link between

Virgil and Dante, especially as we trace the course of the mystic exaltation of the eternal Rome.

And for themselves, these two great spirits may be most profitably studied together. In temperament, they are alike, and diverse. Augustine, as I have said, has very much the mind of Plato, ready for romantic flights, daring raids, into the unknown. These explorations are many; they cover many tracts; but they are too free for system. The explorer is ready to follow a trail, even if it leads him to the absurd or the impossible. The danger's self is lure alone. A mind like that of Aristotle circumnavigates the universe in an orderly and all-inclusive fashion. Nothing escapes him; he belts it all; he is the master of those who know. Such, philosophically, is the mind of Dante, for he has sat at the feet of St. Thomas Aquinas, who travelled Aristotle's journey and more. But Dante, as someone has said, is St. Thomas set to music. He has the poet's vision, into which the *omne scibile* is caught up into the mystery beyond. That is the mind of Lucretius, who left no corners of his cosmos unexplored and yet, though explaining the universe in terms of atoms and void, has not explained the inner depths of his own nature. For the poet and the mystic, the course of their spiritual journeyings is of secondary concern. For Dante and St. Augustine, all roads lead to Rome — that Rome of which Christ is a Roman — *quella Roma onde Cristo è Romano.*

We have come, at last, to our goal. We have seen how in various ways a firm Foundation was laid for the Middle Ages in the early Christian centuries. We have not examined all its parts, yet we have seen enough, I hope, to show us that, despite the decline and fall of the ancient culture, despite the waves of Teutonic invasion from the north and Moslem invasion from the south, the ancient structure had not entirely disappeared.

First, we saw that Christianity, after much searching of heart, had adopted the ancient culture as part of its own. If we begin with the writers of the Middle Ages — Alcuin, John the Scot, Abelard, St. Bernard, St. Thomas Aquinas — and attempt to ascertain the mind of the mediaeval Church about Pagan literature, we shall be balked in our quest if we do not realize that before the Middle Ages the problem had been stated and solved. The views of any mediaeval author about the Classics were formed, not only by what he discovered in his own reading of them and by what authoritative Churchmen of the time might say, but by what was transmitted from the past under the sanction of a Lactantius, an Ambrose, a Jerome, an Augustine, a Boethius. The record thus handed down would of course contain moments of revolt against Pagan culture, questionings of the value of it all, sharp invective, bitter condemnation. But with the whole display before him of the works on which I have touched in these lectures, it is impossible for any reader, whatever his personal sympathies, in mediaeval times or our own, to be blind to one great fact — that before the Middle Ages came on, the Pagan authors were immovably fixed in Christian education.

It may be even that I have dealt too harshly with the great Gregory in this matter. I have regarded him in my text as typically anti-humanistic, though presenting certain qualifying remarks in the footnotes.[73] Perhaps that is the best, or at least a safe, way to treat this complex affair. I now must add that the Middle Ages apparently would not agree with my notion that in the war between theology and humanism Gregory and Cassiodorus were generals in opposing camps.[74] At the beginning of the eleventh century, a certain Iohannes Monachus wrote a work entitled *Liber de Miraculis* — "Short Stories," it would be called to-day, differing in contents, since mediaeval readers liked to hear about something strange and ideal that passes man's wonted experience, while we are fed in short stories with earthly matter that we know only too well. In the introduction to this work,[75] John the Monk speaks of Ambrose, Augustine, Jerome, and Gregory as the four pillars of the church, or, as he puts it, the *four rivers of Paradise*, and calls them all "most learned in both sciences, viz., the human and the divine." No distinction is drawn between St. Gregory and the other three. Whatever his utterances against the Pagan Classics, the Middle Ages apparently discounted his protests and enrolled him *nolens volens* in the noble company of scholars.

Further, when we survey the history of the transmission of the Classics, we are aware, of course, of the services of humanists like St. Jerome and Cassiodorus in that momentous act, but I wonder if we fully appreciate their importance. We speak of the Carolingian Renaissance and the enlightened plans of Charlemagne for the revival of the ancients. As we follow the history of any ancient Latin text, we find evidence of its existence, in most cases, from the author's times down into the sixth century, and then there comes a gap. So far as we can see, the Classics were copied rarely, if at all, during the seventh century and the first half of the eighth. Veritably, the age was dark. Not till Charlemagne is the copying of the ancients, on any large scale, resumed. Our ninth-century texts, so far as we can trace them, descend by no continuous lineage but spring abruptly from books of the sixth century.

Now why should it have occurred to Charlemagne to revive the Classics? He was a man of great sense, of great philological sense. In all of his reforms, his eye was fixed on the original source of things — of dogma, of liturgy, of the text of the Holy Scriptures, and of the Rule of St. Benedict. He might, perhaps, have had his attention called by chance to Virgil's *Aeneid*, to some rare copy, whether old or new, and immediately concluded that the knowledge of Virgil should be spread abroad through the land. Perhaps the impulse to a revival of letters came to Charlemagne from Ireland, where learning may have flourished at the time when it was well-nigh extinguished on the Continent. I say "may have flourished," for many eminent scholars are by no means certain that conditions were radically better in Ireland than elsewhere. I personally incline to what has become the old-fashioned and roseate view about Irish culture in the Early Middle Ages — but that is another story. The point I am coming to is this, that, failing the chance discovery of a Virgil or some other Classic, failing an interview with some cultured monk from the Emerald Isle, Charlemagne's enthusiasm for the Classics might have been aroused by a reading of an ancient Christian book like the *Divine and Human Readings* of Cassiodorus. There would evidently be copies of such a work lying about for the Emperor to see. The influence of Cassiodorus had permeated the learned order, the text of whose Rule the Emperor had restored, or was about to restore, to its pristine integrity. He would find there due commendation of the ancients by its learned author; they are mentioned in his bibliographies. I would not convert a guess into an avowal that it was this very work which stirred Charlemagne's imagination and prompted him to seek out the hidden manuscripts of the Pagan authors, but it is, on the whole, most probable, I believe, that the suggestion came to him from some such work of the Christian centuries before the Middle Ages, that is, from the period of the Foundation.

Similarly, when we consider certain other great and typical achievements of the Middle Ages, we must recall the Founders. The foundations for the monastic scheme of education that prevailed down through the eleventh century were laid in the fourth and the sixth. St. Bernard the mystic recalls the mystic Ambrose. The humanism of John of Salisbury has a model in that of St. Jerome. If St. Anselm and Albertus Magnus can discuss philosophical problems in the terminology of Aristotle, so can Boethius. The making of varied poetry and the outpouring of the soul in Latin hymns spring from rich sources in Ambrose and Prudentius. And when Dante and Beatrice mount to the Empyrean, there is Augustine, amid Francis and Benedict and the blessed John. It is farthest from my purpose to imply that the Middle Ages achieved nothing in letters or in thought that had not been prophesied. It is to understand their originality the better, that we look back from them to their Founders, from the wrought work to the rock whence it was hewn.

LIST OF BOOKS

I mention here merely a few books of general interest accessible in English. The reader will find satisfactory bibliographies in Labriolle. Most of the texts cited will be found in Migne's *Patrologia Latina* (cited as *Migne*), and the *Corpus Scriptorum Ecclesiasticorum Latinorum*, published at Vienna (cited as *C. S. E. L.*).

ALLEN, ALEXANDER VIETS GRISWOLD, *The Continuity of Christian Thought*, Boston, 1884 and 1895.

BURY, JOHN BAGNELL, *History of the Later Roman Empire*, London, 1923.

GIBBON, EDWARD, *The Decline and Fall of the Roman Empire*, ed. J. B. Bury, London, 1901.

GLOVER, TERROT REAVELEY, *Conflict of Religions in the Early Roman Empire*, 3d. ed., London, 1909.
——. *Life and Letters in the Fourth Century*, Cambridge University Press, 1901.

GUIGNEBERT, CHARLES, *Le Christianisme mediéval et moderne*, Paris, 1922. (Translated as "Christianity Past and Present," New York, 1927.)

HALLIDAY, WILLIAM REGINALD, *The Pagan Background of Early Christianity*, Liverpool, 1925.

LABRIOLLE, PIERRE DE, *Histoire de la Littérature Latine Chrétienne*, Paris, 1920. (Translated by Herbert Wilson, London, 1924.)

LAKE, KIRSOPP, *Landmarks in the History of Early Christianity*, New York, 1922.

MERRILL, ELMER TRUESDELL, *Essays in Early Christian History*, London, 1924.

MOORE, CLIFFORD HERSCHEL, *The Religious Thought of the Greeks*, Harvard University Press, 2d. ed., 1925.

MORE, PAUL ELMER, *The Christ of the New Testament*, Princeton, 1924.
——. *Christ the Word*, Princeton, 1927.

SIHLER, ERNEST G., *From Augustus to Augustine*, Cambridge University Press, 1923.

TAYLOR, HENRY OSBORN, *The Classical Heritage of the Middle Ages*, New York, 1911.
——. *The Mediaeval Mind*, 3d. ed., New York, 1919.
——. *Human Values and Verities*, New York, 1928.

NOTES

NOTES

CHAPTER I

1 (3). Lilius Gregorius Gyraldus, *De Poetarum Historia, Dialogus* V (Leyden edition, 1696), II, 304 E: "Quare tu, Pice, tanquam scopulos hos effuge, candorem enim et linguae castitatem inficiunt, magisque nos inquinate et barbare loqui docent; eorumque ideo vobis nonnullos recensebo, ut caveatis potius quam sectemini." In *Dialogus* IV (II, 263), Martianus Capella is the last Roman treated; he is immediately followed by Petrarch and Boccaccio, who are allowed a few sentences of commendation.

2 (3). *Le Lettere di Giovanni Boccaccio,* ed. F. Corazzini, 1877, p. 267: "Post hunc (Virgilium) autem scripserunt et alii sed ignobiles, de quibus nil curandum est, excepto inclyto praeceptore meo Francisco Petrarca, qui stylum praeter solitum paululum sublimavit."

3 (4). The latest discussion of the history of the term "Middle Ages," will be found in a learned and entertaining article, "Mittelalter und Kuchenlatein," by Paul Lehmann, Traube's eminent successor at Munich, in *Historische Zeitschrift,* CXXXVII (1927), 197–213. He would not attribute the decay of Latin as a living language solely to the Italian Humanists (p. 213).

4 (4). C. H. Haskins, *The Renaissance of the Twelfth Century* (Harvard University Press, 1927), p. 129: "Indeed it is this very adaptability and power of absorbing new elements which kept Latin a living language until it was killed by the revival of antique standards in the fifteenth century." See also L. J. Paetow, *Two Mediaeval Satires on the University of Paris,* (University of California Press, 1927), p. 9 and the similar remarks of Eduard Norden there quoted.

5 (4). See the passage at the beginning of the essay on "Pagan and Mediaeval Religious Sentiment," in *Essays in Criticism.*

6 (8). For instance, Tertullian, *De Spectaculis*, 17: "Si et doctrinam saecularis litteraturae et stultitiae apud Deum deputatam aspernamur, satis praescribitur nobis et de illis speciebus spectaculorum quae saeculari litteratura lusoriam vel agonisticam scaenam dispungunt."

7 (11). Paul Elmer More, *The Christ of the New Testament*, p. 293.

8 (12). See Labriolle, *Histoire de la Littérature Chrétienne*, pp. 28 f. (translation, pp. 20 ff.).

9 (12). St. Jerome, *Epist.*, XXII, 29, ed. I. Hilberg, in *Corpus Scriptorum Ecclesiasticorum Latinorum*, LIV, 189; (Migne, *Patrologia Latina*, XXII, 416): "Quae enim communicatio luci ad tenebras? Qui consensus Christo cum Belial? quid facit cum Apostolo Cicero? . . . simul bibere non debemus calicem Christi et calicem daemoniorum."

10 (12). Tertullian, *De Idolatria*, 10 (ed. Reifferscheid and Wissowa, *Corpus Scriptorum Ecclesiasticorum Latinorum*, XX [1890], 39): "Quaerendum autem est etiam de ludimagistris et ceteris professoribus literarum. Immo non dubitandum affines illos esse multimodae idolatriae."

11 (12). Domenico Comparetti, *Virgilio nel Medio Evo*, 1872, 2nd ed., Florence, 1896 (first edition translated by E. F. M. Benecke, London, 1895). See especially chapter 6.

12 (12). Hastings Rashdall, *The Universities of Europe in the Middle Ages* (Oxford, 1895), I, 27: "The tendency of the Church's teaching was to depreciate secular education."

13 (13). See the anonymous *Vita Alcuini*, written not long after his death, edited by W. Arndt in *Monumenta Germaniae Historica, Scriptores*, XV, 1, pp. 185, 193. One will not gather from this *Vita* what Alcuin had done at Tours. It is one of the characteristically Mediaeval "sanctificating" biographies, the exact reverse of the calumniating biographies of our day. See below, p. 72.

14 (13). *Theologia Christiana*, II (Migne, *Patrologia Latina*, CLXXVIII, 1210 D). "Quid ergo episcopi et religionis Christianae doctores poetas a civitate Dei non arcent,

quos a civitate saeculi Plato inhibuit?" As usual, one had better read the whole of Abelard's remarkable discussion.

15 (13). "Pro signo libri scholaris quem aliquis paganus composuit, praemisso signo generali libri, adde ut aurem cum digito tangas, sicut canis cum pede pruriens solet; quia non immerito infidelis tali animali comparatur." Quoted from the Cluniac Order (*Vetus disciplina monastica*, Paris, 1726, p. 172) by Georg Zappert in his extraordinary work, a model of learning and art (which furnished Comparetti with many facts), *Virgils Fortleben im Mittelalter* (*Denkschriften der kaiserlichen Akademie der Wissenschaften*), Vienna, 1851, p. 31.

16 (14). J. B. Bury, *Progress* (London, 1920), pp. 11, 18. He cites the sombre verses with which Horace concludes, with telling effect, his six sermons *virginibus puerisque* (*Odes*, iii, 1–6), and also the protest against the inventions of mankind, particularly the sinful act of navigation, in an ode of genial banter intended to dissuade Virgil from making a voyage to Greece (i, 3). In both cases, Mr. Bury misses the point by failing to take account of the context. He should have considered the poet's *Saecular Hymn*, in which Horace anticipates the progress of Rome under the guidance of Apollo to an ever better age:

Alterum in lustrum meliusque semper
Prorogat aevum.

Mr. Bury does justice to Lucretius and the atomists (p. 15). He does not mention St. Ambrose.

17 (15). Otto Seeck, *Geschichte des Untergangs der antiken Welt*, Berlin, V (1913), 196, 198. The best edition of the *relatio* is that by Seeck, in the works of Symmachus, *Monumenta Germaniae Historica, Auctores Antiquissimi*, VI, 1 (1883), p. 280.

18 (17). See St. Ambrose, *Epist.* XVII and XVIII (Migne, *Patrologia Latina*, XVI, 961–982).

19 (18). In the edition of Prudentius by J. Bergman (*Corpus Scriptorum Ecclesiasticorum Latinorum*, LXI, Vienna, 1926), 215 ff.

20 (25). *Epist.* xi, 54 (Migne, *Patrologia Latina*, LXXVII, 1171 c): "Sed post hoc pervenit ad nos fraternitatem tuam grammaticam quibusdam exponere. Quam rem . . . moleste suscepimus ac sumus vehementius aspernati . . . quia in uno se ore cum Iovis laudibus Christi laudes non capiunt. Et quam grave nefandumque sit episcopis canere quod nec laico religioso conveniat ipse considera. . . . Unde si post hoc evidenter ea quae ad nos perlata sunt falsa esse claruerint nec vos nugis et saecularibus litteris studere constiterit, Deo nostro gratias agimus."

21 (26). *Virgilio nel Medio Evo*, p. 119, n. 1 (translation, p. 89, n. 36). Comparetti's "defence" amounts to the assertion that Gregory was no worse than Christians in general.

22 (26). See Gregory's Exposition of the *First Book of Kings*, V, 30 (Migne, *Patrologia Latina*, LXXXIX, 355 A): "Ad hoc quidem tantum liberales artes discendae sunt ut per instructionem illarum divina eloquia subtilius intelligantur." This utterance, as usual, must be taken with its context. Gregory is allegorizing the war of Israel with the Philistines. He goes on to say that some people, prompted by evil spirits (*maligni spiritus*), show no desire to learn the secular arts, and do not attain the heights of spiritual things either. We go down to prepare for battle against the Philistines, therefore, when we incline our minds to the pursuit of the liberal arts. Matthew Arnold would approve! It is a descent because Christian simplicity dwells on the heights. God has placed secular learning in the plain, that he might make for us the upward slope whereby we should rise to the altitude of Sacred Scripture. ("Hanc quippe scientiam omnipotens Deus in plano anteposuit, ut nobis ascendendi gradum faceret qui nos ad divinae Scripturae altitudinem levare debuisset.") It would thus appear that the liberal arts are a divine ordinance and the refusal to study them a work of devils. President Eliot would not quite agree. Gregory goes on to point out that though Jeremiah and Amos were simple folk, Isaiah had the education of a

gentleman (*nobiliter instructus et urbanus*), and that St. Paul before he was caught up into the third heaven, had sat as a pupil at the feet of Gamaliel.

23 (26). President Eliot's essay was published in the *Century* for 1884. The remark quoted is found on p. 205. The later essay was published with one on "Education for Efficiency," Boston, 1909, Houghton Mifflin Co.; the passage cited is from p. 42. It is unfair to call President Eliot Anti-Classical in this essay. He seeks primarily to put modern languages, English above all, on the same footing as the ancient. In his noble tribute to Professor Goodwin in the proceedings of the Massachusetts Historical Society for 1912, he remarks (p. 22) that Goodwin "did enduring work for human culture." Yet the emphasis of President Eliot's teaching is on modern achievement, with the implication that now that we have become men, we should put away childish things.

24 (27). This much-quoted passage is from Gregory's prefatory letter to his moral exposition of the book of Job (Migne, *Patrologia Latina*, LXXV, 516 B): "Unde et ipsam loquendi artem quam magisteria disciplinae exterioris insinuant, servare despexi. Nam sicut huius quoque epistolae tenor enuntiat, non metacismi collisionem fugio, non barbarismi confusionem devito, situs motusque [modosque?] et praepositionum casus servare contemno, quia indignum vehementer existimo ut verba caelestis oraculi restringam sub regulis Donati. Neque enim haec et ullis interpretibus in scripturae sacrae auctoritate servata sunt. Ex qua nimirum quia nostra expositio oritur, dignum profecto est ut quasi edita soboles speciem suae matris imitetur." The reader will kindly note the sentences which follow the part that I have translated. They contain the chief point that Gregory is making. He is not going to exhibit in his exposition a more ornamental diction than that of the Holy Writ which he expounds; mother and daughter should be attired alike. This is good taste, not illiteracy. Scriptural comments in the "big bow-wow" style of Apuleius and Martianus Capella

would be matter for unquenchable laughter. Once more, critics have damned Gregory for a phrase when, to understand him, they should read at least a paragraph.

25 (28). "Defects in American Education Revealed by the War," Cattell's *School and Society*, 1919, pp. 1 ff.

26 (33). The sources of the quotations are, in their order, Pindar, *Nemean Odes*, viii, 17; Aeschylus, *Prometheus Bound*, l. 1032; Sophocles, *Antigone*, l. 604; Euripides, *Hercules Furens*, l. 1345; *Ion*, l. 440; *Palamedes* (fragment 588); Xenophon, *Memorabilia Socratis*, i, 3, 2; Plato, *Republic*, x, 596 C; Seneca, *Naturales Quaestiones*, ii, 45; *De Vita Beata*, 15, 7; *Epistulae Morales*, 41, 2; 73, 16. These selections, and many others, will be found in E. G. Sihler's *Testimonium Animae* (New York, 1908), an honest and independent work which at times shows the anti-Pagan vehemence of a Tertullian, but which rests on a first-hand study of the ancient authors.

CHAPTER II

1 (34). *Acts*, xvii.

2 (35). The hymn has been often translated, for instance (with Greek text), by E. H. Blakeney for the Society for Promoting Christian Knowledge, London and New York, 1921. There is a good rendering of Aratus by G. R. Mair in his edition (text and translation) of Callimachus in the Loeb series (London, 1920), pp. 359–473.

3 (35). *Christ of the New Testament*, p. 177: "The virus of the Rabbis ran in his blood, and, for all his earnest adherence to Christianity, coloured his ideas to the end."

4 (35). "Evil communications corrupt good manners" (I *Cor.* xv, 33) may come from Menander's *Thais* (218 Kock) or from Euripides (Nauck, fragm. 1013). "The Cretans are always liars, evil beasts, slow bellies" (*Titus*, i, 12) is from Epimenides (H. Diels, *Die Fragmente der Vorsokratiker* [3rd ed., Berlin, 1912], II, 188). "For when the Gentiles, which have not the law, do by nature

the things contained in the law, these, having not the law, are a law unto themselves" (*Rom.* ii, 14) may have some relation (so at least Professor Goodwin thought might be the case) to Aristotle, *Nichomachean Ethics*, IV, 14.

5 (36). *Acts*, xxvi.

6 (36). *The Revival of Learning* (1st ed., 1877), p. 63.

7 (36). For our present purpose, it is obviously unnecessary to reckon with the theories of the decomposing critics about the book of *Acts*. Whether this work is historically reliable, whether it was written by St. Luke the good physician, or by somebody who was not a good physician (or a bad one), matters not. We are here concerned with the character and the interests of St. Paul manifested in the book, and accepted by the Church as authentic and worthy of imitation.

8 (37). E. Lehmann and A. Fridrichsen, *Theologische Studien und Kritiken*, 1922. Sonderheft, pp. 55–95. Finding St. Paul's estimate of gnosis inconsistent with his attitude shown elsewhere, they pronounce the chapter an interpolation. Interpolation is often a useful theory for a small mind that cannot put together all that there is in a great one.

9 (37). *Confessions*, VII, 9.

10 (38). Edited by F. Oehler with *Tertulliani Quae Supersunt Omnia* (Leipzig, 1853), I, 701 ff. Translated in the *Ante-Nicene Christian Library*, XI (Edinburgh, 1869), 304 ff. See particularly chaps. 8 and 13.

11 (40). See above, p. 12, note 10. He says shortly thereafter, in the same chapter (*De Idolatria*, 10): "Videamus igitur necessitatem litteratoriae eruditionis; respiciamus ex parte eam admitti non posse, ex parte vitari." Training in the authors, then, in one respect cannot be admitted (because it is a training in idolatry); in one respect it cannot be avoided (because it is a training in life, — *cum instrumentum sit ad omnem vitam litteratura,* — and a necessary avenue to divine learning — *sine quibus divina non possunt*). The *De Idolatria* is translated in vol. XI of the *Ante-Nicene Christian Library*, pp. 141 ff.

12 (43). Edited by C. Halm in the *Corpus Scriptorum Ecclesiasticorum Latinorum*, vol. II (1867), and by various scholars more recently. On their editions, see Labriolle, *Histoire de la Littérature Latine Chrétienne*, p. 147 (translation, p. 109). A recent translation is by J. H. Freese, in *Translations of Christian Literature Series*, vol. II, published by the Society for Promoting Christian Knowledge (London and New York, 1919). The question of the priority of the work of Minucius Felix or the *Apologeticum* of Tertullian has been hotly debated. Something is sure to be written on this subject at least once a year. Labriolle (p. 173–175; translation, pp. 128–130) argues effectively that the coincidences between the two works must be explained on the ground that Minucius drew from Tertullian, since the latter never borrowed from anybody. And yet?

13 (46). Chap. 19 (Halm, p. 25); Virgil, *Aeneid*, VI, 724–729. Minucius does not quote these lines exactly, but weaves phrases from them into a prose sentence.

14 (46). *Georgics*, IV, 221–223. Minucius misquotes these verses in an interesting way. The last line should be: "hinc pecudes, armenta, viros, genus omne ferarum." Instead he has: "unde homines et pecudes, unde imber et ignes." This is a not quite correct citation of *Aen.* I, 743: "unde hominum genus et pecudes, unde imber et ignes." Minucius again is quoting like a gentleman but not like a scholar — from memory. He has fused two similar passages into one. This is an instructive and typical example. See above, pp. 163 f.

15 (48). For an excellent summary, see Labriolle, pp. 155–171 (translation, pp. 115–127). I had formed my estimate of Minucius Felix years ago, before reading Labriolle, and am glad to note that it is in substantial agreement with his.

16 (49). It should be added that the influence of Minucius Felix on the Middle Ages was slight. In fact, the existence of his dialogue was concealed by its incorporation with the

Adversus Nationes of Arnobius as the eighth book of that work. Queer bedfellows! Evidently in some *Corpus* of Apologetes, Minucius followed Arnobius. In a subsequent copy, *Octavius* was misread *Octavus*, and the rest of the title was dropped. Only two manuscripts of Arnobius and Minucius have come down to us, the one being a direct descendant of the other. See Labriolle, p. 147 (translation, p. 110).

17 (49). René Pichon, *Lactance* (Paris, 1901), p. viii. This is the best account of Lactantius in existence. Labriolle is somewhat belittling. He should not lump Lactantius with Arnobius in the same chapter.

18 (49). "La veritable *Somme* des premieres années du IVᵉ siècle." (R. Thamin, *Saint Ambrose et la Morale Chrétienne au IVᵉ Siècle*, Paris, 1895, p. 147.) The chapter on Lactantius in this admirable book is excellent. The *Divinae Institutiones* is edited by S. Brandt in *Corpus Scriptorum Ecclesiasticorum Latinorum*, vol. XIX (1890); Migne, *Patrologia Latina*, vol. VI. There is a good translation of Lactantius in the *Ante-Nicene Christian Library* (Edinburgh, 1871), vol. XXI, by William Fletcher.

19 (49). I, 1, 13–14 (Migne, VI, 116A–117A). There is some question of the genuineness of this dedication, which Brandt excludes from his text, but it has been satisfactorily defended, in my opinion, by Pichon. See Labriolle, p. 253 (translation, p. 188). It might well have accompanied a second edition of the work.

20 (50). I, 1, 12 (Migne, VI, 116 A).

21 (51). W. Warde Fowler, *Social Life at Rome* (New York, 1909), p. 329. Lucretius says (III, 263) that the four elements in the soul are so conjoined

nil ut secernier unum
possit nec spatio fieri divisa potestas
sed quasi multae vis unius corporis exstant.

One catches a far-away echo of the words of the Athanasian creed: "neque confundentes personas neque substantiam separantes."

22 (52). I, 2, 3 (Migne, VI, 121 A).

23 (53). *Christ the Word*, p. 261.

24 (54). I, 1, 11 (Migne, VI, 115 A–116 A).

25 (54). I, 1, 25 (Migne, VI, 110 A).

26 (56). I, 14, 2–6 (Migne, VI, 190 A–191 A).

27 (58). *Colloquia Familiaria (Convivium Religiosum)*, Leyden edition (1703), I, 683 D: "Profecto mirandus animus in eo [i.e., Socrates] qui Christum ac sacras literas non noverat. Proinde quum hujusmodi quaedam lego de talibus viris, vix mihi tempero, quin dicam, Sancte Socrates, ora pro nobis." This sentiment is attributed to one of the characters in the Dialogue, but it was doubtless shared by the author. I am indebted for the reference to my friend Dr. J. J. Mangan, author of *Life, Character and Influence of Desiderius Erasmus* (New York, 1927).

28 (58). III, 24, 1–2 (Migne, VI, 425 B– 426 A).

29 (59). See Washington Irving, *Life and Voyages of Columbus* (rev. ed., New York, 1849), I, 86 ff. (book II, chap. 3). Tennyson's poem, "Columbus," is virtually a metaphrase of this account. Lactantius and Augustine are naturally registered among the ancients known to Tennyson by W. P. Mustard, *Classical Echoes in Tennyson* (New York, 1904), p. 128, but Tennyson's knowledge in this instance may have extended no further than Washington Irving.

30 (59). *De Rerum Natura*, I, 1052–1082; V, 650–679.

31 (59). IV, 29 (Migne, VI, 538–540).

32 (60). IV, 1, 18 (Migne, VI, 606 B): "recte igitur Flaccus tantum esse dixit innocentiae vim, ut ad tutelam sui non egeat nec armis nec viribus, quacumque iter fecerit." He then quotes the first two strophes of *Integer Vitae*.

33 (60). V, 10, 1–96 (Migne, VI, 580–582). It is noteworthy that Lactantius makes no reference to the experiences of the hero in Carthage; rather, he quotes passages to display his bloodthirstiness in the battles in Latium.

34 (61). VI, 10, 7 (Migne, VI, 667 A): "Itaque non errat Lucretius, cum dicit: denique caelesti sumus omnes

semine oriundi, omnibus ille idem pater est" *De Rerum Natura* (II, 992 f.).

35 (61). VI, 14–15 (Migne, VI, 686–692).

36 (62). VII, 15, 10–12 (Migne, VI, 786 B–788 A).

37 (63). See Brandt in his edition (*C. S. E. L.*, vol. XIX), p. VIII.

38 (64). *Epist.*, LVIII, 10.

39 (64). An impressive list of encomia will be found in Migne VI, 79–82, including a tribute from the critical Lilius Gregorius Gyraldus.

40 (64). Ed. H. M. Bannister, *Henry Bradshaw Society*, vol. LII (1917), p. 25.

41 (65). *Somnium Scipionis*, 3, 6: "Immo vero, inquit, hi vivunt qui e corporum vinclis tamquam e carcere evolaerunt; vestra vero quae dicitur vita mors est."

Tusculan Disputations, I, 40, 95: "totam vim bene vivendi in animi robore ac magnitudine et in omnium rerum humanarum contemptione ac despicientia et in omni virtute ponamus."

42 (65). Eduard Norden, *Die antika Kunstprosa*, 2d ed., (Berlin, 1909), II, 680: "In dieser dienenden Stellung der Wissenschaften liegt der fundamentale Gegensatz des Mittelalters zum Humanismus ausgesprochen."

43 (66). *Tristram Shandy*, vol. VII, chap. 14.

44 (67). Zola, *Rome* (Paris, Charpentier, 1896), chap. 5, p. 195, chap. 7, p. 293.

45 (67). *Sanctissimi Domini Nostri Leonis Papae XIII Allocutiones, Epistolae, Constitutiones, Aliaque Acta Praecipua* (Bruges, 1887), II, 136–139.

46 (68). *Ibid.*, p. 137: "Quarum rerum utilitate perspecta Ecclesia Catholica quemadmodum cetera quae honesta sunt, quae pulchra, quae laudabilia ita etiam humanarum litterarum studia tanti semper facere consuevit quanti debuit in eisque provehendis curarum suarum partem non mediocrem perpetuo collocavit."

CHAPTER III

On St. Ambrose, see, besides Labriolle, book III, chapter 2 the excellent book of R. Thamin, *Saint Ambroise et La Morale Chrétienne au IVe Siècle*, Paris, 1825.

For translations of some of the principal works of St. Ambrose, see *A Select Library of the Nicene and Post-Nicene Fathers*, Second series (New York, 1896), vol. X.

1 (70). See Chapter VIII.

2 (70). *2 Corinthians*, xii, 4.

3 (70). Migne, CLXXXII, 990 c–d.

4 (72). See below, p. 193.

5 (72). Migne, XIV, 27–46.

6 (76). *Christ the Word*, p. 177.

7 (76). Migne, XIV, 75 b, from Theodoret, *Hist. Eccles.* IV, 6 (ed. J. Sirmond, Paris, 1742, III, 667).

8 (76). See Labriolle, p. 366 (translation, p. 275).

9 (77). *Epist.* XXI, 4 (Migne, XVI, 1004): "At certe . . quis est qui abnuat in causa fidei . . . episcopos solere de imperatoribus Christianis, non imperatores de episcopis iudicare?"

10 (77). See above, p. 14.

11 (78). *De Officiis Ministrorum*, I, 1, 4 (Migne, XVI, 24–25)

12 (80). In Migne, XVI, 23–184.

13 (81). I, 28, 131 (Migne, XVI, 62 A). Socrates and Plato had transcended the heathen law. For the tribute of a great Christian humanist to them and to Cicero, see the *Convivium Religiosum* in Erasmus's Colloquies.

14 (81). In his essay on "Paganism and Mr. Lowes Dickinson," in *Heretics*.

15 (82). *De Spectaculis*, 29: "Si scaenicae doctrinae delectant satis nobis litterarum est, satis versuum est, satis sententiarum, satis etiam canticorum, satis vocum, nec fabulae sed veritates, nec strophae sed simplicitates."

16 (82). M. Thamin, *op. cit.*, p. 1.

17 (82). Page 9.

18 (83). III, 15, 92 (Migne, XVI, 171).

19 (84). Migne, XIV, 731–756.

20 (84). *De Elia et Ieiunio*, 15, 59–61 (Migne, XIV, 718).

21 (85). See More, *Christ the Word*, p. 107. Allegory may have started among the Greeks before Theagenes, since there are signs of it in Pherecydes. See Tate, in *Classical Review*, XLI (1927), 214.

22 (85). "Ut posteritas successionum gestis temporis anterioris instructa et praesentia etiam in praeteritis contemplaretur et praeterita nunc quoque in praesentibus veneraretur." *Tractatus Mysteriorum*, II, 14 (ed. A. Feder in *C. S. E. L.*, LXV, p. 37). Labriolle, pp. 323–326 (translation, pp. 242–244), 376–378 (282–283).

23 (86). *Epist.* XIII (X), 7; *Convivio*, II, 1. See also St. Thomas Aquinas, *Summa Theologiae, Pars Prima, Quaest.* I, Art. IX–X; H. Hauvette, *Dante*, 1912 (2d. ed.), pp. 281 ff.

24 (86). XIV, 8 (Migne, XLIX, 962 ff.).

25 (87). I, 2 (Migne, XIV, 420 A–421 A).

26 (88). I, 9, 89 (Migne, XIV, 453 A).

27 (89). I, 9, 87 (Migne, XIV, 452 B).

28 (90). Migne, XIV, 580 ff. and 361 ff.

29 (90). Migne, CLXXVI, 611 ff. and 681 ff.

30 (90). *De Fuga Saeculi* 36 (Migne, XIV, 586, B–C): Ad illud igitur bonum erigamus animos et in illo simus atque in illo vivamus, ipsi adhaereamus, quod est supra omnem mentem et omnem considerationem et pace utitur perpetua ac tranquillitate. Pax autem supra omnem mentem est et supra omnem sensum.

31 (90). See the *Expositio in Apocalysin* (Migne, XVII, 821 A): "Unde et angeli Dei per eam ascendentes et descendentes monstrati sunt; quia sanctos Dei qui per angelos designantur aliquando amor Dei per contemplationis gratiam ad excelsa sublevat, aliquando amor et cura proximorum ad inferiora reducit."

This work is included among the pieces only doubtfully assigned to St. Ambrose, but it is true enough to the spirit of his allegorizings. See, for instance, *De Fuga Saeculi*, 22 (Migne, XIV, 581), again on Jacob: "His ergo virtutibus veluti gradibus quibusdam mens eius ascendit in caelum et Dei secreta cognovit."

32 (90). Edit. C. Schenkl, *C. S. E. L.*, XXXII (1896), 1 ff.; Migne, XIV, 119 ff.

33 (91). See above, pp. 16 f.

34 (91). III, 8, 33–36; 12, 49–52. Compare, for instance, III, 8, 34, with *Cicero, De Senectute* 15, 51. In the praise of flowers, that follows, including the lily of the field (36), St. Ambrose gives us more of his own poetry, and that of our Lord.

35 (92). H. O. Taylor, *The Mediaeval Mind* (2d ed.), I, p. 72; A. Ebert, *Allgemeine Geschichte der Literatur des Mittelalters im Abendlande* (Leipzig, 1889), I, 154.

36 (92). I, 6, 22.

37 (93). Plato, *Phaedo*, 98 c: Cicero, *Academica*, II, 39, 122.

38 (94). V, 15, 53–54 ("Discant homines hospitalia servare iura et ex avibus cognoscant quid religionis hospitibus sit deferendum"); VI, 4, 17 ("Quid autem de canibus loquar, quibus insitum est natura quadam referre gratiam"); V, 16, 55 ("Non recusant aves pascere patrem, quod etiam praescripta necessitate sub terrore poenarum plerique hominum recusant"); V, 9, 24 ("Qui mathematicus, qui astrologus quiue Chaldaeus potest sic siderum cursus, sic caeli motus et signa comprehendere?"); V, 19, 63 ("Optat Paulus in mulieribus quod in turturibus perseverat, et alibi iuniores hortatur nubant, quia mulieres nostrae turturum pudicitiam implere vix possunt.")

The reader will find in books V and VI many other edifying and entertaining descriptions of birds, fish, and beasts that St. Ambrose has known.

39 (94). *De Rerum Natura*, V, 228–234.

40 (94). V, 8, 21 ("fraudulentum illud polypi ingenium ... qui vadoso in litore petram nactus, adfigitur ei atque eius nebuloso ingenio colorem subit ... plurimos piscium sine ulla suspicione fraudis adlapsos ... sinu quodam suae carnis intercipit. ... Isti [i. e. human beings] enim polypi sunt nexus plurimos habentes et callidorum ingeniorum uestigia, quibus inretire possunt quidquid in scopulos suae fraudis inciderit"); 23, 79 ("Doceat igitur nos haec avis vel exemplo sui resurrectionem credere"); 6, 15–16 ("Piscis ergo es, o homo. ... Noli igitur, o bone piscis, Petri hamum timere"); 7, 17 ("Evangelium est in quo licet titubaverit Petrus, quando negavit, tamen per dexteram Christi fidei munimentum, stationis invenit gratiam. ... Evangelium est mare in quo Christi figurantur mysteria").

Ambrose's allegorization of animals is closely akin to that in the curious collection known as *Physiologus*, which exerted so powerful an influence on Mediaeval imagination. On it, see Taylor, *The Mediaeval Mind* (2d ed.), I, 76–77.

41 (94). Hrabanus Maurus, *De Universo*, VIII, 7 (Migne, LXI, 258 c): "Hoc ergo animalis genus [i. e., scinifes] subtilitati haereticae comparatur, quae subtilibus verborum stimulis animas terebrat, tantaque calliditate circumvenit, ut deceptus quisque nec videat nec intelligat unde decipiatur."

42 (95). V, 8, 22.

43 (97). V, 12, 39: "Scientia quam nos rusticani docuerunt."

44 (97). *De Rerum Natura*, V, 999–1006.

45 (97). V, 11, 32–35.

46 (97). E. g., Horace, *Odes*, I, 3 (jocosely); Lucretius V, 1006: "improba navigii ratio" (sincerely).

47 (97). III, 5, 21.

48 (97). *Ibid.*, 23.

49 (98). V, 24, 88.

50 (98). VI, 8, 52.

51 (99). *A Century of Indian Epigrams* (Boston, 1898), p. 111.

52 (100). *Confessions*, VI, 3, 3.

53 (100). The reader will find in Migne, XIV, 113–120, a fine sheaf of eulogies assembled from St. Basil, Gaudentius, St. Jerome, Rufinus, St. Augustine, and others.

54 (100). Migne, XIV, 28 A–B.

55 (101). *De Baptismo*, 2, 8 (Migne, CLXXXII, 1036 c) "Ab his ergo duabus columnis, Augustinum loquor et Ambrosium, crede mihi, difficile avellor. Cum his, inquam, me aut errare aut sapere fateor."

CHAPTER IV

The latest comprehensive work on St. Jerome, and an excellent one, is by F. Cavallera, *St. Jerome, Sa Vie et se. Oeuvres* (*Spicilegium Sacrum Lovaniense*, vol. I), 1922 (only a part has appeared). The best complete study is that by G Grützmacher, *Hieronymus, eine biographische Studie zur alter Kirchengeschichte* (*Studien zur Geschichte der Theologie und der Kirche*, herausg. von N. Bonnwetsch und R. Seeber (Leipzig and Berlin), VI, 3 (1901); X, 1 (1906); X, 2 (1908)

See also Labriolle, book III, chapter 5. For translation of certain works, see *Select Library of Nicene and Post-Nicen Fathers*, 2nd series, VI, New York, 1893.

1 (104). See above, p. 71.

2 (105). *Vita S. Malchi*, I (Migne, XXIII, 53 c): "Christ Ecclesia . . . potentia quidem et divitiis maior sed virtuti bus minor."

3 (106). *Epist.*, XXII, 30. The latest edition of the *Letter.* is by I. Hilberg, *C. S. E. L.*, vols. LIV–LVI (1910–1918) in Migne, vol. XXII.

4 (107). *Epist.*, XXII, 7.

5 (108). *Epist.*, XXII, 34–35; CXXV, 9 (and the whol letter).

6 (109). *Epist.*, CVIII, 20: "Difficile est modum tenere in omnibus. Et vere iuxta philosophorum sententiam in μεσότητες ἀρεταί, ὑπερβολαὶ κακίαι reputantur, quod nos una sententia exprimere possumus: *ne quid nimis.*" Was St. Jerome unaware that Terence (*Andria*, 61) was translating μηδὲν ἄγαν?

7 (109). *Apologia adversus Libros Rufini*, III, 6 (Migne, XXIII, 462).

8 (110). *Epist.*, XL, 3: "In quodcumque vitium stili mei mucro contorquetur, te clamitas designari, conserta manu in ius vocas et satiricum scriptorem in prosa stulte arguis."

9 (110). *Apologia adversus Libros Rufini*, III, 5 (Migne, XXIII, 461): "Ex quo apparet iuxta incliti oratoris elogium, te voluntatem habere mentiendi, artem fingendi non habere." Cf. Cicero, *Pro Fonteio*, 18, 40.

10 (110). *Comment. in Ezechielem Prophetam*, I, prolog. (Migne, XXV, 16): "Scorpiusque inter Enceladum et Porphyrium Trinacriae humo premitur." Perhaps, instead of *Porphyrium*, *Porphyrionem* should be read. Porphyrio was another of the giants who warred on the Gods (Horace, *Odes*, III, 4, 53–56).

11 (110). *De Viris Illustribus*, 124 (ed. E. C. Richardson, Leipzig, 1926, p. 53; Migne, XXIII, 611): "Ambrosius, Mediolanensis episcopus, usque in praesentem diem scribit, de quo, quia superest, meum iudicium subtraham, ne in alterutram partem, aut adulatio in me reprehendatur, aut veritas."

12 (111). See the passages cited from St. Augustine in Chapter III. Rufinus indignantly reprimands Jerome's insidious attacks on St. Ambrose, whom he calls "non solum Mediolanensis Ecclesiae verum omnium ecclesiarum columna quaedam et turris inexpugnabilis." See his *Apologia in Hieronymum*, II, 22–25 (Migne, XXI, 600–604).

13 (111). *Epist.*, CV.

14 (111). *Ibid.*, CV, 5: "Vale, mi amice carissime, aetate fili, dignitate parens."

15 (111). *Epist.*, CXII, 22: "Tu qui iuvenis es et in pontificali culmine constitutus, doceto populos et novis Africae frugibus Romana tecta locupleta. Mihi sufficit cum auditore vel lectore pauperculo in angulo monasterii susurrare.'

16 (113). *Epist.*, XXII, 16.

17 (113). Terence, *Phormio*, 342.

18 (113). *Epist.*, XXII, 32.

19 (114). *Annis pannisque obsita.* Cf. Terence, *Eunuchus*, 236: *pannis annisque obsitum.*

20 (115). *Epist.*, XXII, 28. The account of the young priest has the flavor of Cicero's description of a dandy in his oration *Pro Sexto Roscio Amerino*, 46, 133–135. Jerome and Cicero are brother satirists.

21 (115). "Si ulla in barba sanctitas est, nullus sanctior est hirco." After having had this *bon mot* of St. Jerome's in my notes for years, I cannot now find it in his writings (nor, what is more, can President A. S. Pease). Jerome refers to the *hircorum barba* of false monks in *Epist.*, XXII, 28. For Erasmus, see Μωρίας Ἐγκώμιον, XI (ed. I. B. Kan, The Hague, 1898, p. 14): "barba, insigne sapientiae, etiamsi cum hircis commune."

22 (116). *The History of the Decline and Fall of the Roman Empire* (ed. J. B. Bury, London, 1901), vol. IV, ch. 37, p. 63.

23 (117). See below, p. 273.

24 (117). *Epist.*, LIII, 6–7.

25 (117). Horace, *Epist.*, II, 1, 117:
Scribimus indocti doctique poemata passim.

26 (118). Virgil, *Ecl.*, IV, 6–7.

27 (119). *Epist.*, LXVI, 14: "Nos in ista provincia aedificato monasterio et diversorio propter extructo, ne forte et modo Ioseph cum Maria Bethlehem veniens non inveniat hospitium, tantis de toto orbe confluentibus turbis obruimur monachorum, ut nec coeptum opus deserere nec supra vires ferre valeamus."

28 (119). *Epist.*, CXVII, 1: "quasi vero episcopalem cathe-
dram teneam et non clausus cellula ac procul a turbis
remotus vel praeterita plangam vitia vel vitare nitar
praesentia."

29 (119). *Epist.*, CXXV, 7: "habeto cellulam pro paradiso."
On his satisfaction in his retreat, see, *e. g.*, *Epist.*, L.

30 (119). *Epist.*, XLVI, 12: "In Christi vero, ut supra dixi-
mus, villula tota rusticitas et extra psalmos silentium est.
Quocumque te verteris, arator stivam tenens alleluia
decantat, sudans messor psalmis se avocat et curva ad-
tondens vitem falce vinitor aliquid Davidicum canit.
Haec sunt in hac provincia carmina, hae, ut vuglo dicitur,
amatoriae cantiones, hic pastorum sibilus, haec arma
culturae."

31 (120). *Apologia adversus Libros Rufini*, I, 30–31 (Migne,
XXIII, 421–424).

32 (120). A. S. Pease, "The Attitude of Jerome towards
Pagan Literature," in *Transactions of the American Philological Association*, L (1919), 150–167 (especially p. 157).

33 (121). These lives will be found in Migne, XXIII, 14–60.

34 (121). See above, p. 189.

35 (122). *Dialogus* I, 13. St. Jerome also praises the spiritual
value of a garden, pleasantly quoting Virgil's *Georgics* by
the way (*Epist.*, CXXV, 11).

36 (123). § 10 (Migne, XXIII, 25).

37 (124). § 6 (Migne, XXIII, 31).

38 (124). § 10 (Migne, XXIII, 32): "Capillum semel in anno
die Paschae totondit."

39 (125). See T. R. Glover, *Life and Letters in the Fourth
Century*, ch. 15, "Greek and Early Christian Novels."

40 (125). K. Lake, *Landmarks of Early Christianity*, 1922,
p. 42: "But if the history of religion has any clear lesson,
it is that a nearer approach to truth is always a departure
from orthodoxy."

41 (127). *Adversus Iovinianum*, I, 47 (Migne, XXIII, 276):
"Non est ergo uxor ducenda sapienti. Primum enim im-

pediri studia philosophiae; nec posse quemquam libris et uxori pariter inservire."

42 (127). Horace, *Odes*, II, 1, 7: "incedis per ignes|Suppositos cineri doloso."

43 (128). Livy, *Praefatio*, 5: "Ego contra hoc quoque laboris praemiam petam, ut me a conspectu malorum, quae nostra tot per annos uidit aestas, tantisper certe dum prisca illa tota mente repeto, avertam, omnis expers curae, quae scribentis animum etsi non flectere a vero, sollicitum tamen efficere posset."

44 (128). Migne, XXVII, 40: "Quo fine contentus, reliquum tempus Gratiani et Theodosii latioris historiae stilo reservavi, non quo de viventibus timuerim libere et vere scribere (timor enim Dei hominum timorem expellit) sed quoniam debacchantibus adhuc in terra nostra barbaris, incerta sunt omnia."

45 (128). § 1 (Migne, XXIII, 53): "Scribere enim disposui (si tamen vitam Dominus dederit et si vituperatores mei saltem fugientem me et inclusum persequi desierint) ab adventu Salvatoris usque ad nostram aetatem, id est ab apostolis usque ad nostri temporis faecem, quomodo et per quos Christi ecclesia nata sit et adulta persecutionibus creverit et martyriis coronata sit, et postquam ad Christianos principes venerit potentia quidem et divitiis maior sed virtutibus minor facta sit. Verum haec alias." The pessimistic tone in these remarks may possibly have been somewhat inspired by Livy, who in his *Preface* views the course of Roman history as one of rapid decline (9): "donec ad haec tempora quibus nec vitia nostra nec remedia pati possumus, perventum est."

46 (129). *Epist.*, CXII, 22.

47 (129). For an account of St. Jerome's translation, see M. Schanz, *Geschichte der römischen Literatur*, IV, 1 (2d. ed., 1914), pp. 451–457; Labriolle, pp. 471–473 (translation, pp. 351–353).

48 (130). *Biblia Sacra iuxta Latinam Vulgatam versionem ad codicum fidem iussu Pii XI cura et studio monachorum*

sancti Benedicti . . . edita, Rome, 1926, vol. I, *Genesis*. Whatever criticisms may be passed on Dom Quentin's critical method, they do not apply to the text that he has constructed; indeed, the text is independent of the method. See *The Harvard Theological Review*, XVII (1924), 197–264.

49 (130). *Epist.*, LVII, 4.

50 (132). *Epist.*, CXXXII, 1: "Nam vitiis nemo sine nascitur, optimus ille est | Qui minimis urgetur" (Horace, *Satires*, I, 3, 68).

51 (132). See above, p. 117, and Dom Quentin, *Mémoire sur l'Etablissement du Texte de la Vulgate* (Rome and Paris, 1922), p. 286.

52 (132). *Epist.*, CVIII, 33. This long letter is his tribute to Paula. He applies the proud words of Horace *exegi monumentum aere perennius* (*Odes*, III, 30) to the verses that he composed for Paula's tomb and for the entrance of the cave where her body was buried. Naturally he is thinking of the immortality of Paula's sacred life rather than of the quality of his poetry — at least, we hope so.

53 (132). *Policraticus*, II, 22; VII, 10 (ed. C. C. J. Webb, Oxford, 1909, I, 131; II, 134). The other *testimonia* will be found in Migne, XXII, 213–236.

54 (133). "Deum immortalem, Scotus, Albertus et his impolitiores auctores omnibus in scholis perstrepent et ille unicus religionis nostrae pugil, illustrator ac lumen Hieronymus, qui meruit ut unus celebraretur, unus ex omnibus tacebitur? . . . Ego certe, nisi me sanctissimi viri fallit amor, cum Hieronymianam orationem cum Ciceroniana confero, videor mihi nescio quid in ipso eloquentiae principe desiderare." *Epist.*, V, 19, Leyden edition, III (1703), 67; *Opus Epistolarum Des. Erasmi Roterodami denuo recognitum et auctum per* P. S. Allen, Oxford, I (1906), 332.

55 (133). *Cap.* 21 (Migne, LXX, 1135–1136): "Planus, doctus, dulcis, parata copia sermonum ad quamcumque partem convertit ingenium, modo humilibus suaviter blanditur, modo superborum colla confringit, modo dero-

gatoribus suis vicem necessaria mordacitate restituens, modo virginitatem praedicans, modo matrimonia casta defendens, modo virtutum certamina gloriosa collaudans, modo lapsus in clericis atque monachis probitates accusans; sed tamen ubicumque se locus attulit, Gentilium exempla dulcissima varietate permiscuit, totum explicans, totum exornans, et per diversa disputationum genera disertus semper et aequalis incedens."

56 (134). John of Salisbury even implies that, though the experience was real, it may have been the work of *spiritus maligni* (*Policraticus*, II, 17; ed. Webb, I, 100).

CHAPTER V

For an excellent appreciation of Boethius, see H. F. Stewart, *Boethius, an Essay*, Edinburgh and London, 1891. The most notable account of Boethius's life and works in modern times is Hermann Usener's *Anecdoton Holderi* (*Festschrift zur Begrüssung der XXXII Versammlung deutscher Philologen und Schulmänner zu Wiesbaden*), 1877. Alfred Holder, librarian at Karlsruhe, had found in a manuscript of Cassiodorus, at that place, a fragment of a work of that author on certain eminent writers of his day, including Boethius. This fragment is the *Anecdoton Holderi*, interpreted by Usener in masterly style. See also Labriolle, pp. 665–673 (translation, pp. 499–505, "First of the Scholastics").

The *Consolation of Philosophy* and the *Opuscula Sacra* are edited with translations, by H. F. Stewart and E. K. Rand, in the *Loeb Classical Library*, London and New York, 1918 (reprinted 1926). On the genuineness of the theological tractates, see the writer's thesis, "Der dem Boethius zugeschriebene Traktat De Fide Catholica" (*Jahrbücher für klassische Philologie*, XXVI, Supplementband, 1901). I will refer to this work as *Jahrbb.*, XXVI. See also "On the Composition of Boethius' *Consolatio Philosophiae*," *Harvard Studies in Classical Philology*, XV (1904), 1–28.

1 (136). *Chaucer's Translation of Boethius's "De Consolatione Philosophiae,"* edited by Richard Morris (*Early English Text Society*, Extra Series, no. V, 1868), p. ii.

2 (137). Glareanus, in his edition of the *Opera* of Boethius (Basle, 1546), fol. a 2^v: "Ego igitur, ut ingenue fatear id quod res est (etsi scio quam magnam mihi moveam hac opinione invidiam . . .) mihi quidem magis Philosophicum opus videtur, quam Christianum, nec tamen indignum quod a Christiano homine legatur, sed indignum, ut ab eo scriptum credatur, qui ipsi Christo, dato in sacro baptismate nomine, ipsum antescriptis professus." He points out that many regard the prose as not by the same hand as the poems, the latter having the better quality: "Multis sane (e quorum numero me facile dixero) prosa illa cum carmine non unius hominis esse videntur, longe maiorem gratiam habet carmen, quam ieiuna illa prosa." See O. F. Fritzsche, *Glarean, sein Leben und seine Schriften*, Frauenfeld, 1890, p. 111.

3 (137). *Edictum Theoderici Regis*, ed. F. Bluhme, 1870 (*Monumenta Germaniae Historica, Leges*, V, 145–179).

4 (137). *Ibid.*, § 35, p. 155: "Is qui quasi sub specie utilitatis publicae, ut sic necessarie faciat, delator existit, quem tamen nos execrari omnino profitemur, quamvis vel dicens legibus prohibeatur audiri: tamen si ea quae ad aures publicas detulerit, inter acta constitutus non potuerit adprobare, flammis debet absumi."

5 (138). *Ibid.*, § 108, p. 164: "Si quis pagano ritu sacrificare fuerit deprehensus, arioli etiam atque umbrarii, si reperti fuerint, sub iusta aestimatione convicti, capite puniantur; malarum artium conscii, id est malefici, nudatis rebus omnibus, quas habere possunt, honesti perpetuo damnantur exilio, humiliores capite puniendi sunt."

6 (138). *Odes*, III, 24, 35: "Quid leges sine moribus | Vanae proficiunt?"

7 (138). *Edictum Theoderici Regis*, § 155, p. 168: "Quia quod omnium provincialium securitate provisum est, universitatis debet servare devotio."

8 (139). Edward Zeller, *Grundriss der Geschichte der griechischen Philosophie*, Leipzig, 1883, pp. 309 f.: "Der letzte Vertreter der alten Philosophie ist hier der edle Anicius Manilius Severinus Boethius. . . . Denn wiewohl er aüsserlich der christlichen Kirche angehörte, ist doch seine eigentliche Religion die Philosophie." This remark gives the gist of Zeller's discussion in his larger work (*Die Philosophie der Griechen*, 1868, III, 776–783), in the later editions of which essentially the same point of view is expressed.

9 (139). William Turner, *History of Philosophy* (Boston, 1903), p. 235.

10 (140). *Anecdoton Holderi*, p. 4, l. 16: "condidit et carmen bucolicum." Boethius implies his early writing of elegies in the opening verses of the *Consolation of Philosophy*:

Carmina qui quondam studio florente peregi,
Flebilis heu maestos cogor inire modos.

11 (140). *Anecdoton Holderi*, pp. 38–40. Part of our information about these varied accomplishments of Boethius comes from a letter of Cassiodorus (*Variae*, I, 45), an interesting document in the history of mechanics. See p. 147, n. 22.

12 (143). On the probable order of the works of Boethius, see A. P. McKinlay, "Stylistic Texts and the Chronology of the Works of Boethius," *Harvard Studies in Classical Philology*, XVIII (1907), 123–156. In this article he takes issue with S. Brandt, "Entstehung und Zeitliche Folge der Werke von Boethius" (*Philologus*, LXII (1903), 141–154, 234–279), who regards the *Arithmetica* as the first of Boethius's works. Brandt edits the two commentaries on Porphyry's *Isagoge*, in an exemplary fashion, in *C. S. E. L.*, XXXXVIII (1906).

13 (144). *In Isagogen Porphyrii Commentorum Ed.*, Sec. i, 1 (Brandt, p. 135): "Secundus hic arreptae expositionis labor nostrae seriem translationis expediet, in qua quidem uereor ne subierim fidi interpretis culpam, cum uerbum uerbo expressum comparatumque reddiderim." Horace,

Art of Poetry, 133: "nec uerbum uerbo curatis reddere fidus | Interpres." See *Jahrbb.*, XXVI, 431.

14 (144). The source of this quotation, which has long been among my notes, escapes me.

15 (144). *Academica Priora*, II, 10, 31: "istam κατάληψιν quam, ut dixi, uerbum e uerbo exprimentes comprensionem dicemus." Cf. II, 6, 17, and various other specimens of Cicero's philosophical novelties in this work. One of the connecting links between Boethius and Cicero in this invention of philosophical terms is Marius Victorinus; see Labriolle p. 350 (translation, p. 262). His achievements, however, are far less significant than those of Boethius. Someone should write the entire history of the Latin philosophical vocabulary from Cicero to St. Thomas Aquinas.

16 (144). *Comment. in Epist. ad Galatas*, i, v. 12 (*Migne* XXVI, 323 B): "Si itaque hi qui disertos saeculi legere consueverunt, coeperint nobis de novitate et vilitate sermonis illudere, mittamus eos ad Ciceronis libros, qui de quaestionibus philosophiae praenotantur, et videant, quanta ibi necessitate compulsus sit, tanta verborum portenta proferre, quae numquam Latini hominis auris audivit: et hoc cum de Graeco, quae lingua vicina est, transferret in nostram. Quid patiuntur illi, qui de Hebraeis difficultatibus proprietates exprimere conantur? et tamen multo pauciora sunt in tantis voluminibus Scripturarum quae novitatem sonent, quam ea quae ille in parvo opere congessit."

17 (145). Cicero, *Academica Posteriora*, I, 7, 25: "Qualitates igitur appellari, quas ποιότητας Graeci appellant, quod ipsum apud Graecos non est vulgi uerbum sed philosophorum. Cf. *De Natura Deorum*, II, 37, 94. On *specificus* (for εἰδοποιός), see *Jahrb.*, XXVI, p. 429.

18 (145). *In Isagogen Porph. Ed. Sec* i, 10 (Brandt, p. 159): "Altissimum enim negotium est et maioris egens inquisitionis." C. C. J. Webb, *A History of Philosophy* (London, 1915), p. 115, fittingly remarks that this passage "is a

good example of the way in which what is called elementary logic may attract attention to great philosophical problems."

19 (145). The verses are quoted by B. Haureau, *Histoire de la Philosophie Scholastique* (Paris, 1872), i, 120, and by Stewart, *Boethius*, p. 254.

20 (146). In his first commentary (Brandt, p. 24), he had ventured to add after the quotation from Porphyry: "de his sese, quoniam altior esset disputatio, facere promisit, nos autem adhibito moderationis freno mediocriter unum quodque tangamus." The following discussion is of a Platonic cast, and the argument of the *Consolation of Philosophy* is definitely Platonic. See *Harv. Stud.*, XV, 26.

21 (146). See *Jahrbb.*, XXVI, pp. 434 f.; McKinley, *op. cit.*, pp. 148 f.

22 (147). Cassiodorus *Variae*, I, 45, 4 (ed. Mommsen, *Mon. Hist. Germ.*, *Auctores Antiquissimi*, XII, 40): "Translationibus enim tuis Pythagoras musicus, Ptolomaeus astronomus leguntur Itali: Nicomachus arithmeticus, geometricus Euclides audiuntur Ausonii: Plato theologus, Aristoteles logicus Quirinali voce disceptant: mechanicum etiam Archimeden Latialem Siculis reddidisti. Et quascumque disciplinas vel artes facunda Graecia per singulos viros edidit, te uno auctore patrio sermone Roma suscepit." This letter, evidently the work of Cassiodorus, was sent by Theodoric to Boethius. It is a highly interesting document, particularly in the interest in science and machinery that it shows.

23 (147). R. H. M. Bosanquet in *Encyclopaedia Britannica*, 9th ed., XVII, 80 (*s. v. Music*).

24 (147). Sir F. A. Gore Ouseley, as quoted by R. C. Hope, *Mediaeval Music* (London, 1894), pp. 1 f.

25 (147). *De Institutione Musica*, I, 34 (ed. G. Friedlein, Leipzig, 1867, pp. 224 f.).

26 (148). *Ibid.*, p. 225: "Quod scilicet quoniam totum in ratione ac speculatione positum est, hoc proprie musicae deputabitur, isque est musicus, cui adest facultas secun-

dum speculationem rationemue propositam ac musicae convenientem de modis ac rythmis deque generibus cantilenarum ac de permixtionibus ac de omnibus, de quibus posterius explicandum est, ac de poetarum carminibus iudicandi."

27 (149). *Academica Posteriora*, I, 4, 17–18: "Platonis autem auctoritate, qui varius et multiplex et copiosus fuit, una et consentiens duobus vocabulis philosophiae forma instituta est, Academicorum et Peripateticorum, qui rebus congruentes nominibus differebant. . . . Abundantia quodam ingenii praestabat, ut mihi quidem videtur, Aristoteles, sed idem fons erat utrisque et eadem rerum expetendarum fugiendarumque partitio." *Academica Priora*, ii, 5, 15: "Plato . . . quia reliquit perfectissiman disciplinam, Peripateticos et Academicos, nominibus differentes, re congruentes."

28 (149). The long debate over the genuineness of the theological tractates was virtually settled by Usener in *Anecdoton Holderi*. The *Anecdoton* contains the statement (p. l. 4, 14): "Scripsit librum de sancta trinitate et capita quaedam dogmatica et librum contra Nestorium." In my thesis, I produced further arguments for the genuineness of Tractates I, II, III, and V, but sought to show that Tractate IV was spurious. I should now say that it is directly referred to by Cassiodorus in the phrase *capita quaedam dogmatica*. See below, pp. 156 f.

29 (150). Tr. v, 57 (Stewart and Rand): "natura est unam quamque rem informans specifica differentia." *Ibid.*, iii, 4: "reperta personae est definitio: naturae rationabilis indiuidua substantia.'"

30 (150). C. C. J. Webb, *God and Personality* (Aberdeen, 1919), p. 47: "To Boethius at the beginning of the sixth century, we owe the definition of *persona* which became the standard definition for the writers of the Middle Ages and which is still, perhaps, take it all in all, the best that we have." Mr. Webb uses Boethius's definition as the starting-point of his argument throughout the book. In

his earlier work, *Studies in the History of Natural Theology* (Oxford, 1915), he had made similar remarks (p. 143), but was unable to accept the genuineness of the fifth Tractate, since "it was written at the time of the Council of Chalcedon, about twenty years before Boethius was born." But it might have been written at any time up to 518 or 519 (see Usener, *Anecdoton Holderi*, p. 54). The particular assembly to which Boethius refers was probably that to which a letter on the two heresies was read, that had been sent to Pope Symmachus by certain Oriental bishops in 1512. See A. Hildebrand, *Boethius und seine Stellung zum Christentume* (Regensburg, 1885), p. 251. Mr. Webb in his later statement withdrew his chief objection, and finds that "the weight of the evidence is, I think, on the whole in favour of the genuineness of the Tractate."

31 (150). See E. K. Rand, *Johannes Scottus* (Traube's *Quellen und Untersuchungen zur lateinischen Philologie des Mittelalters*), i (1906), 19.

32 (151). Tract. V, 1, 31: "Tuli aegerrime, fateor, compressusque indoctorum grege conticui metuens ne iure uiderer insanus, si sanus inter furiosos haberi contenderem."

33 (151). *Christ the Word*, p. 75. I would not imply that Dr. More is insensible to the achievements of the Western Church, especially if we weigh the words in his preface to this book. His general point of view, however, I think it is fair to say, is anti-scholastic .

34 (152). *Ibid.*, pp. 194, 244. There is much uncertainty as to the date of Leontios's writings and of the events in his life. He may have been in Rome in 519. See K. Krumbacher, *Geschichte der byzantinischen Literatur*, 2d ed., (1897), p. 55. We need a careful comparison of his Christological argument with that of Boethius. Krumbacher remarks (p. 54): "Man hat ihn mit Recht den ersten Scholastiker genannt und wir halten dafür, dass damit ein Fortschritt in der Erforschung des Christusgeheimnisses gegeben war."

35 (154). *Tract.* II, 68: "Haec si se recte et ex fide habent, ut me instruas peto; aut si aliqua re forte diversus es, diligentius intuere quae dicta sunt et fidem si poterit rationemque coniunge."

36 (155). K. Prantl, *Geschichte der Logik* (2d ed. Leipzig, 1885), II, pp. 22, 108 f. Prantl repeats the views expressed in the first edition (1855), not convinced by the arguments of Usener in *Anecdoton Holderi.*

37 (156). See *Jahrbb.*, pp. 409, 437: *Harv. Stud.*, XV, pp. 27 f.; *Johannes Scottus*, p. 97. The more recent historians of scholastic philosophy do ample justice to this point of view. See especially M. Grabmann, *Die Geschichte der scholastischen Methode* (Freiburg im Breisgau, 1909) III[er] Abschnitt, "Boethius, der letzte Römer — der erste Scholastiker" (pp. 148–177). M. de Wulf, *Histoire de la Philosophie Mediévale* (Paris-Louvain, 1925), p. 84. So Labriolle; see above, p. 314. Apparently the title has come to stay.

38 (156). *Tract.* IV, 29: "De qua velut arce religionis nostrae multi diversa et humaniter atque ut ita dicam carnaliter sentientes adversa locuti sunt, ut Arrius," etc. The simile of the citadel we also note in the *Consolatio;* see I, 3, 44 (and above p. 166); IV, 6, 25: "Haec [i.e., *divina mens*] in suae simplicitatis arce composita". Boethius, like Lucretius (II, 8) and Horace (*Sat.*, II, 6, 16, *Odes*, II, 6, 21), liked to view life from a citadel, above the boorish and the maddened crowd.

39 (156). See Stewart and Rand, *Boethius* (Loeb series), pp. xi, 52.

40 (158). Apollinaris Sidonius, *Epistulae*, IV, 11: "vir siquidem fuit providus prudens, doctus, eloquens, acer et hominum aevi loci populi sui ingeniosissimus quique indesinenter salva religione philospharetur."

41 (158). *De Syllogismis Hypotheticis* (Migne, LXIV, 831 B): "Cum in omnibus philosophiae disciplinis ediscendis atque tractandis summum vitae positum solamen existimen . . ."

42 (158). *In Categorias Aristotelis*, II, *init.* (*Ibid.*, 201 B): "Et si nos curae officii consularis impediunt quominus in his studiis omne otium plenamque operam consumimus, pertinere tamen videtur hoc ad aliquam reipublicae curam, elucubratae rei doctrina cives instruere. Nec male de civibus meis merear, si cum prisca hominum virtus urbium ceterarum ad hanc unam rem publicam, dominationem imperiumque transtulerit, ego id saltem quod reliquum est, Graecae sapientiae artibus mores nostrae civitatis instruxero. Quare ne hoc quidem ipsum consulis vacat officio, cum Romani semper fuerit moris quod ubicumque gentium pulchrum esset atque laudabile, id magis ac magis imitatione honestare. Aggrediar igitur et propositi sententiam ordinemque contexam."

43 (158). *Tusc. Disp.*, I, 1: "hoc [i. e., *studium philosophiae*] mihi Latinis litteris inlustrandum putavi, non quia philosophia Graecis et litteris et doctoribus percipi non posset, sed meum semper iudicium fuit omnia nostros aut invenisse per se sapientius quam Graecos aut accepta ab illis fecisse meliora, quae quidem digna statuissent in quibus elaborarent." Boethius plainly has this very passage in mind. He has happily relieved it of a certain national egotism that makes Cicero's words unpalatable.

44 (159). *Cons. Phil.*, I, pr. 4, 89: "Nam de compositis falso litteris quibus libertatem arguor sperasse Romanam quid attinet dicere?"

45 (159). *Ibid.*, 143: "Nec conueniebat uilissimorum me spirituum praesidia captare quem tu in hanc excellentiam componebas ut consimilem deo faceres."

46 (160). See above, p. 202.

47 (160). "The Soveraignty and Goodness of God, together with the Faithfulness of His Promises Displayed; Being a Narrative of the Captivity and Restauration of Mrs. Mary Rowlandson," Cambridge, 2d ed., 1682. Reprinted in *Genealogy of the Descendants of John White* (Haverhill, Mass., 1900), I, 763–810.

48 (161). *The History of the Decline and Fall of the Roman Empire* (ed. J. B. Bury, London, 1901), IV, ch. 39, p. 201. Gibbon accepts the genuiness of the theological tractates (*Ibid.*, p. 198).

49 (162). Martial, *Epigrammata*, I, 16:
Sunt bona, sunt quaedam mediocria, sunt mala plura
Quae legis hic: aliter non fit, Avite, liber.

50 (163). *Vergilii Vita Donatiana* (ed. J. Brummer, Leipzig, 1912), pp. 11, 189: "cur non illi quoque eadem furta temptarent? verum intellecturos facilius esse Herculi clavam quam Homero versum subripere."

51 (163). *Cons. Phil.*, I, pr., 4, 10: "Haecine est bibliotheca, quam certissimam tibi sedem nostris in laribus ipsa delegeras?" Cf. I, pr., 5, 20.

52 (164). See H. Hüttinger, *Studia in Boetii Carmina Collata;* Stadtamhof, *Pars Prior*, 1900, *Pars Posterior*, 1902; and above all, the work of F. Klingner (see below, note 74), with my review of the same, *American Journal of Philology*, XLIV (1923), 86–87.

53 (164). See below, n. 74.

54 (164) *Anecdoton Holderi*, pp. 51–52.

55 (165). *Ibid.,*: "Dort ein kind des vi jh., hier einen denker grösserer zeit." The work thus falls into three parts, according to Usener: A. The Aristotelian Part, II, pr. 4, 41 (Stewart and Rand, p. 190) to IV, pr. 6, 20 (S. and R., p. 339); B. The Neoplatonic Part, IV, pr. 6, 21 (S. and R., p. 340), to the end of the work; C. The additions of Boethius, I, pr. 1 to II, pr. 4, 41 (S. and R., p. 190), and the poems.

56 (165). A fuller analysis, from which the present one is excerpted, with a few changes, will be found in *Harvard Studies*, XV, pp. 5–24.

57 (166). *Cons. Phil.*, I, pr. 3, 37–48, p. 140: "Itaque nihil est quod admirer, si in hoc uitae salo circumflantibus agitemur procellis, quibus hoc maxime propositum est pessimis displicere. Quorum quidem tametsi est numerosus exercitus, spernendus tamen est, quoniam nullo duce

regitur, sed errore tantum temere ac passim lymphante raptatur. Qui si quando contra nos aciem struens ualentior incubuerit, nostra quidem dux copias suas in arcem contrahit, illi uero circa diripiendas inutiles sarcinulas occupantur. At nos desuper inridemus uilissima rerum quaeque rapientes securi totius furiosi tumultus eoque uallo muniti quo grassanti stultitiae adspirare fas non sit."

58 (167). *Ibid.*, I, pr. 3, 21, p. 138: "Cuius hereditatem cum deinceps Epicureum uulgus ac Stoicum ceterique pro sua quisque parte raptum ire molirentur meque reclamantem renitentemque uelut in partem praedae traherent, uestem quam meis texueram manibus, disciderunt abreptisque ab ea panniculis totam me sibi cessisse credentes abiere."

59 (167). For Cicero, Aristotle is far ahead of all other philosophers with the sole exception of Plato. *Tusc.*, I, 10, 22: "Aristoteles longe omnibus (Platonem semper excipio) praestans et ingenio et diligentia." He would rather err with Plato (*Ibid.*, 17, 30) than be right with those of the lesser schools, whom he calls the plebeian philosophers (*Ibid.*, 23, 55). Boethius would entirely agree.

60 (168). *Cons. Phil.*, II, pr. 1, 21 (p. 174): "Rhetoricae suadela dulcedinis." Cf. ii, pr. 3, 4–6 (p. 182).

61 (168). II, pr. 3, 7: "Sed miseris malorum altior sensus est." See the note in *Harvard Studies*, XV, p. 9.

62 (169). II, pr. 7. See *Harvard Studies*, XV, pp. 111–2.

63 (170). II, pr. 7. See *Harvard Studies*, XV, p. 4, n. 7, and "Mediaeval Gloom and Mediaeval Uniformity," *Speculum*, I (1926), 253 ff.

64 (170). II, 19, 13.

65 (172). III, m. 12, 55:

> Nam qui tartareum in specus
> Victus lumina flexerit,
> Quidquid praecipuum trahit
> Perdit, dum uidet inferos.

But Orpheus was looking back at Eurydice, not at Hell.

66 (173). See *Harvard Studies*, XV, p. 15.

67 (173). *Tract.*, I, 6, 30 (p. 30): "Quod si sententiae fidei fundamentis sponte firmissimae opitulante gratia divina idonea argumentorum adiumenta praestitimus . . ."

68 (174). IV, pr. 6, 21 (p. 340): "Tum uelut ab alio orsa principio ita disseruit."

69 (174). *De Divinatione*, II, 49, 101: "Quae cum ille dixisset, tum ego rursus quasi ab alio principio sum exorsus dicere." See President Pease's note on this passage in his monumental edition (*University of Illinois Studies in Language and Literature*, VIII [1923], 520).

70 (175). IV, pr. 6, (p. 129): "et uictricem quidem causam dis, uictam uero Catoni placuisse familiaris noster Lucanus [*Pharsalia*, I, 126] admonuit." See *Harvard Studies*, XV, p. 17.

71 (177). For a further analysis, see *Harvard Studies*, XV, pp. 20–24. Boethius saves one human quality, freedom of the will, by sacrificing another, the sense of time.

72 (177). Boethius's dualism should commend itself to Dr. More, whose defence of the old-fashioned dualistic point of view is timely and refreshing. See his remarks on "the twin paradox which rationalism is always busy in explaining away" (that of mind and Ideas, that of good and evil, and also that of mind and body), in *The Christ of the New Testament*, pp. 5 ff. The same dualism confronts us in the dogma of the Incarnation, which proclaims the union of two natures, human and divine (*Ibid.*, p. 24). The paradox of human freedom and divine omniscience is merely one of those antinomies that Christian theology hospitably entertains. In general, the attitude of theology is to accept the dualisms that a critical analysis discovers to exist. The attitude of rationalism is to build a universe out of one of the contradictory elements, thus constructing a theory logical and self-contained, but true to only a half of human experience.

73 (177). Magna nobis est, si dissimulare non uultis, necessitas indicta probitatis, cum ante oculos agitis iudicis cuncta cernentis.

74 (178). Such is the argument of my article in *Harvard Studies*, XV, repeated independently, with a far greater wealth of detail, by F. Klingner, *De Boethii Consolatione Philosophiae (Philologische Untersuchungen* herausg. von A. Kiessling und U. v. Wilamowitz-Moellendorf, Berlin, XXVII (1921), 1–120. See *American Journal of Philology*, XLIV (1923), 86–87.

75 (179). On the causes of the arraignment of Boethius, with a consideration of the ancient sources at our disposal, see Stewart, *Boethius*, pp. 29–54. The importance of the theological aspects of the case has become ever plainer in recent years. Thus Bury, in his edition of Gibbon (London, 1901), could remark in a note (IV, 201): "The condemnation of Boethius and Symmachus had nothing to do with religion, so that they are in no sense martyrs." But in his *History of the Later Roman Empire* (London, 1923), I, 156, he admits that the execution of Boethius and Symmachus probably "had some connection with an Imperial edict which was issued about this time, threatening Arians with severe penalties." He adds that the decree was possibly not issued till after the death of Boethius, and insists in a foot-note that "in the prosecution of Boethius there was no anti-Catholic tendency," since his opponents, Cyprian and the rest, were Catholics. Even so, this latest discussion of the case by Bury indicates a noteworthy modification of his earlier point of view. I should say that politicians like Cyprian are the exceptions that prove the rule. Boethius's case is bound up with that of the Senate as a whole. The gist of the matter is contained, I believe, in the following passage in the *Cambridge Mediaeval History*, I (Cambridge University Press, 1911), 453: "The Anonymus declares, besides, that the king was angry with the Romans; and it is difficult to see why he should have been thus angry unless the Romans had been approving of Justin's religious decrees.

On the other hand, if any plot had existed in the real sense of the term, it is not probable that such a man as Boethius, the master of the offices, that is to say one of the chief officers of the Crown, would have endeavoured to shield Albinus by saying, 'Cyprian's accusation is false, but if Albinus has written to Constantinople, he has done so with my consent and that of the whole Senate.' He might perhaps have spoken in such a manner for the purpose of expressing his own and his colleagues' approval of a religious decree promulgated by a sovereign to whom they owed allegiance. Boethius, indeed, had himself just published a work against Arianism, entitled *De Trinitate*, but it does not seem likely that he would have talked in this fashion had a conspiracy really been brewing." I thoroughly agree with the writer of this chapter, M. Dumoulin, that the tractates on the Holy Trinity may have been written not long before. In any case Boethius's Catholicity is given an emphatic expression in Tractate V, written possibly as late as 519 (see above, p. 150, n. 30).

F. W. Bussell, *The Roman Empire* (London, 1910), I, 223 f., well remarks that the passing from Arianism to Catholicism meant "much more than a mere personal conversion; it meant the permeation of Roman and Hellenic ideas, the advance of administrative centralising, the capture of the monarchy, still confined to a Teutonic family, by Roman influences; it implied subservience to central clerical authority at Rome."

76 (179). *Vita*, VI (R. Peiper, in his edition of the *Consolatio* and *Opuscula Sacra*, Leipzig, 1871, p. xxxv): "et uocatur Sanctus Seuerinus a prouintialibus."

77 (179). Abelard makes an excellent statement about the theological tractates at the end of Book I of his *Theologia Christiana* (Migne, CLXXVIII, 1165–1166). He declares that in these works Boethius "fidem . . . nostram et suam ne in aliquo vacillaret . . . inexpugnabiliter astruxit." He adds: "Constat hunc egregium senatorem Romanum . . . in illa persecutione Christianorum qua in Ioannem papam ceterosque Christianos Theodericus saeviit una cum prae-

dicto Symmacho occubuisse." He quotes as sources *Gesta Pontificum* and *Liber Miraculorum beati Benedicti*.

78 (179). *Paradiso*, X, 125:

L'anima santa, che il mondo fallace
Fa manifesto a chi di lei ben ode.
Lo corpo ond'ella fu cacciata giace
Giuso in Cieldauro, ed essa da martiro
E da esilio venne a questa pace.

79 (179). *Acta Sanctorum, Maii*, VI (1688), 702–710: "De S. Johanne Papa I Mart. . . . Quo etiam agitur de Symmacho & S. Severino Boethio Patriciis & Exconsulibus Romanis." The recent editors of the *Acta Sanctorum* repeat in substance the earlier account: see VI (1866), 694, by Carnandet. But in the *Bibliotheca Hagiographica Latina Antiquae et Mediae Aetatis*, published by the *Socii Bollandiani* (Brussels, 1898–1901), one looks in vain for the name of the philosopher under either Boethius or Severinus.

80 (179). His name nowhere appears in the *Martyrologium Romanum Gregorii* XIII, edited from time to time under Pontifical supervision. In S. Baring-Gould's *The Lives of the Saints*, V, *May* (London, 1873), 395–398, St. John I, Martyr, is duly chronicled, and a paragraph on Boethius is tucked in at the end. The author remarks of the *Consolation of Philosophy* that "its religion is no higher than Theism, almost the whole might have been written by Cicero in exile." He states further that Boethius's "name has found its way into some Martyrologies, which commemorate S. Severianus [*sic*] Boethius on October 23. On that day he is venerated in the church of S. Peter at Pavia; but as a modern biographer (Dom Guérin, *Vie des Saints*, V, p. 514) remarks, 'Before giving the biography of Boethius among the saints, I wait till history has determined that he was a Christian.'" How long, oh Lord, how long!

CHAPTER VI

A convenient account of Christian Latin poetry, with good bibliographies, is given by F. J. E. Raby, *A History of Christian-Latin Poetry from the Beginnings to the Close of the Middle Ages*, Oxford, 1927. See also Labriolle, for the different poets here treated. A standard history of the subject is by M. Manitius, *Geschichte der christlich-lateinischen Poesie*, Stuttgart, 1891. For various details, see C. Weyman, *Beiträge zur Geschichte der christlich-lateinischen Poesie*, Munich, 1926.

1 (182). The best edition of Prudentius is by J. Bergman, in *C. S. E. L.*, LXI (1926). For an interesting chapter on Prudentius, see Glover, *Life and Letters in the Fourth Century*, pp. 249 ff. I have drawn freely from my previous paper on the poet (*Transactions of the American Philological Society*, LI [1920], 71–83).

2 (182). Commodian's poems are edited by B. Dombart, *C. S. E. L.*, XV (1887).

3 (182). (*Ibid.*, p. 8):

Saturnusque senex si deus, deus quando senescit?
Aut si deus erat, cur natos ille uorabat?
Terroribus actus, sed quia deus non erat ille,
Viscera natorum rabie monstruosa sumebat.
Rex fuit in terris, in monte natus Olympo,
Nec erat diuinus, sic deum esse dicebat.
Venit inops animi, lapidem pro filio surpsit.
Sic deus euasit; dicitur modo Iuppiter ille.

4 (184). M. Thamin. See above, p. 82.

5 (184). See especially, E. B. Lease, *A syntactic, stylistic and metrical study of Prudentius*, Baltimore, 1895.

6 (185). *Hamartigenia*, 1:

Quo te praecipitat rabies tua, perfide Cain
Divisor blaspheme Dei?

7 (186). *Ibid.*, 126 ff.

8 (186). *Ibid.*, 99:
> Inventor uitii non est Deus, angelus illud
> Degener infami conceptum mente creauit.

9 (186). *Ibid.*, 250:
> Exemplum dat uita hominum, quo cetera peccent.

10 (187). *Ibid.*, 406:
> Heu quantis mortale genus premit improbus hostis
> Armigeris, quanto ferrata satellite ductor
> Bella gerit, quanta uictos dicione triumphat!

11 (188). *Ibid.*, 958:
> At mihi Tartarei satis est si nulla ministri
> Occurrat facies auidae nec flamma Gehennae
> Deuoret hanc animam mersam fornacibus imis.
> Esto cauernoso, quia sic pro labe necesse est
> Corporea, tristis me sorbeat ignis Auerno,
> Saltem mitificos incendia lenta uapores
> Exhalent aestuque calor languente tepescat.
> Lux immensa alios et tempora iuncta coronis
> Glorificent, me poena leuis clementer adurat.

12 (188). G. A. Simcox, *A History of Latin Literature from Ennius to Boethius* (New York, 1883), II, 363. After all, the edge is taken off the absurdity of the plea, when we become aware that it is an *anima naturaliter Horatiana* that speaks. The *ego* of Horace's *Odes* is typical, like that of the coryphaeus in a Greek drama, not individual. Precisely so our poet is not thinking primarily of what is coming to Aurelius Prudentius in the next world. He is speaking for the race.

13 (189). See above, pp. 121 ff.

14 (189). The lapidary poems of Damasus (*Damasi Epigrammata*) are edited by M. Ihm, Leipzig, 1895.

15 (189). Included by Ihm in the *Pseudodamasiana*, No. 71 (p. 75).

16 (190). *Peristeph.*, XI, 9:
> Sunt et muta tamen tacitas claudentia tumbas
> Marmora, quae solum significant numerum.

17 (191). *L'Ile des Pingouins*, ch. 5 (ed. Paris, 1909, p. 152): "Pour se consoler de ton absence, Virgile, ils ont trois poètes: Commodien, Prudence et Fortunat, qui naquirent tous trois en des jours ténébreux où l'on ne savait plus ni la prosodie ni la grammaire."

18 (193). See A. Ebert, *Allgemeine Geschichte der Literatur des Mittelalters im Abendlande* (Leipzig, 1887), I, 263; III, 179–181.

19 (194). IX, 27:
Doctor amarus enim discenti semper ephebo,
Nec dulcis ulli disciplina infantiae est.

20 (195). *Paradise Regained*, II, 340:
A table richly spread in regal mode
. . . all fish, from sea or shore,
Freshet or purling brook, if shell or fin,
And exquisitest name, for which was drained
Pontus, and Lucrine bay, and Afric coast.

21 (196). Juvencus's poem is edited by J. Huemer in *C. S. E. L.*, XXIV (1891).

22 (196). IV, 553:
Adiurabo tamen summi per regna Tonantis;
Praefatio, 24:
Iudex, altithroni genitoris gloria, Christus.

23 (196). *Matthew*, 27, 1.

24 (196). III, 1:
Fuderat in terras roseum iubar ignicomus sol.

25 (197). Juvencus's adaptations of the Classical poets are noticed in Huemer's edition.

26 (197). III, 56.

27 (198). On this author and other writers of Biblical Epic, see Labriolle, pp. 415–444 (translation, pp. 310–332), Manitius and Raby, *Index*, under the names of the different authors.

28 (198). The cento of Proba is published with the *Poetae Christiani Minores*, edited by C. Schenkl in *C. S. E. L.*, XVI (1888).

29 (198). See above, pp. 117 f.

30 (199). V, 172–219. Even the schoolboy will find familiar echoes in the last lines of this passage, for instance, 210–215:

> At non haec nullis hominum / rerumque repertor
> Obseruans oculis / caedes et facta tyranni
> Praesensit / notumque furens quid femina posset.
> Continuo inuadit: / 'procul o procul este profani'
> Conclamat, / caelum ac terras qui numine firmat.

31 (200). *De Viris Illustribus*, 18 (Migne, LXXXIII, 1093 a): "cuius quidem non miramur studium sed laudamus ingenium. Quod tamen opusculum inter apocryphas scripturas inseritur."

32 (201). The *Harvard Lampoon* for May 31, 1922, p. 182, prints a modified cento from various familiar masterpieces entitled "A Poem that Every Child Should Know." The writer was possibly not aware that he was continuing an ancient tradition.

33 (201). II, 25; IV, 801.

34 (201). Dracontius is edited by F. Vollmer, *Monumenta Germaniae Historica, Auctores Antiquissimi*, XIV (1905).

35 (202). See above, pp. 159 f.

36 (202). I, 417.

> Mirata diem, discedere solem
> Nec lucem remeare putat terrena propago
> Solanturque graves lunari luce tenebras,
> Sidera cuncta notant caelo radiare sereno.
> Ast ubi purpureo surgentem ex aequore cernunt
> Luciferum vibrare iubar flammasque ciere
> Et reducem super astra diem de sole rubente,
> Mox revocata fovent hesterna in gaudia mentes;
> Temporis esse vices noscentes luce divina
> Coeperunt sperare dies, ridere tenebras.

As Vollmer notes, Dracontius may possibly have taken a suggestion from Manilius, I, 69. Perhaps he also knew Lucretius, V, 973–976. In any case, the main part of the imagination is his own.

37 (203). Avitus is edited by R. Peiper, *Monumenta Germaniae Historica, Auctores Antiquissimi*, VI, 2 (1883).

38 (204). II, 418:
> Nec deus in vobis, quamquam formaverit ante,
> Iam plus iuris habet: teneat quod condidit ipse;
> Quod docui, mecum est; maior mihi portio restat.
> Multa creatori debetis, plura magistro.

39 (204). *Purgatorio*, II, 46:
> *In exitu Israel de Aegypto*
> Cantavan tutti insieme ad una voce,
> Con quanto di quel salmo e poscia scripto.

40 (204). See above, p. 86.

41 (205). V, 720:
> Nosque tubam stipula sequimur numerumque tenentes
> Hoc tenui cumbae ponemus litore portum.

42 (205). Gennadius, *De Viris Illustribus*, 13 (ed. E. C. Richardson, Leipzig, 1896, p. 66): "Commentatus est et in morem Graecorum *Hexemeron* de mundi fabrica usque ad condicionem primi hominis et praevaricationem eius."

43 (206). See above, pp. 17 ff.

44 (206). *Psychomachia*, ll. 310 ff.

45 (206). On the hymn, see the books mentioned by Labriolle, Index, *s. v.* "Hymnes Chrétiennes" and by Raby, pp. 28–41, 45–49.

46 (207). Arator, *Epistola ad Parthenium*, 45 (Migne, LXVIII, 250):
> Qualis in Hyblaeis Ambrosius eminet hymnis
> Quos positi cunis significastis apes.

A most important discussion of the hymns of St. Ambrose is by G. M. Dreves, S. J., "Aurelius Ambrosius, der Vater des Kirchengesanges" (*Ergänzungsheft zu den Stimmen aus Marialaach*), Freiburg-im-Breisgau, 1893. He gives good reasons for attributing to Ambrose, not only the four hymns which the "higher criticism" had allowed the saint, but fourteen more.

47 (207). Much of the following account is repeated from the writer's paper on Prudentius. See above, p. 182, n. 1.

48 (212). *Cath.* 3, 26:

> Sperne, Camena, leues hederas,
> Cingere tempora quis solita es,
> Sertaque mystica dactylico
> Texere docta liga strophio
> Laude Dei redimita comas.

49 (212). *Odes*, IV, 5, 5.

50 (212). *Cath.* 5, 125:

> Sunt et spiritibus saepe nocentibus
> Poenarum celebres sub Styge feriae
> Illa nocte sacer qua rediit Deus
> Stagnis ad superos ex Acherunticis.

51 (213). *Cath.* 12, 125.

52 (214). For the entire poem, see the edition by E. Dümm-ler, *Monumenta Germaniae Historica, Poetae Latini Aevi Carolini,* I (1881), 558–559. A convenient text of the part excerpted for a hymn will be found in the admirable little volume of selections by W. A. Merrill (*Latin Hymns,* Boston, 1904), p. 29.

53 (215). Matthew Britt, O. S. B., *The Hymns of the Breviary and the Missal,* New York, 1922. See also *Ecclesia Orans,* herausg. vom Abt Ildefons Herwegen: I (1920), *Vom Geist der Liturgie;* IX (1923), H. Rosenberg, *Die Hymnen des Breviers;* Ulysse Chevalier, *Poésie Liturgique Traditionelle de l'Église Catholique en Occident,* Tournai, 1894. I cannot refrain from adding here a welcome *regalo di Befania* of this year from my friend Professor H. H. Yeames of Hobart College.

Epiphania

> Oriens ex alto stella,
>   funde lumen mentibus
> Hac in valle lacrimarum
>   nocte caligantibus,
> Ut videntes Salvatorem
>   pacem invenerimus.

Luce nova dissipentur
    animarum tenebrae,
Super nubes peccatorum
    surge, Sol Justitiae,
Vitam nobis et salutem
    ferens alis hodie.

Te petentes sapientes
    dona tria tibi dant:
Aurum regi, tus ut deo,
    atque myrrham dedicant
Morituro quem victorem
    mortis fore consciant.

Ecce, stabulo in obscuro,
    Mundi Lux, puerulus;
Inter asinum et bovem
    Angelorum Dominus;
Ecce, Verbum caro factum
    infans jacet parvulus!

Nobis quoque dona danda
    tibi, Rex puerule:
Laudes, honor, fides, amor,
    sine fine gratiae,
Corda nostra, vitae nostrae,
    corpora et animae.

Regna, Regum Rex, in nobis;
    corda rege hominum,
Pedes nostros duc in viam
    pacis, Lumen Luminum;
Verbum Dei, monstra nobis
    verum evangelium.

54 (215). For recent papers on these poets, see J. C. Rolfe, "Claudian," *Transactions of the American Philological Association*, L (1919), 135–149, and the writer's "Ausonius, the First French Poet," *Proceedings of the Classical Association* (British), XXIV (1927), 28–41.

55 (216). *Les Fleurs du Mal, précédées d'une notice par Théophile Gautier*, Paris, 1869, p. 18: "Dans cette merveilleuse langue, le solécisme et le barbarisme me paraissent rendre les négligences forcées d'une passion qui s'oublie et se moque des régles."

56 (216). *Ibid.*

CHAPTER VII

For an excellent monograph on education in the Roman Empire, see G. Rauschen, *Das griech-römische Schulwesen zur Zeit des ausgehenden antiken Heidentums* (Programme of the Königliches Gymnasium zu Bonn), Bonn, 1900. Also C. Barbagallo, *Lo Stato e l'Instruzione Publica nell' Impero Romano*, Catania, 1911. Dr. J. W. H. Walden's admirable work, *The Universities of Ancient Greece* (New York, 1909), also contains important information about the western part of the Empire. On monasticism, consult the careful bibliography given by L. J. Paetow, *Guide to the Study of Mediaeval History* (Berkeley, California, 1917), pp. 117–121. On Trivium and Quadrivium, see a valuable article by Pio Rajna, *Studi Medievali*, I, N. S. (1928), 4–36.

1 (218). The chief source of information about these deities is Varro, quoted by various later writers, particularly by St. Augustine. See *De Civitate Dei*, IV, 11, 21, 34.

2 (219). On the Alexandrian Libraries and the Museum, see J. E. Sandys, *A History of Classical Scholarship* (Cambridge, England), I (2d. ed., 1906), 105–108.

3 (219). Timon of Phlius, cited by Sandys, *loc. cit.*

4 (219). On Roman libraries see A. Langie, *Les Bibliothèques dans l'ancienne Rome et dans L'Empire Romain*, Fribourg (Suisse), 1908; C. E. Boyd, *Public Libraries and Literary Culture in Ancient Rome*, Chicago, 1916.

5 (220). *Res Gestae*, XIV, 6, 18: "bybliothecis sepulchrorum ritu in perpetuum clausis." One must not press these words unduly; they occur in the historian's "arraignment of his age," which suffers from exaggeration. At the same time, some libraries were certainly turned into churches,

notably in the case of the Santa Maria Antiqua. See
Boyd, *op. cit.*, p. 2.

6 (220). *Epist.*, XLVIII (XLIX), 3 (*C. S. E. L.*, LIV, 3):
"revolue omnium, quos supra memoraui, commentarios et
ecclesiarum bibliothecis fruere."

7 (220). On the desolate condition of Rome in the times of
Gregory the Great, see Gibbon (ed. Bury, London, 1901),
V, Ch. 45, pp. 30–38. Some libraries still existed, we know
from Gregory, though he did not find in them the copy of
Eusebius for which he was looking. (*Epist.*, VIII, 29,
Migne, LXXVII, 231 A): "nulla in archivo huius nostrae
Ecclesiae, vel in Romanae urbis bibliothecis esse cognovi."

8 (220). *Theodosiani Libri XVI* . . . . edidit adsumpto
apparatu P. Kruegeri, Th. Mommsen, Berlin, 1905. See
in particular Book XIII, 3: *De Medicis et Professoribus*.

9 (220). *Ibid.*, XIII, 3, 1 and 11 (a decree of Valens, Gratian
and Valentinian): "Trevirorum vel clarissimae civitati
uberius aliquid putavimus deferendum, rhetori ut tri-
ginta, item viginti grammatico Latino, Graeco etiam,
si qui dignus repperiri potuerit, duodecim praebeantur
annonae."

10 (221). *Ibid.*, 2, 10: "Medicis et magistris urbis Romae
sciant omnes immunitatem esse concessam, ita ut etiam
uxores eorum ab omni inquietudine tribuantur inmunes
et a ceteris oneribus publicis vacent, eosdemque ad mi-
litiam minime conprehendi placeat, sed nec hospites
militares recipiant."

11 (221). *Ibid.*, 5: "Magistros studiorum doctoresque ex-
cellere oportet moribus primum, deinde facundia. Sed
quia singulis civitatibus adesse ipse non possum, iubeo,
quisque docere vult, non repente nec temere prosiliat ad
hoc munus, sed iudicio ordinis probatus decretum curia-
lium mereatur optimorum conspirante consensu. Hoc
enim decretum ad me tractandum referetur, ut altiore
quodam honore nostro iudicio studiis civitatum accedant.

12 (221). See Walden, *The Universities of Ancient Greece*,
p. 85. I am aware that my friend Professor Paetow pro-

tests, with good reason, against the indiscriminate use of the term "university" (*op. cit.*, p. 437). See also Haskins, *The Renaissance of the Twelfth Century*, p. 369. The institutions of the later empire differed at notable points from those of the Middle Ages, as the latter do from our own. And yet there are certain common bonds that seem to me to justify "university" as a general term applicable to them all. With its liberal use in our country, there is not much objection to extending it to include the ancient institutions of higher learning. See Rauschen, *op. cit.*, p. 2: "Mit Überraschung nimmt man in diesen Quellenschriften wahr, welch eine grosse Ähnlichkeit zwischen den damaligen Universitätsverhältnissen und den heutigen besteht." He points to similarities in matriculation, student-regulations, and clubs. On the organization of the ancient university, see his work, p. 20, and on the chief universities of the empire, p. 19.

13 (221). In particular, see *Codex Theodosianus*, XIV, 9.

14 (222). *Ibid.*, 1: "Idem immineant censuales, ut singuli eorum tales se in conventibus praebeant, quales esse debeant, qui turpem inhonestamque famam et consociationes, quas proximas putamus esse criminibus, aestiment fugiendas neve spectacula frequentius adeant aut adpetant vulgo intempestiva convivia."

15 (222). On the regulations governing students, including various matters of interest not treated here, see Rauschen, *op. cit.*, pp. 24–30.

16 (222). See Sandys, *History of Classical Scholarship*, I, 670; K. A. Schmid, *Geschichte der Erziehung* (Stuttgart, 1892), II, 1, pp. 114 ff.

17 (223). Irving Babbitt, "The Critic and American Life," *Forum*, February, 1928.

18 (223). Flavel S. Thomas, *A Dictionary of University Degrees* (Syracuse, N. Y., 1898), p. 29.

19 (224). *Republic*, VII, 521 D.

20 (224). *Ibid.*, 526 B: τόδε ἤδη ἐπεσκέψω, ὡς οἵ τε φύσει λογιστικοὶ εἰς πάντα τὰ μαθήματα ὡς ἔπος εἰπεῖν ὀξεῖς

φύονται, οἵ τε βραδεῖς ἂν ἐν τούτῳ παιδευθῶσι καὶ γυμνά-
σωνται, κἂν μηδὲν ἄλλο ὠφεληθῶσιν, ὅμως εἴς γε τὸ
ὀξύτεροι αὐτοὶ αὐτῶν γίγνεσθαι πάντες ἐπιδιδόασιν.

21 (224). *Ibid.*, 532 A–533 E.

22 (224). *Ibid.*, 537 B–540 B.

23 (225). See J. Adam, *Classical Review*, XV (1901), 220.

24 (225). *De Oratore*, III, 127: "has artis quibus liberales
doctrinae atque ingenuae continerentur, geometriam,
musicam, litterarum cognitionem et poetarum, atque illa,
quae de naturis rerum, quae de hominum moribus, quae
de rebus publicis dicerentur."

25 (226). *Ibid.*, I, 42, 187: "in grammaticis [inclusa sunt]
poetarum pertractatio, historiarum cognitio, verborum
interpretatio, pronuntiandi quidam sonus."

26 (226). *Ibid.*, 187–188. See also, for instance, I, 3, 9; and
Tusculan Disputations, I, 1, 1: "cum omnium artium quae
ad rectam vivendi rationem pertinerent, ratio et disciplina
studio sapientiae, quae philosophia dicitur, contineretur";
I, 26, 64: "Philosophia vero, omnium mater artium, quid
est aliud nisi, ut Plato, donum, ut ego, inventum deorum?"

27 (226). Only fragments of Varro's *Disciplinarum Libri IX*
remain. See M. Schanz, *Geschichte der römischen Literatur*,
§ 188.

28 (227). *Or.*, XLIII, 23. See Walden, *The Universities of
Ancient Greece*, p. 196.

29 (228). St. Augustine himself informs us about his encyclopaedia of the *arts*. See *Retractationes*, I, 6 (ed. Knöll,
C. S. E. L., XXXVI, 1902, p. 27).

30 (228). *De Doctrina Christiana*, II, 16, 44 (Migne, XXXII,
1015): "Cum enim artes illae omnes liberales, partim ad
usum vitae, partim ad cognitionem rerum contemplati-
onemque discantur, usum earum assequi difficilimum est
nisi ei qui ab ipsa pueritia ingeniosissimus instantissime
atque constantissime operam dederit."

31 (228). *Retractationes*, III, 2 (*C. S. E. L.*, XXXVI, p. 19): "displicet mihi . . . quod multum tribui liberalibus disciplinis, quas multi sancti multum nesciunt, quidam etiam sciunt et sancti non sunt."

32 (228). See *Retractationes*, II, 30 (Knoll, pp. 135 f.).

33 (228). The work of Martianus Capella is most recently edited by A. Dick, Leipzig, 1925.

34 (230). John the Scot's commentary on Martianus Capella still awaits a complete publication, even after the additions made by Manitius (*Didaskaleion* I [1912], 157 ff.; II, 43 ff.), to what Hauréau had published. See the writer's *Johannes Scottus* (Traube's *Quellen und Untersuchungen*, I, 1906), p. 97.

35 (230). *Gargantua*, ch. 23.

36 (230). J. E. Sandys, *A History of Classical Scholarship*, II (1908), 290, and other passages noted in the index.

37 (230). See Frontispiece.

38 (231). See above, p. 26.

39 (233). See "The Outlook for the American College," *Harvard Alumni Bulletin*, January 19, 1928, pp. 475–478.

40 (233). See above, p. 105.

41 (235). Cassian's work is edited by M. Petschenig, *C. S. E. L.*, XVII (1888).

42 (235). *Ibid.*, VI, 1: "Sextum nobis certamen est, quod Graeci ἀκηδίαν, quam nos taedium siue anxietatem cordis possumus nuncupare."

43 (235). *Ad Atticum*, XII, 45, 1: "'Ακηδία tua me mouet, etsi scribis nihil esse."

44 (235). St. Thomas Aquinas, *Summa Theologiae*, *Prima*, *Qu.* LXIII, Art. 2: "Acedia vero est quaedam tristitia qua homo redditur tardus ad spirituales actus propter corporalem laborem."

45 (235). *Persones Tale*, 53: "Envye and Ire maken bitternesse in herte; which bitternesse is moder of Accidie."

46 (236). *De Imitatione Christi*, I, 24, 3: "Ibi acediosi ardentibus stimulis perurgentur."

47 (236). *Ecclus.*, X, 15.

48 (236). *Inst. Coen.*, IV, 17: "Illud autem ut reficientibus fratribus sacrae lectiones in coenobiis recitentur, non de Aegyptiorum typo processisse, sed de Cappadocum noverimus, quos nulli dubium est non tam spiritalis exercitationis causa, quam conpescendae superfluae otiosaeque confabulationis gratia et maxime contentionum, quae plerumque solent in conuiuiis generari, hoc statuere uoluisse, uidentes eas aliter apud se non posse cohiberi."

49 (237). *Ibid.*: "tantaque uescentibus eis silentii huius disciplina seruatur, ut cucullis ultra oculorum palpebras demissis, ne scilicet liber aspectus habeat copiam curiosius evagandi, nihil amplius intueantur quam mensam et adpositos in ea uel quos ex ea capiunt cibos, ita ut, quemadmodum uel quantum reficiat alius, nullus inuicem notet."

50 (237). *Ibid.*, V, 29: "Uidimus senem Machaten . . . hanc a domino gratiam diuturnis precibus inpetrasse, ut quotquot diebus ac noctibus agitaretur conlatio spiritalis, numquam somni torpore penitus laxaretur. Si quis uero detractationis uerbum seu otiosum temptasset inferre, in somnium protinus concidebat, ac ne usque ad aurium quidem eius pollutionem uirus obloquii poterat peruenire.

51 (237). *Ibid.*, V, 33–34: "ait, monachum scripturarum notitiam pertingere cupientem nequaquam debere labores suos erga commentatorum libros inpendere, sed potius omnem mentis industriam et intentionem cordis erga emundationem uitiorum carnalium detinere."

52 (237). Gibbon (ed. Bury, London, 1901), vol. IV, ch. 37, pp. 57 ff.

53 (239). Marcus Cassinensis, *Carmen de S. Benedicto* (Migne, LXXX, 184 c):
"Arxque modo vitae est, quae fuit ante necis."

54 (239). *Dialogi*, II, *praef.* (Migne, LXI, 126): "scienter nescius et sapienter indoctus."

55 (239). On Mabillon and the question of St. Benedict's learning, see Roger, *L'Enseignement des Lettres Classiques*

d'Ausone à Alcuin (Paris, 1905), pp. 173–175, and the literature cited by Schanz, *Römische Litteraturgeschichte*, § 1241 (IV, 11, [1920], p. 593).

56 (239). Regula Benedicti, 38, 48, 57.

57 (239). Gregory, *Dialogi*, II, *praef.* (Migne, LXI, 126): "Qui . . . Romae liberalibus litterarum studiis traditus fuerat. Sed cum in eis multos ire per abrupta vitiorum cerneret, eum quem quasi in ingressu mundi posuerat, retraxit pedem."

58 (240). Edited by Mommsen, *Monumenta Germaniae Historica, Scriptores Antiquissmi*, XII. Hodgkin, *The Letters of Cassiodorus*, being a condensed translation of the *Variae Epistulae*, London, 1886.

59 (240). *Variae*, II, 27 (Mommsen, p. 62): "damus quidem permissum, sed errantium votum laudabiliter improbamus; religionem imperare non possumus, quia nemo cogitur ut credat invitus." The Jews of Genoa had asked permission to repair their synagogue, and Theodoric allowed them at least to put on a new roof.

60 (241). Cassiodorus, *Inst. Div. Lect., praef.* (Migne, LXX, 1105): "Nisus sum cum Agapito papa urbis Romae, ut sicut apud Alexandriam multo tempore fuisse traditur institutum . . . collatis expensis in urbe Romana professos doctores scholae potius acciperent Christianae." See Traube, *Vorlesungen und Abhandlungen*, II (1911), 128–130.

61 (241). See Rauschen, *op. cit.*, pp. 18, 31.

62 (241). See above, pp. 165, 168.

63 (243). *Inst. Div. Lect.*, 30 (Migne, LXX, 1144 D): "Felix intentio, laudanda sedulitas, manu hominibus praedicare, digitis linguas aperire, salutem mortalibus tacitam dare, et contra diaboli subreptiones illicitas calamo atramentoque pugnare. Tot enim vulnera Satanas accipit quod antiquarius Domini verba describit."

64 (244). *De topicis.* See *Inst. Hum. Lect.* (Migne, LXX, 1190–1192).

65 (244). *Inst. Div. Lect.*, 28 (Migne, LXX, 1142 c): "Quod si alicui fratrum (ut meminit Virgilius)
Frigidus obstiterit circum praecordia sanguis,
ut nec humanis nec divinis litteris perfecte possit erudiri, aliqua tamen scientiae mediocritate suffultus, eligat certe quod sequitur:
Rura mihi et rigui placeant in vallibus amnes."

66 (245). *Ibid.*, 29 (Migne, LXX, 1143 c): "Maria quoque vobis ita subiacent, ut piscationibus variis pateant; et captus piscis, cum libuerit, vivariis possit includi. Fecimus enim illic (iuvante Domino) grata receptacula, ubi sub claustro fideli vagetur piscium multitudo; ita consentanea montium speluncis, ut nullatenus se sentiat captum, cui libertas est escas sumere, et per solitas se cavernas abscondere. Balnea quoque congruenter aegris praeparata corporibus iussimus aedificari, ubi fontium perspicuitas decenter illabitur, quae et potui gratissima cognoscitur et lavacris. Ita fit ut monasterium vestrum potius quaeratur ab aliis, quam vos extranea loca iuste desiderare possitis."

67 (246). *De Anima*, 10 (Migne, LXX, 1298): "Malis nubilus vultus est in qualibet gratia corporali; maesti etiam, cum laetanter agunt, cum paulo post paeniteant deserti impetu voluptatis suae, subito in tristitiam redeunt; oculi interdum supra quam necesse est commoventur; iterumque cogitantes infixi sunt, incerti, vagi, fluctuantes, ad omnia trepidi, de cunctorum voluntate suspensi, curis anxii, suspicionibus inquieti; aliena de se iudicia sollicite perscrutantur, quia dementer propria perdiderunt."

68 (247). *Ibid.*, 11 (1300 D): "Hilaris illi semper vultus est et quietus, macie validus, pallore decoratus, lacrimis assiduis laetus, promissa barba reverendus, nullo cultu mundissimus. Sic per iustitiam mentis de rebus contrariis redduntur homines pulchriores: oculi laeti et honeste blandi: sermo veriloquus, bonorum pectorum penetrabilis, cupiens amorem Dei omnibus suadere, quo plenus est: vox ipsa mediocris, nec debilis vicino silentio, nec robusto clamore dilatata."

69 (247). Gibbon (ed. Bury, London, 1901), IV, ch. 37, p. 69.

70 (248). M. Roger, *op. cit.*, p. 189.

71 (248). See E. Norden in *Die Kultur der Gegenwart*, herausg. von P. Hinneberg, Teil I, Abt. VIII (ed. 3, Berlin and Leipzig, 1912), 412: "So verdient Cassiodor den Ehrentitel den ihm ein französischen Gelehrter gegeben hat, le héros et le restaurateur de la science au VI siècle."

72 (249). *Policraticus*, II, 26 (ed. Webb, [Oxford, 1909], I, 142); VIII, 19 (II, 370): "Fertur tamen beatus Gregorius bibliothecam combusisse gentilium, quo divinae paginae gratior esset locus et maior auctoritas et diligentia studiosior." The use of *fertur* here (and of *traditur a maioribus* in the first passage) suggests that John himself was a bit uncertain about the story.

73 (249). In one disconsolate letter, full of his own woes and those of the world, Gregory finds comfort in the thought that the end of the world is drawing nigh. *Epist.*, IX, 123 (Migne, LXXVII, 105 A): "In his itaque omnibus quia, appropinquante fine mundi, generalem percussionem esse cognoscitis, affligi nimis de propriis molestiis non debetis."

74 (249). *Republic*, X, 8, 607 B: ὅτι παλαιὰ μέν τις διαφορὰ φιλοσοφίᾳ τε καὶ ποιητικῇ.

CHAPTER VIII

An excellent brief treatment of the life and works of St. Augustine is given by Labriolle, pp. 519–578 (translation, pp. 389–432), with a well-selected bibliography. I refrained from much searching in the recent discussions of Dante until this lecture had been written and delivered. The reader can extensively supplement what I have said here by the admirable chapter, "Dante and St. Augustine," in E. G. Gardner's *Dante and the Mystics* (London, 1913), pp. 44–76. Dr. Edward Moore, *Studies in Dante*, I (Oxford, 1896), pp. 291–294, had paved the way, though he merely mentions the *De Quantitate Animae* (p. 292). These two scholars between them have probably amassed most of the significant connections in imagery and thought between St. Augustine and Dante.

Translations of a number of the works of St. Augustine will be found in *A Select Library of the Nicene and Post-Nicene Fathers of the Christian Church*, I–VII (Buffalo, 1886–1888).

1 (251). See above, pp. 132 f.

2 (251). *Epistulae*, lib. VI, *epist. ultima*, ad Aloysium Crottum (quoted in Migne, XXII, 225): "Caeterum puto utrumque ucro pulcherrime divinarum rerum omnium scientiam tenuisse. Sed quoad reliquas omnes partes philosophiae, Augustinus unus est longe tum acutior et peritior, tum etiam subtilior. Dialecticus Augustinus fuit egregius, et idem physicus atque mathematicus. Huic Hieronymus plurimum praestitit dicendi elegantia potius, quam doctrina: id quod ex utriusque oratione licet intueri. Graecam litteraturam Hieronymus perpulchre calluit; Augustinus minus perfecte. Ille Hebraice quoque habetur eruditus, et Augustinus illius linguae ignarus omnino. Vita horridus Hieronymus, Augustinus autem mitis. Quod si ex iis duobus unum effici potuisset, nihil natura absolutius edidisset." (In the Venice edition of 1489, by Bernardinus Corius Cremonensis, this letter is found on folio iii. Harvard College Library has a copy, Inc. 5009).

3 (252). *Convivio*, i, 2, 14 (*Le Opere di Dante, Testo Critico della Società Dantesca Italiana*, Florence, 1921): "L'altra è quando, per ragionare di sè, grandissima utilitade ne seque altrui per via di dottrina; e questa ragione mosse Agustino ne le sue Confessioni a parlare di sè, chè per lo processo de la sua vita, lo quale fu di [non] buono in buono, e di buono in migliore, e di migliore in ottimo, ne diede essemplo e dottrina, la quale per sè vero testimonio ricevere non si potea."

4 (252). This sermon is relegated to the Appendix (No. CLXXVII) in the Benedictine edition (Migne, XXXIX, 2082).

5 (252). See *Alfred Lord Tennyson, a Memoir, by his Son*, Hallam, Lord Tennyson (London, 1924), II, 391.

6 (254). An attractive way to read the *Confessions* is in the recent edition by Labriolle in *Collection des Universités de France* (published by the Association Guillaume Budé), Paris, 2 vols., 1925–26, with the Latin text confronted by a French translation. So in English, with the translation of William Watts, 1631, used by W. H. D. Rouse in his edition in the *Loeb Classical Library*, London, 1912.

7 (254). Since this lecture was delivered, Mr. Bradford has published his wise and stimulating book, "Life and I" (Boston, 1928), which contains various references to St. Augustine, and which itself, in some respects, suggests Augustine, as well as Boethius and certain works of the Middle Ages. See *Speculum*, III (1928), 276 ff.

8 (255). *Vorlesungen und Abhandlungen*, II (1911), 113.

9 (256). *Contra Academicos*, I, 1, 4 (ed. P. Knöll, *C. S. E. L.*, LXIII, 1922): "adhibito itaque notario, ne aurae laborem nostrum discerperent, nihil perire permisi." For other references to this little Academy, see *De Ordine*, I, 3, 6–4, 11; 8, 22, and Labriolle, pp. 537 (translation, p. 402).

10 (257). See for instance, the description in *Contra Academicos*, II, 4, 10.

11 (257). *De Beata Vita*, 35: "foue precantes trinitas" (from Ambrose's hymn, *Deus creator omnium*).

12 (257). *Inferno*, IV, 106 ff.

13 (257). See above, pp. 227 f.

14 (258). *Paradiso*, XXXII, 35.

15 (258). *Paradiso*, X. Dr. Gardner, *Dante and the Mystics*, pp. 74–77, would regard Augustine as typifying theology. But why should he then not be placed with St. Thomas? With some misgivings, I would still adhere to what seems to me a simpler explanation. There may be grades among

the mystics, but Augustine is one of them. Dr. Moore (*op. cit.*, p. 291) thinks that Augustine is selected for this exalted position "rather from his traditional connexion with the great monastic order of Augustinians, and with hermits and solitaries in particular, than for his eminence as a theologian." Change "hermits and solitaries" to "mystics," and, I think, we have the right answer — supplied by the *De Quantitate Animae*.

16 (259). *Paradiso*, I, 7 ff.

17 (259). *Epist.*, XIII (X), 28: "Et ubi ista invidis non sufficiant, legant Richardum de sancto Victore in libro *De Contemplatione*; legant Bernardum in libro *De Consideratione*; legant Augustinum in libro *De Quantitate Animae*, et non invidebunt."

18 (259). *De Quantitate Animae*, 33, 76 (Migne, XXXII, 1076): "Iam vero in ipsa visione atque contemplatione veritatis qui septimus atque ultimus animae gradus est . . . vel summum principium rerum omnium, vel si quo alio modo res tanta congruentius appellari potest." See C. Witte, *Dantis Alligherii Epistolae* (Padua, 1827), p. 99; P. Toynbee, *Dantis Alagherii Epistolae*, (Oxford, 1920), p. 192; E. G. Gardner, *op. cit.*, p. 46.

19 (259). Dr. Gardner, naturally, appreciates its importance. (*Op. cit.*, pp. 44–48.)

20 (260). § 71 (Migne, XXXII, 1074): "Non enim audienda est nescio quae impietas rusticana plene, magisque lignea quam sunt ipsae arbores quibus patrocinium praebet, quae dolere vitem quando uva decerpitur et non solum sentire ista cum creduntur, sed etiam videre atque audire credit, de quo errore sacrilego alius est disserendi locus."

The Benedictine editors call this fancy *Manichaeorum error*. See Augustine's *De Moribus Manichaeorum*. II. xvii, 54 — xviii, 66 (*Ibid.*, 1368–1373).

21 (260). Cicero, *Tusculan Disputations*, I, 24, 56.

22 (261). § 72 (Migne, XXXII, 1074): "Ergo attollere in tertium gradum, qui iam est homini proprius, et cogita

memoriam non consuetudine inolitarum sed animadver-
sione atque signis commendatarum ac retentarum rerum
innumerabilium, tot artes opificum, agrorum cultus, ex-
stinctiones urbium . . . inventiones tot signorum in litteris,
in verbis, in gestu, in cuiuscemodi sono, in picturis atque
figmentis, tot gentium linguas . . . tantamque curam
posteritatis; officiorum, potestatum, honorum dignitatum-
que ordines, sive in familiis, sive domi militiaeque in re
publica, sive in profanis, sive in sacris apparatibus; vim
ratiocinandi et excogitandi, fluvios eloquentiae, carminum
varietates, ludendi ac iocandi causa milleformes simula-
tiones, modulandi peritiam, dimetiendi subtilitatem,
numerandi disciplinam, praeteritorum ac futurorum ex
praesentibus coniecturam."

23 (261). *Tusculan Disputations*, I, 24, 57–27, 67.

24 (262). The same mystic progress of the Soul is described
in *Confessions*, VII, 17.

25 (263). *Tusculan Disputations*, I, 19, 44: "quodque nunc
facimus, cum laxati curis sumus, ut spectare aliquid veli-
mus et visere, id multo tum faciemus liberius totosque nos
in contemplandis rebus perspiciendisque ponemus, propterea quod et natura inest in mentibus nostris insatiabilis
quaedam cupiditas veri videndi et orae ipsae locorum
illorum, quo peruenerimus, quo faciliorem nobis cognitionem rerum caelestium, eo maiorem cognoscendi cupidi-
tatem dabunt."

26 (263). § 79 (Migne, XXXII, 1079): "Ascendentibus igitur
sursum versus, primus actus, docendi causa, dicatur animatio; secundus, sensus; tertius, ars; quartus, virtus;
quintus, tranquillitas; sextus, ingressio; septimus, con-
templatio."

27 (263). *Ibid.*: "de corpore; per corpus; circa corpus; ad
seipsam; in seipsa; ad Deum; apud Deum."

28 (264). *Ibid.*: "pulchre de alio; pulchre per aliud; pulchre
circa aliud; pulchre ad pulchrum; pulchre in pulchro;
pulchre ad pulchritudinem; pulchre apud pulchritudinem."

29 (264). All the more, perhaps, because he had said something like it in one of his early works (*Contra Academicos*, II, 3, 7), where he called the love of beauty (*philocalia*), and the love of truth (*philosophia*), two sisters. In the *Retractations* (I, 1, 7), he pronounced all that a pointless and silly fable (*prorsus inepta est et insulsa illa quasi fabula de philocalia et philosophia*). The aestheticism of the *De Quantitate Animae*, however, is not reproved in the *Retractations*.

30 (264). See above, p. 177, n. 72.

31 (265). See above, p. 70.

32 (266). See above, p. 65.

33 (266). Dr. Gardner (*op. cit.*, p. 45), following Lubin, works out the correspondence in all parts of the poem. He finds the first three stages illustrated in the *Inferno*, the fourth in the *Purgatorio*, the fifth in the Earthly Paradise, the sixth in the ascent through the nine spheres, and the seventh in the Empyrean. If that is so, as seems likely, the final abiding-place of St. Augustine in the Empyrean is natural enough, since he had discovered it for Dante.

34 (266). *Inferno*, IV, 141.

35 (267). Notably in the poem of Prudentius. See above, p. 18.

36 (267). *De Civitate Dei*, VIII, 8.

37 (267). *De Civitate Dei*, II, 14: "Hunc Platonem . . . non heroibus tantum, sed etiam diis ipsis praeferendum esse non dubito."

38 (267). See the passage quoted above (p. 37) from *Confessions*, VII, 9, and *De Civitate Dei*, VIII, 9. See Labriolle, p. 526 (translation, 394). In the *Retractations*, Augustine carefully purges his earlier works of Platonic flavorings that are not quite Christian, such as the theory that the soul recollects something of its former existence. See, for instance, 4, 8 (*C. S. E. L.*, XXXVI, 24).

39 (268). *Comment. in Epist. ad Galatas*, III, *praef.* (Migne, XXVI, 399): "Nostis enim et ipsae, quod plus quam quin-

decim anni sunt, ex quo in manus meas numquam Tullius, numquam Maro, numquam gentilium litterarum quilibet auctor ascendit: et si quid forte inde dum loquimur, obrepit, quasi antiqui per nebulam somnii recordamur."

40 (269). See above, p. 228.

41 (269). E. Norden, "Die lateinische Literatur im Übergang vom Altertum zum Mittelalter" (*Die Kultur des Gegenwart*, herausg. von P. Hinneberg, Berlin and Leipzig, 1907), p. 419: "Augustinus war der grösste Dichter der alten Kirche, mag er auch in Versen so weniges geschrieben wie Plato."

42 (270). *De Doctrina Christiana*, II, 18, 28 (Migne, XXXIV, 49): "Quisquis bonus verusque Christianus est, Domini sui esse intelligat, ubicumque invenerit veritatem."

43 (270). The matter is well discussed by Norden, *op. cit.*, pp. 422–423. On Prudentius see above, pp. 17 ff.

44 (270). *Republic*, IX, 592 B.

45 (271). In *Republic*, VIII. See the note by J. Adam in his edition (Cambridge, England, 1907), II, p. 196.

46 (272). Professor D. L. Drew discusses this aspect of Virgil's poetry in his book, *The Allegory of the Aeneid* (Oxford, 1927). He makes many acute suggestions, but goes much too far, it seems to me, in his identifications.

47 (273). Περὶ τοῦ ἐν Ὀδυσσείᾳ τῶν Νυμφῶν ἄντρου. (*Odyssey*, XIII, 102–112).

48 (273). E. Norden, *P. Vergilius Maro Aeneis Buch VI* (Leipzig, 1903), p. 29. This idea was followed further by Norden's pupil, F. Bitsch, *De Platonicorum Quaestionibus quibusdam Vergilianis*, Berlin, 1911.

49 (273). See D. Comparetti, *Virgilio nel Medio Evo* (2d ed. Florence, 1896), pp. 129–138; 1st ed. trans. by E. F. M. Benecke (London, 1899), pp. 96–103.

50 (273). See R. Pichon, *Lactance* (Paris, 1901), pp. 448 f.

51 (273). See above, p. 118.

52 (273). *Epistolae ad Romanos Inchoata Expositio* (Migne, XXXV, 2089): "quod non facile crederem nisi quod po-

etarum quidam in Romana lingua nobilissimus, antequam diceret ea de innovatione saeculi, quae in Domini nostri Iesu Christi satis concinere et convenire videantur, praeposuit versum, dicens:

Ultima Cumaei iam venit carminis aetas."

53 (274). *Epist.*, CCLVIII, 5 (Migne, XXXIII, 1073): "Nam omnino non est cui alteri praeter Dominum Christum dicat genus humanum:

Te duce si qua manent sceleris vestigia nostri,
Irrita perpetua solvent formidine terras.

Quod ex Cumaeo, id est, ex Sibyllino carmine se fassus est transtulisse Virgilius; quoniam fortassis etiam illa vates aliquid de unico Salvatore in spiritu audierat, quod necesse habuit confiteri." See also *Epist.*, CXXXVII, 12 (*Ibid.*, p. 521). The same two verses are also quoted in *De Civitate Dei*, X, 27.

54 (274). *De Civitate Dei*, X, 27: "Nam utique non hoc a se ipso se dixisse Vergilius in eclogae ipsius quarto ferme versu indicat, ubi ait:

Ultima Cumaei venit iam carminis aetas."

55 (274). St. Augustine's references to Virgil (in *De Civitate Dei*, I–X) are collected by S. Angus, *The Sources of the first Ten Books of Augustine's De Civitate Dei* (Princeton, 1906), p. 12. For specimens of criticism, see *De Civitate Dei*, XIII, 19; XIV, 3 and 8; XXI, 13.

56 (275). E. g., X, 27.

57 (275). *Confessions*, I, 21.

58 (275). *De Civitate Dei*, I, 3: "Nempe apud Vergilium quem propterea parvuli legunt, ut videlicet poeta magnus omniumque praeclarissimus atque optimus teneris ebibitus animis non facile oblivione possit oboleri, secundum illud Horatii [*Epist.*, I, 2, 69]:

Quo semel est imbuta recens servabit odorem
Testa diu."

59 (275). XXI, 27, where *Aen.*, VI, 664 follows *St. Luke* 16, 9 and *St. Matthew* 10, 41.

60 (275). III, 14. He takes the destruction of Alba as typical of Roman brutality. After quoting Virgil (*Aen.*, VI, 814), he adds: *Libido ista dominandi magnis malis agitat et conterit humanum genus.*

61 (275). II, 29; IV, 11.

62 (276). III, 10 (here he quotes *Aen.*, VIII, 326 f.); XIX, 12, 13. For an important study of Augustine's ideas, see H. Fuchs, *Augustin und der antike Friedensgedanke (Neue Philologische Untersuchungen*, herausg. v. W. Jaeger, Berlin, III, 1926). Virgil is mentioned in several places, but he might have figured more prominently in this discussion.

63 (276). See F. Schneider, *Rom und Romgedanke im Mittelalter* (Munich, 1926), pp. 55–68.

64 (276). Moribus antiquis res stat Romana virisque. Augustine quotes Ennius's verse and also Sallust's remarks about it (*De Civ. Dei*, II, 21).

65 (276). Here he quotes, with two other passages, the famous lines from *Aen.*, VI, 646 ff.:
Excudent alii spirantia mollius aera . . .
Parcere subiectis et debellare superbos.

66 (276). V, 24–25.

67 (276). II, 29: "Illic enim tibi non Vestalis focus non lapis Capitolinus, sed Deus unus et verus
Nec metas rerum nec tempora possit,
Imperium sine fine dabit." (*Aen.*, I, 278).

68 (277). Einhard, *Vita Caroli*, 24: "Inter cenandum aut aliquod acroama aut lectorem audiebat. Legebantur ei historiae et antiquorum res gestae. Delectabatur et libris sancti Augustini, praecipueque his qui *De Civitate Dei* praetitulati sunt."

69 (277). III, 12 (ed. 1820, vol. I, p. 367).

70 (277). See the edition of Fulgentius by R. Helm (Leipzig, 1898), p. 87. An important article concerning the mediaeval vogue of Fulgentius is that of M. L. W. Laistner,

"Fulgentius in the Carolingian Age," *Festschrift zu Ehren Prof. M. Hruschewsky* (*Ukrainian Academy of Science*, Kiev, 1928), 445-466.

71 (278). A portion is printed from a Paris manuscript of the fifteenth century, by V. Cousin, *Ouvrages Inédits d'Abélard* (Paris, 1836), pp. 639-644.

72 (278). *Epist.*, XIII (X), 24 [8]: "Est ergo subiectum totius operis, litteraliter tantum accepti, status animarum post mortem simpliciter sumptus; nam de illo et circa illum totius operis versatur processus. Si vero accipiatur opus allegorice, subiectum est homo prout merendo et demerendo per arbitrii libertatem iustitie premiandi et puniendi obnoxius est."

73 (281). See above, pp. 292-294, the notes on pp. 25-27.

74 (281). See above, pp. 248 ff.

75 (281). Iohannes Monachus, *Liber de Miraculis, prolog.* (ed. M. Huber, O. S. B., in A. Hilka's *Sammlung mittellateinischer Texte*, 7, Heidelberg, 1913, p. 1): "Ambrosius, Augustinus, Hieronimus atque Gregorius, qui fuerunt doctissimi in utraque sciencia, divina scilicet et humana, et fuerunt in eloquentia ueluti quatuor paradisi flumina." On the date of Iohannes, see Huber, p. xxi.

INDEX

INDEX

Abelard, Peter, 13, 43, 155, 179, 280, 290 n. 14, 323 n. 77.

Aeschylus, 33.

Aetas Ciceroniana (the 4th century), 255.

Agatha, St., 189.

Agapetus, Pope, 241.

Agnes, St., 191.

Agrippa, King, 35.

Alaric, 276.

Albertus Magnus, 284.

Alcuin, 13, 132, 280, 290 n. 13.

Alexandria, library at, 219, 332 n. 2.

Alfred, King, 136.

Allegorical method of interpretation, popularized in the West by St. Ambrose, 85, 86 ff., 300 n. 21; use of, by Eastern writers, 85; St. Thomas and Dante on, 86; and Cassian, 86, 87; and mysticism, 90.

Allegory, and the problem of evil, 96; Jerome's dislike of, 117, 118.

Allen, Alexander V. G., *The Continuity of Christian Thought*, 7, 9, 10, 38, 285.

Altar of Victory, the, 14 ff.

Alypius, 256.

Ambrose, St., and the Altar of Victory, 15, 16, 17; not always a mystic, 70; as administrator, 71, 72, 77, 100; of noble birth, 73; trained in the law, 73, 74; how he became Bishop of Milan, 74, 75; his death and funeral, 77; his intellectual training, 77, 78; philosophers quoted by, 78, 79; influence of Cicero on, 79 ff.; certain similarities in their careers, 79; his style, 79; his interpretation of Cicero in his *De Officiis Ministrarum*, 79 ff., 83; significance of the title, 80; his *De Paradiso*, 82; a satirist, 83-85; the road to mysticism, 85 ff.; first to popularize allegorical method of interpretation in the West, 85 ff.; his *De Abraham*, 87-89; his *De Fuga Saeculi*, 90; the *Hexaemeron*, 90 ff., 96 ff.; his fondness for the old authors, 91; why he never mentioned Cicero, 91; his interest in Science, 92, 93, 94; and the higher life of beasts, 94, 95, 302 n. 38, 303 n. 40; fascinated by the sea, actual and spiritual, 97, 98; on the nature and needs of man, 98, 99; how regarded by contemporaries and others, 100; St. Bernard on, 101; his hymns, 207, 208, 209, 213; *Expositio in Apocalypsum*, 301 n. 31; mentioned, 7, 22, 29, 104, 110, 111, 117, 140, 206, 255, 257, 265, 280, 281, 284.

Ammianus Marcellinus, 220, 332 n. 5.

Angus, S., *Sources of the First Ten Books of Augustine's* Civitate Dei, 347 n. 55.

Anselm, St., 284.

ORIENTAL RELIGIONS IN ROMAN PAGANISM
by Franz Cumont

This study by the great Belgian historian Franz Cumont describes one aspect of the cultural meeting of east and west in the Early Roman Empire. It describes the great pagan religions of the orient, and tells how their religious thought and ceremonial permeated, altered, and revivified Roman paganism.

It provides a coverage of all the more important eastern religions of the time, from their first appearance in Rome, 204 B.C., when the great Mother of the Gods was first imported from Syria:

The ecstatic cults of Phrygia and Syria; the worship of Cybele, the Magna Mater, Attis, Adonis; their orgies and mutilatory rites.
The mysteries of Egypt; the worship of Serapis, Isis, Osiris, their closely hidden secret rites, redemption ceremonies.
The dualism of Persia; the elevation of cosmic evil to a full and equal partnership with the deity; the mysteries of Mithra.
The worship of Hermes Trismegistos, and the documents ascribed to him; Sabazios, Ishtar, Astarte.
The magic, thaumaturgy, judicial astrology of the ancient near east.
The emotional and intellectual impact of the great civilized traditions of Egypt and Babylonia upon still barbarian Europe.

Cumont's ORIENTAL RELIGIONS IN ROMAN PAGANISM is the best general picture, on an intermediate level, of this important moment in cultural history. It is also of great value in analyzing an era which shared certain cultural problems with our own time.

Introduction by Grant Showerman. 55pp. of notes, with extensive evaluated bibliography. Translated from 2nd French edition. Index. xxiv + 298pp. 5⅜ x 8.   Paperbound **$1.75**

AN INTRODUCTION TO SCHOLASTIC PHILOSOPHY
(Formerly published under the title: Scholasticism Old & New)
By Maurice de Wulf

In this corrected edition of a standard work, Professor Maurice de Wulf, great authority on medieval philosophy, examines the scholastic tradition. After a careful and discriminating examination of the true nature and definition of scholasticism, in which he sifts modern interpretations and misinterpretations of the scholastic spirit, he analyzes

the scholastic method

scholastic philosophy in its relations

to medieval philosophy in general,

to ancient philosophy, to medieval science

scholastic metaphysics, theodicy, general physics,

celestial and terrestrial physics, psychology,

moral philosophy and logic

The decline of medieval scholasticism is then treated. Examination is not so much in terms of individual thinkers, as is usual in histories of philosophy, as in terms of a "Philosophia communis" of the scholastic tradition.

The second part of this work examines the modern scholastic revival, with a discussion of the relations of neoscholasticism and neothomism to history of philosophy, religion, and modern science; and an examination of the neoscholastic doctrines. Considerable information is included on the neoscholastic estimation of various trends in modern philosophy.

Written by one of the very greatest historians of medieval philosophy, this book is useful both as a corrective to earlier histories and as an excellent exposition and evaluation of the scholastic position.

Newly corrected edition. Translated with introduction by P. Coffey. Index. 281 footnotes, mostly bibliographical. xvi + 271pp. 5⅜ x 8.

T283 Paperbound $1.75

CHRISTIAN AND ORIENTAL PHILOSOPHY OF ART
by Ananda K. Coomaraswamy

The late A. K. Coomaraswamy was a unique fusion of art historian, philosopher, orientalist, linguist, expositor. Here he discusses the true function of aesthetics in art, the importance of symbolism, the importance of intellectual and philosophic background for the artist. He analyzes the role of a traditional culture in enriching art, and demonstrates that modern abstract art and primitive art, despite superficial resemblances, are completely divergent. Other topics discussed are the common philosophy which pervades all truly great art; the beauty inherent in such forms of activity as mathematics; the union of traditional symbolism and individual portraiture in premodern cultures.

2 illustrations. Bibliography for the study of medieval and oriental art. 114 bibliographic notes. 148pp. 5⅜ x 8.

T378 Paperbound **$1.25**

ARISTOTLE
by A. E. Taylor

Here is a brilliantly written popular account of the great Greek philosopher and his thought. It is not simply a listing and abstract discussion of Ideas, but a searching analysis of Aristotle's thought, both in terms of its contemporary and historical background, and its present application. Written by one of the very greatest Platonic scholars of our day, it is provocative enough to stimulate the expert, and lucid and instructive for the beginner.

Dr. Taylor covers the life and works of Aristotle; classification of the sciences; scientific method; formal logic; induction; theory of knowledge; first philosophy; matter and form; the potential and the actual; the four causes; motion and eternity; God; physics; terrestrial bodies; biology; psychology; grades of psychical life; sensation; common sensibles and the common sense organ; thought; active intelligence; practical philosophy; ethics; society; the theory of the state; music and literature.

Revised edition printed from new plates. New index specially compiled for this edition. 118pp. 5⅜ x 8.

T280 Paperbound $1.00

Best introduction to classical philosophy

HISTORY OF ANCIENT PHILOSOPHY
by W. Windelband

Windelband's HISTORY OF ANCIENT PHILOSOPHY has served generations of scholars as the best introduction and survey volume to Greek and Roman philosophy. It combines rigorously exact scholarship, insight into the difficulties of the student, a genius for easily followed presentation with a remarkably complete coverage of persons, movements, and ideas.

After an introduction discussing ancient philosophy in general and the intellectual life of Greece in the 7th and 6th centuries B.C., the author discusses the Ionian speculators and Pythagoras. He then analyzes the Milesians (Thales, Anaximander, Anaximenes), Heraclitus, the Eleatics, Empedocles, Anaxagoras, Leucippus, the Pythagoreans, the Sophists, Socrates, and other early schools and personalities. 20 pages are then devoted to an analysis of Democritus, 50 pages to Plato, and 70 pages to Aristotle.

The remainder of the book discusses later classical philosophy. The Peripatetics, Stoics, Epicureans are covered in detail, as are the Skeptics and the Middle Platonists. Neoplatonism is described in terms of Plotinus, Jamblichus and Proclus, while a special chapter gives a brief discussion of those Christian Apologists who used philosophic techniques, the more important Gnostics, and Origen.

Background information is supplied for each philosopher and his thought, while an evaluated bibliography of thousands of entries is given in separate sections within the text. It covers all the basic work in the historiography of philosophy up to 1900.

Translated by H. E. Cushman, from 2nd German edition. xv + 393pp. 5⅜ x 8. Paperbound **$1.75**

THE GUIDE FOR THE PERPLEXED by Moses Maimonides

This is the full unabridged text of one of the greatest philosophic works of all time. Written by a 12th century thinker who was equally preeminent as an original philosopher and as a Biblical and Talmudic scholar, it is both a classic of great historical importance and a work of living significance today.

THE GUIDE FOR THE PERPLEXED was written for scholars who were bewildered by the conflict between religion and the scientific and philosophic thought of the day. It is concerned, basically, with finding a concord between the religion of the Old Testament and its commentaries, and Aristotelian philosophy. After analyzing the ideas of the Old Testament by means of "homonyms" Maimonides examines other reconciliations of religion and philosophy (the Moslem rationalists) and then proposes his own resolution with contemporary Aristotelianism.

THE GUIDE FOR THE PERPLEXED was at once recognized as a masterwork, and it influenced Jewish, Christian, and Moslem thought of the Middle Ages. It is necessary reading for a comprehension of the thought of such scholastics as Aquinas and Scotus, and indispensable for everyone interested in the Middle Ages, Judaism, medieval philosophy, or the larger problems which Maimonides discusses.

Unabridged reproduction of 2nd revised edition of Friedländer's translation. 55pp. introduction discusses Maimonides' life, editions, mss., translations, and provides a summary of the GUIDE. Special and general indexes. lix + 414pp. 5⅜ x 8.

Paperbound **$1.85**

Catalog
of
DOVER BOOKS

BOOKS EXPLAINING SCIENCE

(Note: The books listed under this category are general introductions, surveys, reviews, and non-technical expositions of science for the interested layman or scientist who wishes to brush up. Dover also publishes the largest list of inexpensive reprints of books on intermediate and higher mathematics, mathematical physics, engineering, chemistry, astronomy, etc., for the professional mathematician or scientist. For our complete Science Catalog, write Dept. catrr., Dover Publications, Inc., 180 Varick Street, New York 14, N. Y.)

CONCERNING THE NATURE OF THINGS, Sir William- Bragg. Royal Institute Christmas Lectures by Nobel Laureate. Excellent plain-language introduction to gases, molecules, crystal structure, etc. explains "building blocks" of universe, basic properties of matter, with simplest, clearest examples, demonstrations. 32pp. of photos; 57 figures. 244pp. 5⅜ x 8.
T31 Paperbound **$1.35**

MATTER AND LIGHT, THE NEW PHYSICS, Louis de Broglie. Non-technical explanations by a Nobel Laureate of electro-magnetic theory, relativity, wave mechanics, quantum physics, philosophies of science, etc. Simple, yet accurate introduction to work of Planck, Bohr, Einstein, other modern physicists. Only 2 of 12 chapters require mathematics. 300pp. 5⅜ x 8.
T35 Paperbound **$1.60**

THE COMMON SENSE OF THE EXACT SCIENCES, W. K. Clifford. For 70 years, Clifford's work has been acclaimed as one of the clearest, yet most precise introductions to mathematical symbolism, measurement, surface boundaries, position, space, motion, mass and force, etc. Prefaces by Bertrand Russell and Karl Pearson. Introduction by James Newman. 130 figures. 249pp. 5⅜ x 8.
T61 Paperbound **$1.60**

THE NATURE OF LIGHT AND COLOUR IN THE OPEN AIR, M. Minnaert. What causes mirages? haloes? "multiple" suns and moons? Professor Minnaert explains these and hundreds of other fascinating natural optical phenomena in simple terms, tells how to observe them, suggests hundreds of experiments. 200 illus; 42 photos. xvi + 362pp.
T196 Paperbound **$1.95**

SPINNING TOPS AND GYROSCOPIC MOTION, John Perry. Classic elementary text on dynamics of rotation treats gyroscopes, tops, how quasi-rigidity is induced in paper disks, smoke rings, chains, etc, by rapid motion, precession, earth's motion, etc. Contains many easy-to-perform experiments. Appendix on practical uses of gyroscopes. 62 figures. 128pp.
T416 Paperbound **$1.00**

A CONCISE HISTORY OF MATHEMATICS, D. Struik. This lucid, easily followed history of mathematics from the Ancient Near East to modern times requires no mathematical background itself, yet introduces both mathematicians and laymen to basic concepts and discoveries and the men who made them. Contains a collection of 31 portraits of eminent mathematicians. Bibliography. xix + 299pp. 5⅜ x 8.
T255 Paperbound **$1.75**

THE RESTLESS UNIVERSE, Max Born. A remarkably clear, thorough exposition of gases, electrons, ions, waves and particles, electronic structure of the atom, nuclear physics, written for the layman by a Nobel Laureate. "Much ·more thorough and deep than most attempts . . . easy and delightful," CHEMICAL AND ENGINEERING NEWS. Includes 7 animated sequences showing motion of molecules, alpha particles, etc. 11 full-page plates of photographs. Total of nearly 600 illus. 315pp. 6⅛ x 9¼.
T412 Paperbound **$2.00**

WHAT IS SCIENCE?, N. Campbell. The role of experiment, the function of mathematics, the nature of scientific laws, the limitations of science, and many other provocative topics are explored without technicalities by an eminent scientist. "Still an excellent introduction to scientific philosophy," H. Margenau in PHYSICS TODAY. 192pp. 5⅜ x 8.
S43 Paperbound **$1.25**

FADS AND FALLACIES IN THE NAME OF SCIENCE, Martin Gardner. The standard account of the various cults, quack systems and delusions which have recently masqueraded as science: hollow earth theory, Atlantis, dianetics, Reich's orgone theory, flying saucers, Bridey Murphy, psionics, irridiagnosis, many other fascinating fallacies that deluded tens of thousands. "Should be read by everyone, scientist and non-scientist alike," R. T. Birge, Prof. Emeritus, Univ. of California; Former President, American Physical Society. Formerly titled, "In the Name of Science." Revised and enlarged edition. x + 365pp. 5⅜ x 8.
T394 Paperbound **$1.50**

THE STUDY OF THE HISTORY OF MATHEMATICS, THE STUDY OF THE HISTORY OF SCIENCE, G. Sarton. Two books bound as one. Both volumes are standard introductions to their fields by an eminent science historian. They discuss problems of historical research, teaching, pitfalls, other matters of interest to the historically oriented writer, teacher, or student. Both have extensive bibliographies. 10 illustrations. 188pp. 5⅜ x 8.   T240 Paperbound **$1.25**

THE PRINCIPLES OF SCIENCE, W. S. Jevons. Unabridged reprinting of a milestone in the development of symbolic logic and other subjects concerning scientific methodology, probability, inferential validity, etc. Also describes Jevons' "logic machine," an early precursor of modern electronic calculators. Preface by E. Nagel. 839pp. 5⅜ x 8.   S446 Paperbound **$2.98**

SCIENCE THEORY AND MAN, Erwin Schroedinger. Complete, unabridged reprinting of "Science and the Human Temperament" plus an additional essay "What is an Elementary Particle?" Nobel Laureate Schroedinger discusses many aspects of modern physics from novel points of view which provide unusual insights for both laymen and physicists. 192 pp. 5⅜ x 8.
T428 Paperbound **$1.35**

BRIDGES AND THEIR BUILDERS, D. B. Steinman & S. R. Watson. Information about ancient, medieval, modern bridges; how they were built; who built them; the structural principles employed; the materials they are built of; etc. Written by one of the world's leading authorities on bridge design and construction. New, revised, expanded edition. 23 photos; 26 line drawings, xvii + 401pp. 5⅜ x 8.   T431 Paperbound **$1.95**

HISTORY OF MATHEMATICS, D. E. Smith. Most comprehensive non-technical history of math in English. In two volumes. Vol. I: A chronological examination of the growth of mathematics from primitive concepts up to 1900. Vol. II: The development of ideas in specific fields and areas, up through elementary calculus. The lives and works of over a thousand mathematicians are covered; thousands of specific historical problems and their solutions are clearly explained. Total of 510 illustrations, 1355pp. 5⅜ x 8. Set boxed in attractive container.   T429, T430 Paperbound, the set **$5.00**

PHILOSOPHY AND THE PHYSICISTS, L. S. Stebbing. A philosopher examines the philosophical implications of modern science by posing a lively critical attack on the popular science expositions of Sir James Jeans and Arthur Eddington. xvi + 295pp. 5⅜ x 8.
T480 Paperbound **$1.65**

ON MATHEMATICS AND MATHEMATICIANS, R. E. Moritz. The first collection of quotations by and about mathematicians in English. 1140 anecdotes, aphorisms, definitions, speculations, etc. give both mathematicians and layman stimulating new insights into what mathematics is, and into the personalities of the great mathematicians from Archimedes to Euler, Gauss, Klein, Weierstrass. Invaluable to teachers, writers. Extensive cross index. 410pp. 5⅜ x 8.
T489 Paperbound **$1.95**

NATURAL SCIENCE, BIOLOGY, GEOLOGY, TRAVEL

A SHORT HISTORY OF ANATOMY AND PHYSIOLOGY FROM THE GREEKS TO HARVEY, C. Singer. A great medical historian's fascinating intermediate account of the slow advance of anatomical and physiological knowledge from pre-scientific times to Vesalius, Harvey. 139 unusually interesting illustrations. 221pp. 5⅜ x 8.   T389 Paperbound **$1.75**

THE BEHAVIOUR AND SOCIAL LIFE OF HONEYBEES, Ronald Ribbands. The most comprehensive, lucid and authoritative book on bee habits, communication, duties, cell life, motivations, etc. "A MUST for every scientist, experimenter, and educator, and a happy and valuable selection for all interested in the honeybee," AMERICAN BEE JOURNAL. 690-item bibliography. 127 illus.; 11 photographic plates. 352pp. 5⅜ x 8⅜.   S410 Clothbound **$4.50**

TRAVELS OF WILLIAM BARTRAM, edited by Mark Van Doren. One of the 18th century's most delightful books, and one of the few first-hand sources of information about American geography, natural history, and anthropology of American Indian tribes of the time. "The mind of a scientist with the soul of a poet," John Livingston Lowes. 13 original illustrations, maps. Introduction by Mark Van Doren. 448pp. 5⅜ x 8.   T326 Paperbound **$2.00**

STUDIES ON THE STRUCTURE AND DEVELOPMENT OF VERTEBRATES, Edwin Goodrich. The definitive study of the skeleton, fins and limbs, head region, divisions of the body cavity, vascular, respiratory, excretory systems, etc., of vertebrates from fish to higher mammals, by the greatest comparative anatomist of recent times. "The standard textbook," JOURNAL OF ANATOMY. 754 illus. 69-page biographical study. 1186-item bibliography. 2 vols. Total of 906pp. 5⅜ x 8.
Vol. I: S449 Paperbound **$2.50**
Vol. II: S450 Paperbound **$2.50**

DOVER BOOKS

THE BIRTH AND DEVELOPMENT OF THE GEOLOGICAL SCIENCES, F. D. Adams. The most complete and thorough history of the earth sciences in print. Covers over 300 geological thinkers and systems; treats fossils, theories of stone growth, paleontology, earthquakes, vulcanists vs. neptunists, odd theories, etc. 91 illustrations, including medieval, Renaissance wood cuts, etc. 632 footnotes and bibliographic notes. 511pp. 308pp. 5⅜ x 8. T5 Paperbound **$2.00**

FROM MAGIC TO SCIENCE, Charles Singer. A close study of aspects of medical science from the Roman Empire through the Renaissance. The sections on early herbals, and "The Visions of Hildegarde of Bingen," are probably the best studies of these subjects available. 158 unusual classic and medieval illustrations. xxvii + 365pp. 5⅜ x 8. T390 Paperbound **$2.00**

SAILING ALONE AROUND THE WORLD, Captain Joshua Slocum. Captain Slocum's personal account of his single-handed voyage around the world in a 34-foot boat he rebuilt himself. A classic of both seamanship and descriptive writing. "A nautical equivalent of Thoreau's account," Van Wyck Brooks. 67 illus. 308pp. 5⅜ x 8. T326 Paperbound **$1.00**

TREES OF THE EASTERN AND CENTRAL UNITED STATES AND CANADA, W. M. Harlow. Standard middle-level guide designed to help you know the characteristics of Eastern trees and identify them at sight by means of an 8-page synoptic key. More than 600 drawings and photographs of twigs, leaves, fruit, other features. xiii + 288pp. 4⅝ x 6½. T395 Paperbound **$1.35**

FRUIT KEY AND TWIG KEY ("Fruit Key to Northeastern Trees," "Twig Key to Deciduous Woody Plants of Eastern North America"), **W. M. Harlow.** Identify trees in fall, winter, spring. Easy-to-use, synoptic keys, with photographs of every twig and fruit identified. Covers 120 different fruits, 160 different twigs. Over 350 photos. Bibliographies. Glossaries. Total of 143pp. 5⅝ x 8⅜. T511 Paperbound **$1.25**

INTRODUCTION TO THE STUDY OF EXPERIMENTAL MEDICINE, Claude Bernard. This classic records Bernard's far-reaching efforts to transform physiology into an exact science. It covers problems of vivisection, the limits of physiological experiment, hypotheses in medical experimentation, hundreds of others. Many of his own famous experiments on the liver, the pancreas, etc., are used as examples. Foreword by I. B. Cohen. xxv + 266pp. 5⅜ x 8. T400 Paperbound **$1.50**

THE ORIGIN OF LIFE, A. I. Oparin. The first modern statement that life evolved from complex nitro-carbon compounds, carefully presented according to modern biochemical knowledge of primary colloids, organic molecules, etc. Begins with historical introduction to the problem of the origin of life. Bibliography. xxv + 270pp. 5⅜ x 8. S213 Paperbound **$1.75**

A HISTORY OF ASTRONOMY FROM THALES TO KEPLER, J. L. E. Dreyer. The only work in English which provides a detailed picture of man's cosmological views from Egypt, Babylonia, Greece, and Alexandria to Copernicus, Tycho Brahe and Kepler. "Standard reference on Greek astronomy and the Copernican revolution," SKY AND TELESCOPE. Formerly called "A History of Planetary Systems From Thales to Kepler." Bibliography. 21 diagrams. xvii + 430pp. 5⅜ x 8. S79 Paperbound **$1.98**

URANIUM PROSPECTING, H. L. Barnes. A professional geologist tells you what you need to know. Hundreds of facts about minerals, tests, detectors, sampling, assays, claiming, developing, government regulations, etc. Glossary of technical terms. Annotated bibliography. x + 117pp. 5⅜ x 8. T309 Paperbound **$1.00**

DE RE METALLICA, Georgius Agricola. All 12 books of this 400 year old classic on metals and metal production, fully annotated, and containing all 289 of the 16th century woodcuts which made the original an artistic masterpiece. A superb gift for geologists, engineers, libraries, artists, historians. Translated by Herbert Hoover & L. H. Hoover. Bibliography, survey of ancient authors. 289 illustrations of the excavating, assaying, smelting, refining, and countless other metal production operations described in the text. 672pp. 6¾ x 10¾. Deluxe library edition. S6 Clothbound **$10.00**

DE MAGNETE, William Gilbert. A landmark of science by the man who first used the word "electricity," distinguished between static electricity and magnetism, and founded a new science. P. F. Mottelay translation. 90 figures. lix + 368pp. 5⅜ x 8. S470 Paperbound **$2.00**

THE AUTOBIOGRAPHY OF CHARLES DARWIN AND SELECTED LETTERS, Francis Darwin, ed. Fascinating documents on Darwin's early life, the voyage of the "Beagle," the discovery of evolution, Darwin's thought on mimicry, plant development, vivisection, evolution, many other subjects Letters to Henslow, Lyell, Hooker, Wallace, Kingsley, etc. Appendix. 365pp. 5⅜ x 8. T479 Paperbound **$1.65**

A WAY OF LIFE AND OTHER SELECTED WRITINGS OF SIR WILLIAM OSLER. 16 of the great physician, teacher and humanist's most inspiring writings on a practical philosophy of life, science and the humanities, and the history of medicine. 5 photographs. Introduction by G. L. Keynes, M.D., F.R.C.S. xx + 278pp. 5⅜ x 8. T488 Paperbound **$1.50**

CATALOG OF

LITERATURE

WORLD DRAMA, B. H. Clark. 46 plays from Ancient Greece, Rome, to India, China, Japan. Plays by Aeschylus, Sophocles, Euripides, Aristophanes, Plautus, Marlowe, Jonson, Farquhar, Goldsmith, Cervantes, Molière, Dumas, Goethe, Schiller, Ibsen, many others. One of the most comprehensive collections of important plays from all literature available in English. Over ⅓ of this material is unavailable in any other current edition. Reading lists. 2 volumes. Total of 1364pp. 5⅜ x 8. Vol. I, T57 Paperbound **$2.00**
Vol. II, T59 Paperbound **$2.00**

MASTERS OF THE DRAMA, John Gassner. The most comprehensive history of the drama in print. Covers more than 800 dramatists and over 2000 plays from the Greeks to modern Western, Near Eastern, Oriental drama. Plot summaries, theatre history, etc. "Best of its kind in English," NEW REPUBLIC. 35 pages of bibliography. 77 photos and drawings. Deluxe edition. xxii + 890pp. 5⅜ x 8. T100 Clothbound **$5.95**

THE DRAMA OF LUIGI PIRANDELLO, D. Vittorini. All 38 of Pirandello's plays (to 1935) summarized and analyzed in terms of symbolic techniques, plot structure, etc. The only authorized work. Foreword by Pirandello. Biography. Bibliography. xiii + 350pp. 5⅜ x 8.
T435 Paperbound **$1.98**

ARISTOTLE'S THEORY OF POETRY AND THE FINE ARTS, S. H. Butcher, ed. The celebrated "Butcher translation" faced page by page with the Greek text; Butcher's 300-page introduction to Greek poetic, dramatic thought. Modern Aristotelian criticism discussed by John Gassner. lxxvi + 421pp. 5⅜ x 8.
T42 Paperbound **$2.00**

EUGENE O'NEILL: THE MAN AND HIS PLAYS, B. H. Clark. The first published source-book on O'Neill's life and work. Analyzes each play from the early THE WEB up to THE ICEMAN COMETH. Supplies much information about environmental and dramatic influences. ix + 182pp. 5⅜ x 8. T379 Paperbound **$1.25**

INTRODUCTION TO ENGLISH LITERATURE, B. Dobrée, ed. Most compendious literary aid in its price range. Extensive, categorized bibliography (with entries up to 1949) of more than 5,000 poets, dramatists, novelists, as well as historians, philosophers, economists, religious writers, travellers, and scientists of literary stature. Information about manuscripts, important biographical data. Critical, historical, background works not simply listed, but evaluated. Each volume also contains a long introduction to the period it covers.

Vol. I: **THE BEGINNINGS OF ENGLISH LITERATURE TO SKELTON, 1509, W. L. Renwick. H. Orton.** 450pp. 5⅛ x 7⅛. T75 Clothbound **$3.50**
Vol. II: **THE ENGLISH RENAISSANCE, 1510-1688, V. de Sola Pinto.** 381pp. 5⅛ x 7⅛.
T76 Clothbound **$3.50**
Vol. III: **THE AUGUSTANS AND ROMANTICS, 1689-1830, H. Dyson, J. Butt.** 320pp. 5⅛ x· 7⅛.
T77 Clothbound **$3.50**
Vol. IV: **THE VICTORIANS AND AFTER, 1830-1914, E. Batho, B. Dobrée.** 360pp. 5⅛ x 7⅛.
T78 Clothbound **$3.50**

EPIC AND ROMANCE, W. P. Ker. The standard survey of Medieval epic and romance by a foremost authority on Medieval literature. Covers historical background, plot, literary analysis, significance of Teutonic epics, Icelandic sagas, Beowulf, French chansons de geste, the Niebelungenlied, Arthurian romances, much more. 422pp. 5⅜ x 8. T355 Paperbound **$1.95**

THE HEART OF EMERSON'S JOURNALS, Bliss Perry, ed. Emerson's most intimate thoughts, impressions, records of conversations with Channing, Hawthorne, Thoreau, etc., carefully chosen from the 10 volumes of The Journals. "The essays do not reveal the power of Emerson's mind . . .as do these hasty and informal writings," N. Y. TIMES. Preface by B. Perry. 370pp. 5⅜ x 8. T447 Paperbound **$1.85**

A SOURCE BOOK IN THEATRICAL HISTORY, A. M. Nagler. (Formerly, "Sources of Theatrical History.") Over 300 selected passages by contemporary observers tell about styles of acting, direction, make-up, scene designing, etc., in the theatre's great periods from ancient Greece to the Théâtre Libre. "Indispensable complement to the study of drama," EDUCATIONAL THEATRE JOURNAL. Prof. Nagler, Yale Univ. School of Drama, also supplies notes, references. 85 illustrations. 611pp. 5⅜ x 8. T515 Paperbound **$2.75**

THE ART OF THE STORY-TELLER, M. L. Shedlock. Regarded as the finest, most helpful book on telling stories to children, by a great story-teller. How to catch, hold, recapture attention; how to choose material; many other aspects. Also includes: a 99-page selection of Miss Shedlock's most successful stories; extensive bibliography of other stories. xxi + 320pp. 5⅜ x 8. T245 Clothbound **$3.50**

THE DEVIL'S DICTIONARY, Ambrose Bierce. Over 1000 short, ironic definitions in alphabetical order, by America's greatest satirist in the classical tradition. "Some of the most gorgeous witticisms in the English language," H. L. Mencken. 144pp. 5⅜ x 8. T487 Paperbound **$1.00**

MUSIC

A DICTIONARY OF HYMNOLOGY, John Julian. More than 30,000 entries on individual hymns, their authorship, textual variations, location of texts, dates and circumstances of composition, denominational and ritual usages, the biographies of more than 9,000 hymn writers, essays on important topics such as children's hymns and Christmas carols, and hundreds of thousands of other important facts about hymns which are virtually impossible to find anywhere else. Convenient alphabetical listing, and a 200-page double-columned index of first lines enable you to track down virtually any hymn ever written. Total of 1786pp. 6¼ x 9¼. 2 volumes. **T133. The Set, Clothbound $15.00**

STRUCTURAL HEARING, TONAL COHERENCE IN MUSIC, Felix Salzer. Extends the well-known Schenker approach to include modern music, music of the middle ages, and Renaissance music. Explores the phenomenon of tonal organization by discussing more than 500 compositions, and offers unusual new insights into the theory of composition and musical relationships. "The foundation on which all teaching in music theory has been based at this college," Leopold Mannes, President, The Mannes College of Music. Total of 658pp. 6½ x 9¼. 2 volumes. **S418 The set, Clothbound $8.00**

A GENERAL HISTORY OF MUSIC, Charles Burney. The complete history of music from the Greeks up to 1789 by the 18th century musical historian who personally knew the great Baroque composers. Covers sacred and secular, vocal and instrumental, operatic and symphonic music; treats theory, notation, forms, instruments; discusses composers, performers, important works. Invaluable as a source of information on the period for students, historians, musicians. "Surprisingly few of Burney's statements have been invalidated by modern research . . . still of great value," NEW YORK TIMES. Edited and corrected by Frank Mercer. 35 figures. 1915pp. 5½ x 8½. 2 volumes. **T36 The set, Clothbound $12.50**

JOHANN SEBASTIAN BACH, Phillp Spitta. Recognized as one of the greatest accomplishments of musical scholarship and far and away the definitive coverage of Bach's works. Hundreds of individual pieces are analyzed. Major works, such as the B Minor Mass and the St. Matthew Passion are examined in minute detail. Spitta also deals with the works of Buxtehude, Pachelbel, and others of the period. Can be read with profit even by those without a knowledge of the technicalities of musical composition. "Unchallenged as the last word on one of the supreme geniuses of music," John Barkham, SATURDAY REVIEW SYNDICATE. Total of 1819pp. 5⅜ x 8. 2 volumes. **T252 The set, Clothbound $10.00**

HISTORY

THE IDEA OF PROGRESS, J. B. Bury. Prof. Bury traces the evolution of a central concept of Western civilization in Greek, Roman, Medieval, and Renaissance thought to its flowering in the 17th and 18th centuries. Introduction by Charles Beard. xl + 357pp. 5⅜ x 8.
T39 Clothbound $3.95
T40 Paperbound $1.05

THE ANCIENT GREEK HISTORIANS, J. B. Bury. Greek historians such as Herodotus, Thucydides, Xenophon; Roman historians such as Tacitus, Caesar, Livy; scores of others fully analyzed in terms of sources, concepts, influences, etc., by a great scholar and historian. 291pp. 5⅜ x 8. **T397 Paperbound $1.50**

HISTORY OF THE LATER ROMAN EMPIRE, J. B. Bury. The standard work on the Byzantine Empire from 395 A.D. to the death of Justinian in 565 A.D., by the leading Byzantine scholar of our time. Covers political, social, cultural, theological, military history. Quotes contemporary documents extensively. "Most unlikely that it will ever be superseded," Glanville Downey, Dumbarton Oaks Research Library. Genealogical tables. 5 maps. Bibliography. 2 vols. Total of 965pp. 5⅜ x 8. **T398, T399 Paperbound, the set $4.00**

GARDNER'S PHOTOGRAPHIC SKETCH BOOK OF THE CIVIL WAR, Alexander Gardner. One of the rarest and most valuable Civil War photographic collections exactly reproduced for the first time since 1866. Scenes of Manassas, Bull Run, Harper's Ferry, Appomattox, Mechanicsville, Fredericksburg, Gettysburg, etc.; battle ruins, prisons, arsenals, a slave pen, fortifications; Lincoln on the field, officers, men, corpses. By one of the most famous pioneers in documentary photography. Original copies of the "Sketch Book" sold for $425 in 1952. Introduction by E. Bleiler. 100 full-page 7 x 10 photographs (original size). 244pp. 10¾ x 8½ **T476 Clothbound $6.00**

THE WORLD'S GREAT SPEECHES, L. Copeland and L. Lamm, eds. 255 speeches from Pericles to Churchill, Dylan Thomas. Invaluable as a guide to speakers; fascinating as history past and present; a source of much difficult-to-find material. Includes an extensive section of informal and humorous speeches. 3 indices: Topic, Author, Nation. xx + 745pp. 5⅜ x 8.
T468 Paperbound $2.49

FOUNDERS OF THE MIDDLE AGES, E. K. Rand. The best non-technical discussion of the transformation of Latin paganism into medieval civilization. Tertullian, Gregory, Jerome, Boethius, Augustine, the Neoplatonists, other crucial figures, philosophies examined. Excellent for the intelligent non-specialist. "Extraordinarily accurate," Richard McKeon, THE NATION. ix + 365pp. 5⅜ x 8. **T369 Paperbound $1.85**

THE POLITICAL THOUGHT OF PLATO AND ARISTOTLE, Ernest Barker. The standard, comprehensive exposition of Greek political thought. Covers every aspect of the "Republic" and the "Politics" as well as minor writings, other philosophers, theorists of the period, and the later history of Greek political thought. Unabridged edition. 584pp. 5⅜ x 8.
T521 Paperbound **$1.85**

PHILOSOPHY

THE GIFT OF LANGUAGE, M. Schlauch. (Formerly, "The Gift of Tongues.") A sound, middle-level treatment of linguistic families, word histories, grammatical processes, semantics, language taboos, word-coining of Joyce, Cummings, Stein, etc. 232 bibliographical notes. 350pp. 5⅜ x 8.
T243 Paperbound **$1.85**

THE PHILOSOPHY OF HEGEL, W. T. Stace. The first work in English to give a complete and connected view of Hegel's entire system. Especially valuable to those who do not have time to study the highly complicated original texts, yet want an accurate presentation by a most reputable scholar of one of the most influential 19th century thinkers. Includes a 14 x 20 fold-out chart of Hegelian system. 536pp. 5⅜ x 8.
T254 Paperbound **$2.00**

ARISTOTLE, A. E. Taylor. A lucid, non-technical account of Aristotle written by a foremost Platonist. Covers life and works; thought on matter, form, causes, logic, God, physics, metaphysics, etc. Bibliography. New index compiled for this edition. 128pp. 5⅜ x 8.
T280 Paperbound **$1.00**

GUIDE TO PHILOSOPHY, C. E. M. Joad. This basic work describes the major philosophic problems and evaluates the answers propounded by great philosophers from the Greeks to Whitehead, Russell. "The finest introduction," BOSTON TRANSCRIPT. Bibliography, 592pp. 5⅜ x 8.
T297 Paperbound **$2.00**

LANGUAGE AND MYTH, E. Cassirer. Cassirer's brilliant demonstration that beneath both language and myth lies an unconscious "grammar" of experience whose categories and canons are not those of logical thought. Introduction and translation by Susanne Langer. Index. x + 103pp. 5⅜ x 8.
T51 Paperbound **$1.25**

SUBSTANCE AND FUNCTION, EINSTEIN'S THEORY OF RELATIVITY, E. Cassirer. This double volume contains the German philosopher's profound philosophical formulation of the differences between traditional logic and the new logic of science. Number, space, energy, relativity, many other topics are treated in detail. Authorized translation by W. C. and M. C. Swabey. xii + 465pp. 5⅜ x 8.
T50 Paperbound **$2.00**

THE PHILOSOPHICAL WORKS OF DESCARTES. The definitive English edition, in two volumes, of all major philosophical works and letters of René Descartes, father of modern philosophy of knowledge and science. Translated by E. S. Haldane and G. Ross. Introductory notes. Total of 842pp. 5⅜ x 8.
T71 Vol. 1, Paperbound **$2.00**
T72 Vol. 2, Paperbound **$2.00**

ESSAYS IN EXPERIMENTAL LOGIC, J. Dewey. Based upon Dewey's theory that knowledge implies a judgment which in turn implies an inquiry, these papers consider such topics as the thought of Bertrand Russell, pragmatism, the logic of values, antecedents of thought, data and meanings. 452pp. 5⅜ x 8.
T73 Paperbound **$1.95**

THE PHILOSOPHY OF HISTORY, G. W. F. Hegel. This classic of Western thought is Hegel's detailed formulation of the thesis that history is not chance but a rational process, the realization of the Spirit of Freedom. Translated and introduced by J. Sibree. Introduction by C. Hegel. Special introduction for this edition by Prof. Carl Friedrich, Harvard University. xxxix + 447pp. 5⅜ x 8.
T112 Paperbound **$1.85**

THE WILL TO BELIEVE and HUMAN IMMORTALITY, W. James. Two of James's most profound investigations of human belief in God and immortality, bound as one volume. Both are powerful expressions of James's views on chance vs. determinism, pluralism vs. monism, will and intellect, arguments for survival after death, etc. Two prefaces. 429pp. 5⅜ x 8.
T294 Clothbound **$3.75**
T291 Paperbound **$1.65**

INTRODUCTION TO SYMBOLIC LOGIC, S. Langer. A lucid, general introduction to modern logic, covering forms, classes, the use of symbols, the calculus of propositions, the Boole-Schroeder and the Russell-Whitehead systems, etc. "One of the clearest and simplest introductions," MATHEMATICS GAZETTE. Second, enlarged, revised edition. 368pp. 5⅜ x 8.
S164 Paperbound **$1.75**

MIND AND THE WORLD-ORDER, C. I. Lewis. Building upon the work of Peirce, James, and Dewey, Professor Lewis outlines a theory of knowledge in terms of "conceptual pragmatism," and demonstrates why the traditional understanding of the a priori must be abandoned. Appendices. xiv + 446pp. 5⅜ x 8.
T359 Paperbound **$1.95**

THE GUIDE FOR THE PERPLEXED, M. Maimonides One of the great philosophical works of all time, Maimonides' formulation of the meeting-ground between Old Testament and Aristotelian thought is essential to anyone interested in Jewish, Christian, and Moslem thought in the Middle Ages. 2nd revised edition of the Friedlander translation. Extensive introduction. lix + 414pp. 5⅜ x 8.
T351 Paperbound **$1.85**

DOVER BOOKS

THE PHILOSOPHICAL WRITINGS OF PEIRCE, J. Buchler, ed. (Formerly, "The Philosophy of Peirce.") This carefully integrated selection of Peirce's papers is considered the best coverage of the complete thought of one of the greatest philosophers of modern times. Covers Peirce's work on the theory of signs, pragmatism, epistemology, symbolic logic, the scientific method, chance, etc. xvi + 386pp. 5 ⅜ x 8.
T216 Clothbound **$5.00**
T217 Paperbound **$1.95**

HISTORY OF ANCIENT PHILOSOPHY, W. Windelband. Considered the clearest survey of Greek and Roman philosophy. Examines Thales, Anaximander, Anaximenes, Heraclitus, the Eleatics, Empedocles, the Pythagoreans, the Sophists, Socrates, Democritus, Stoics, Epicureans, Sceptics, Neo-platonists, etc. 50 pages on Plato; 70 on Aristotle. 2nd German edition tr. by H. E. Cushman. xv + 393pp. 5⅜ x 8.
T357 Paperbound **$1.75**

INTRODUCTION TO SYMBOLIC LOGIC AND ITS APPLICATIONS, R. Carnap. A comprehensive, rigorous introduction to modern logic by perhaps its greatest living master. Includes demonstrations of applications in mathematics, physics, biology. "Of the rank of a masterpiece," Z. für Mathematik und ihre Grenzgebiete. Over 300 exercises. xvi + 241pp. 5⅜ x 8.
Clothbound **$4.00**
S453 Paperbound **$1.85**

SCEPTICISM AND ANIMAL FAITH, G. Santayana. Santayana's unusually lucid exposition of the difference between the independent existence of objects and the essence our mind attributes to them, and of the necessity of scepticism as a form of belief and animal faith as a necessary condition of knowledge. Discusses belief, memory, intuition, symbols, etc. xii + 314pp. 5⅜ x 8.
T235 Clothbound **$3.50**
T236 Paperbound **$1.50**

THE ANALYSIS OF MATTER, B. Russell. With his usual brilliance, Russell analyzes physics, causality, scientific inference, Weyl's theory, tensors, invariants, periodicity, etc. in order to discover the basic concepts of scientific thought about matter. "Most thorough treatment of the subject," THE NATION. Introduction. 8 figures. viii + 408pp. 5⅜ x 8.
T231 Paperbound **$1.95**

THE SENSE OF BEAUTY, G. Santayana. This important philosophical study of why, when, and how beauty appears, and what conditions must be fulfilled, is in itself a revelation of the beauty of language. "It is doubtful if a better treatment of the subject has since appeared," PEABODY JOURNAL. ix + 275pp. 5⅜ x 8.
T238 Paperbound **$1.00**

THE CHIEF WORKS OF SPINOZA. In two volumes. Vol. I: The Theologico-Political Treatise and the Political Treatise. Vol. II: On the Improvement of Understanding, The Ethics, and Selected Letters. The permanent and enduring ideas in these works on God, the universe, religion, society, etc., have had tremendous impact on later philosophical works. Introduction. Total of 862pp. 5⅜ x 8.
T249 Vol. I, Paperbound **$1.50**
T250 Vol. II, Paperbound **$1.50**

TRAGIC SENSE OF LIFE, M. de Unamuno. The acknowledged masterpiece of one of Spain's most influential thinkers. Between the despair at the inevitable death of man and all his works, and the desire for immortality, Unamuno finds a "saving incertitude." Called "a masterpiece," by the ENCYCLOPAEDIA BRITANNICA. xxx + 332pp. 5⅜ x 8.
T257 Paperbound **$1.95**

EXPERIENCE AND NATURE, John Dewey. The enlarged, revised edition of the Paul Carus lectures (1925). One of Dewey's clearest presentations of the philosophy of empirical naturalism which reestablishes the continuity between "inner" experience and "outer" nature. These lectures are among the most significant ever delivered by an American philosopher. 457pp. 5⅜ x 8.
T471 Paperbound **$1.85**

PHILOSOPHY AND CIVILIZATION IN THE MIDDLE AGES, M. de Wulf. A semi-popular survey of medieval intellectual life, religion, philosophy, science, the arts, etc. that covers feudalism vs. Catholicism, rise of the universities, mendicant orders, and similar topics. Bibliography. viii + 320pp. 5⅜ x 8.
T284 Paperbound **$1.75**

AN INTRODUCTION TO SCHOLASTIC PHILOSOPHY, M. de Wulf. (Formerly, "Scholasticism Old and New.") Prof. de Wulf covers the central scholastic tradition from St. Anselm, Albertus Magnus, Thomas Aquinas, up to Suarez in the 17th century; and then treats the modern revival of. scholasticism, the Louvain position, relations with Kantianism and positivism, etc. xvi + 271pp. 5⅜ x 8.
T296 Clothbound **$3.50**
T283 Paperbound **$1.75**

A HISTORY OF MODERN PHILOSOPHY, H. Höffding. An exceptionally clear and detailed coverage of Western philosophy from the Renaissance to the end of the 19th century. Both major and minor figures are examined in terms of theory of knowledge, logic, cosmology, psychology. Covers Pomponazzi, Bodin, Boehme, Telesius, Bruno, Copernicus, Descartes, Spinoza, Hobbes, Locke, Hume, Kant, Fichte, Schopenhauer, Mill, Spencer, Langer, scores of others. A standard reference work. 2 volumes. Total of 1159pp. 5⅜ x 8.
T117 Vol. 1, Paperbound **$2.00**
T118 Vol. 2, Paperbound **$2.00**

LANGUAGE, TRUTH AND LOGIC, A. J. Ayer. The first full-length development of Logical Positivism in English. Building on the work of Schlick, Russell, Carnap, and the Vienna school, Ayer presents the tenets of one of the most important systems of modern philosophical thought. 160pp. 5⅜ x 8.
T10 Paperbound **$1.25**

ORIENTALIA AND RELIGION

THE MYSTERIES OF MITHRA, F. Cumont. The great Belgian scholar's definitive study of the Persian mystery religion that almost vanquished Christianity in the ideological struggle for the Roman Empire. A masterpiece of scholarly detection that reconstructs secret doctrines, organization, rites. Mithraic art is discussed and analyzed. 70 illus. 239pp. 5⅜ x 8.
T323 Paperbound **$1.85**

CHRISTIAN AND ORIENTAL PHILOSOPHY OF ART. A. K. Coomaraswamy. The late art historian and orientalist discusses artistic symbolism, the role of traditional culture in enriching art, medieval art, folklore, philosophy of art, other similar topics. Bibliography. 148pp. 5⅜ x 8.
T378 Paperbound **$1.25**

TRANSFORMATION OF NATURE IN ART, A. K. Coomaraswamy. A basic work on Asiatic religious art. Includes discussions of religious art in Asia and Medieval Europe (exemplified by Meister Eckhart), the origin and use of images in Indian art, Indian Medieval aesthetic manuals, and other fascinating, little known topics. Glossaries of Sanskrit and Chinese terms. Bibliography. 41pp. of notes. 245pp. 5⅜ x 8.
T368 Paperbound **$1.75**

ORIENTAL RELIGIONS IN ROMAN PAGANISM, F. Cumont. This well-known study treats the ecstatic cults of Syria and Phrygia (Cybele, Attis, Adonis, their orgies and mutilatory rites); the mysteries of Egypt (Serapis, Isis, Osiris); Persian dualism; Mithraic cults; Hermes Trismegistus, Ishtar, Astarte, etc. and their influence on the religious thought of the Roman Empire. Introduction. 55pp. of notes; extensive bibliography. xxiv + 298pp. 5⅜ x 8.
T321 Paperbound **$1.75**

ANTHROPOLOGY, SOCIOLOGY, AND PSYCHOLOGY

PRIMITIVE MAN AS PHILOSOPHER, P. Radin. A standard anthropological work based on Radin's investigations of the Winnebago, Maori, Batak, Zuni, other primitive tribes. Describes primitive thought on the purpose of life, marital relations, death, personality, gods, etc. Extensive selections of original primitive documents. Bibliography. xviii + 420pp. 5⅜ x 8.
T392 Paperbound **$2.00**

PRIMITIVE RELIGION, P. Radin. Radin's thoroughgoing treatment of supernatural beliefs, shamanism, initiations, religious expression, etc. in primitive societies. Arunta, Ashanti, Aztec, Bushman, Crow, Fijian, many other tribes examined. "Excellent," NATURE. New preface by the author. Bibliographic notes. x + 322pp. 5⅜ x 8. T393 Paperbound **$1.85**

SEX IN PSYCHO-ANALYSIS, S. Ferenczi. (Formerly, "Contributions to Psycho-analysis.") 14 selected papers on impotence, transference, analysis and children, dreams, obscene words, homosexuality, paranoia, etc. by an associate of Freud. Also included: THE DEVELOPMENT OF PSYCHO-ANALYSIS, by Ferenczi and Otto Rank. Two books bound as one. Total of 406pp. 5⅜ x 8. T324 Paperbound **$1.85**

THE PRINCIPLES OF PSYCHOLOGY, William James. The complete text of the famous "long course," one of the great books of Western thought. An almost incredible amount of information about psychological processes, the stream of consciousness, habit, time perception, memory, emotions, reason, consciousness of self, abnormal phenomena, and similar topics. Based on James's own discoveries integrated with the work of Descartes, Locke, Hume, Royce, Wundt, Berkeley, Lotse, Herbart, scores of others. "A classic of interpretation," PSYCHIATRIC QUARTERLY. 94 illus. 1408pp. 2 volumes. 5⅜ x 8.
T381 Vol. 1, Paperbound **$2.50**
T382 Vol. 2, Paperbound **$2.50**

THE POLISH PEASANT IN EUROPE AND AMERICA, W. I. Thomas, F. Znaniecki. Monumental sociological study of peasant primary groups (family and community) and the disruptions produced by a new industrial system and emigration to America, by two of the foremost sociologists of recent times. One of the most important works in sociological thought. Includes hundreds of pages of primary documentation; point by point analysis of causes of social decay, breakdown of morality, crime, drunkenness, prostitution, etc. 2nd revised edition. 2 volumes. Total of 2250pp. 6 x 9. T478 2 volume set, Clothbound **$12.50**

FOLKWAYS, W. G. Sumner. The great Yale sociologist's detailed exposition of thousands of social, sexual, and religious customs in hundreds of cultures from ancient Greece to Modern Western societies. Preface by A. G. Keller. Introduction by William Lyon Phelps. 705pp. 5⅜ x 8. S508 Paperbound **$2.49**

BEYOND PSYCHOLOGY, Otto Rank. The author, an early associate of Freud, uses psychoanalytic techniques of myth-analysis to explore ultimates of human existence. Treats love, immortality, the soul, sexual identity, kingship, sources of state power, many other topics which illuminate the irrational basis of human existence. 291pp. 5⅜ x 8. T485 Paperbound **$1.75**

ILLUSIONS AND DELUSIONS OF THE SUPERNATURAL AND THE OCCULT, D. H. Rawcliffe. A rational, scientific examination of crystal gazing, automatic writing, table turning, stigmata, the Indian rope trick, dowsing, telepathy, clairvoyance, ghosts, ESP, PK, thousands of other supposedly occult phenomena. Originally titled "The Psychology of the Occult." 14 illustrations. 551pp. 5⅜ x 8. T503 Paperbound **$2.00**

DOVER BOOKS

YOGA: A SCIENTIFIC EVALUATION, Kovoor T. Behanan. A scientific study of the physiological and psychological effects of Yoga discipline, written under the auspices of the Yale University Institute of Human Relations. Foreword by W. A. Miles, Yale Univ. 17 photographs. 290pp. 5⅜ x 8.   T505 Paperbound **$1.65**

HOAXES, C. D. MacDougall. Delightful, entertaining, yet scholarly exposition of how hoaxes start, why they succeed, documented with stories of hundreds of the most famous hoaxes. "A stupendous collection . . . and shrewd analysis, "NEW YORKER. New, revised edition. 54 photographs. 320pp. 5⅜ x 8.   T465 Paperbound **$1.75**

CREATIVE POWER: THE EDUCATION OF YOUTH IN THE CREATIVE ARTS, Hughes Mearns. Named by the National Education Association as one of the 20 foremost books on education in recent times. Tells how to help children express themselves in drama, poetry, music, art, develop latent creative power. Should be read by every parent, teacher. New, enlarged, revised edition. Introduction. 272pp. 5⅜ x 8.   T490 Paperbound **$1.50**

LANGUAGES

NEW RUSSIAN-ENGLISH, ENGLISH-RUSSIAN DICTIONARY, M. A. O'Brien. Over 70,000 entries in new orthography! Idiomatic usages, colloquialisms. One of the few dictionaries that indicate accent changes in conjugation and declension. "One of the best," Prof. E. J. Simmons, Cornell. First names, geographical terms, bibliography, many other features. 738pp. 4½ x 6¼.
T208 Paperbound **$2.00**

MONEY CONVERTER AND TIPPING GUIDE FOR EUROPEAN TRAVEL, C. Vomacka. Invaluable, handy source of currency regulations, conversion tables, tipping rules, postal rates, much other travel information for every European country plus Israel, Egypt and Turkey. 128pp. 3½ x 5¼.
T260 Paperbound **60¢**

MONEY CONVERTER AND TIPPING GUIDE FOR TRAVEL IN THE AMERICAS (including the United States and Canada), **C. Vomacka.** The information you need for informed and confident travel in the Americas: money conversion tables, tipping guide, postal, telephone rates, etc. 128pp. 3½ x 5¼.   T261 Paperbound **65¢**

DUTCH-ENGLISH, ENGLISH-DUTCH DICTIONARY, F. G. Renier. The most convenient, practical Dutch-English dictionary on the market. New orthography. More than 60,000 entries: idioms, compounds, technical terms, etc. Gender of nouns indicated. xviii + 571pp. 5½ x 6¼.
T224 Clothbound **$2.50**

LEARN DUTCH!, F. G. Renier. The most satisfactory and easily-used grammar of modern Dutch. Used and recommended by the Fulbright Committee in the Netherlands. Over 1200 simple exercises lead to mastery of spoken and written Dutch. Dutch-English, English-Dutch vocabularies. 181pp. 4¼ x 7¼.   I441 Clothbound **$1.75**

PHRASE AND SENTENCE DICTIONARY OF SPOKEN RUSSIAN, English-Russian, Russian-English. Based on phrases and complete sentences, rather than isolated words; recognized as one of the best methods of learning the idiomatic speech of a country. Over 11,500 entries, indexed by single words, with more than 32,000 English and Russian sentences and phrases, in immediately usable form. Probably the largest list ever published. Shows accent changes in conjugation and declension; irregular forms listed in both alphabetical place and under main form of word. 15,000 word introduction covering Russian sounds, writing, grammar, syntax. 15-page appendix of geographical names, important signs, given names, foods, special Soviet terms, etc. Travellers, businessmen, students, government employees have found this their best source for Russian expressions. Originally published as U.S. Government Technical Manual TM 30-944. iv + 573pp. 5⅝ x 8⅜.   T496 Paperbound **$2.75**

PHRASE AND SENTENCE DICTIONARY OF SPOKEN SPANISH, Spanish-English, English-Spanish. Compiled from spoken Spanish, emphasizing idiom and colloquial usage in both Castilian and Latin-American. More than 16,000 entries containing over 25,000 idioms—the largest list of idiomatic constructions ever published. Complete sentences given, indexed under single words —language in immediately usable form, for travellers, businessmen, students, etc. 25-page introduction provides rapid survey of sounds, grammar, syntax, with full consideration of irregular verbs. Especially apt in modern treatment of phrases and structure. 17-page glossary gives translations of geographical names, money values, numbers, national holidays, important street signs, useful expressions of high frequency, plus unique 7-page glossary of Spanish and Spanish-American foods and dishes. Originally published as U.S. Government Technical Manual TM 30-900. iv + 513pp. 5⅝ x 8⅜.   T495 Paperbound **$1.75**

SAY IT language phrase books

"SAY IT" in the foreign language of your choice! We have sold over ½ million copies of these popular, useful language books. They will not make you an expert linguist overnight, but they do cover most practical matters of everyday life abroad.

Over 1000 useful phrases, expressions, with additional variants, substitutions.

Modern! Useful! Hundreds of phrases not available in other texts: "Nylon," "air-conditioned," etc.

The ONLY inexpensive phrase book **completely indexed.** Everything is available at a flip of your finger, ready for use.

Prepared by native linguists, travel experts.

Based on years of travel experience abroad.

This handy phrase book may be used by itself, or it may supplement any other text or course; it provides a living element. Used by many colleges and institutions: Hunter College; Barnard College; Army Ordnance School, Aberdeen; and many others.

Available, 1 book per language:

Danish (T818) 75¢
Dutch T(817) 75¢
English (for German-speaking people) (T801) 60¢
English (for Italian-speaking people) (T816) 60¢
English (for Spanish-speaking people) (T802) 60¢
Esperanto (T820) 75¢
French (T803) 60¢
German (T804) 60¢
Modern Greek (T813) 75¢
Hebrew (T805) 60¢

Italian (T806) 60¢
Japanese (T807) 60¢
Norwegian (T814) 75¢
Russian (T810) 75¢
Spanish (T811) 60¢
Turkish (T821) 75¢
Yiddish (T815) 75¢
Swedish (T812) 75¢
Polish (T808) 75¢
Portuguese (T809) 75¢

LISTEN & LEARN language record sets

LISTEN & LEARN is the only language record course designed especially to meet your travel needs, or help you learn essential foreign language quickly by yourself, or in conjunction with any school course, by means of the automatic association method. Each set contains three 33⅓ rpm long- playing records — 1½ hours of recorded speech by eminent native speakers who are professors at Columbia, N.Y.U., Queens College and other leading universities. The sets are priced far below other sets of similar quality, yet they contain many special features not found in other record sets:

* Over 800 selected phrases and sentences, a basic vocabulary of over 3200 words.
* Both English and foreign language recorded; with a pause for your repetition.
* Designed for persons with limited time; no time wasted on material you cannot use immediately.
* Living, modern expressions that answer modern needs: drugstore items, "air-conditioned," etc.
* 128-196 page manuals contain everything on the records, plus simple pronunciation guides.
* Manual is fully indexed; find the phrase you want instantly.
* High fidelity recording—equal to any records costing up to $6 each.

The phrases on these records cover 41 different categories useful to the traveller or student interested in learning the living, spoken language: greetings, introductions, making yourself understood, passing customs, planes, trains, boats, buses, taxis, nightclubs, restaurants, menu items, sports, concerts, cameras, automobile travel, repairs, drugstores, doctors, dentists, medicines, barber shops, beauty parlors, laundries, many, many more.

"Excellent . . . among the very best on the market," Prof. Mario Pei, Dept. of Romance Languages, Columbia University. "Inexpensive and well-done . . . an ideal present," CHICAGO SUNDAY TRIBUNE. "More genuinely helpful than anything of its kind which I have previously encountered," Sidney Clark, well-known author of "ALL THE BEST" travel books. Each set contains 3 33⅓ rpm pure vinyl records, 128- 196 page with full record text, and album. One language per set. LISTEN & LEARN record sets are now available in—

FRENCH	the set $4.95		**GERMAN**	the set $4.95
ITALIAN	the set $4.95		**SPANISH**	the set $4.95
RUSSIAN	the set $5.95		**JAPANESE** *	the set $5.95

* Available Sept. 1, 1959

UNCONDITIONAL GUARANTEE: Dover Publications stands behind every Listen and Learn record set. If you are dissatisfied with these sets for any reason whatever, return them within 10 days and your money will be refunded in full.

ART HISTORY

STICKS AND STONES, Lewis Mumford. An examination of forces influencing American architecture: the medieval tradition in early New England, the classical influence in Jefferson's time, the Brown Decades, the imperial facade, the machine age, etc. "A truly remarkable book," SAT. REV. OF LITERATURE. 2nd revised edition. 21 illus. xvii + 228pp. 5⅜ x 8.
T202 Paperbound **$1.60**

THE AUTOBIOGRAPHY OF AN IDEA, Louis Sullivan. The architect whom Frank Lloyd Wright called "the master," records the development of the theories that revolutionized America's skyline. 34 full-page plates of Sullivan's finest work. New introduction by R. M. Line. xiv + 335pp. 5⅜ x 8.
T281 Paperbound **$1.85**

THE MATERIALS AND TECHNIQUES OF MEDIEVAL PAINTING, D. V. Thompson. An invaluable study of carriers and grounds, binding media, pigments, metals used in painting, al fresco and al secco techniques, burnishing, etc. used by the medieval masters. Preface by Bernard Berenson. 239pp. 5⅜ x 8.
T327 Paperbound **$1.85**

PRINCIPLES OF ART HISTORY, H. Wölfflin. This remarkably instructive work demonstrates the tremendous change in artistic conception from the 14th to the 18th centuries, by analyzing 164 works by Botticelli, Dürer, Hobbema, Holbein, Hals, Titian, Rembrandt, Vermeer, etc., and pointing out exactly what is meant by "baroque," "classic," "primitive," "picturesque," and other basic terms of art history and criticism. "A remarkable lesson in the art of seeing," SAT. REV. OF LITERATURE. Translated from the 7th German edition. 150 illus. 254pp. 6⅛ x 9¼.
T276 Paperbound **$2.00**

FOUNDATIONS OF MODERN ART, A. Ozenfant. Stimulating discussion of human creativity from paleolithic cave painting to modern painting, architecture, decorative arts. Fully illustrated with works of Gris, Lipchitz, Léger, Picasso, primitive, modern artifacts, architecture, industrial art, much more. 226 illustrations. 368pp. 6⅛ x 9¼.
T215 Paperbound **$1.95**

HANDICRAFTS, APPLIED ART, ART SOURCES, ETC.

WILD FOWL DECOYS, J. Barber. The standard work on this fascinating branch of folk art, ranging from Indian mud and grass devices to realistic wooden decoys. Discusses styles, types, periods; gives full information on how to make decoys. 140 illustrations (including 14 new plates) show decoys and provide full sets of plans for handicrafters, artists, hunters, and students of folk art. 281pp. 7⅞ x 10¾. Deluxe edition.
T11 Clothbound **$8.50**

METALWORK AND ENAMELLING, H. Maryon. Probably the best book ever written on the subject. Tells everything necessary for the home manufacture of jewelry, rings, ear pendants, bowls, etc. Covers materials, tools, soldering, filigree, setting stones, raising patterns, repoussé work, damascening, niello, cloisonné, polishing, assaying, casting, and dozens of other techniques. The best substitute for apprenticeship to a master metalworker. 363 photos and figures. 374pp. 5½ x 8½.
T183 Clothbound **$7.50**

SHAKER FURNITURE, E. D. and F. Andrews. The most illuminating study of Shaker furniture ever written. Covers chronology, craftsmanship, houses, shops, etc. Includes over 200 photographs of chairs, tables, clocks, beds, benches, etc. "Mr. & Mrs. Andrews know all there is to know about Shaker furniture," Mark Van Doren, NATION. 48 full-page plates. 192pp. Deluxe cloth binding. 7⅞ x 10¾.
T7 Clothbound **$6.00**

PRIMITIVE ART, Franz Boas. A great American anthropologist covers theory, technical virtuosity, styles, symbolism, patterns, etc. of primitive art. The more than 900 illustrations will interest artists, designers, craftworkers. Over 900 illustrations. 376pp. 5⅜ x 8.
T25 Paperbound **$1.95**

ON THE LAWS OF JAPANESE PAINTING, H. Bowie. The best possible substitute for lessons from an oriental master. Treats both spirit and technique; exercises for control of the brush; inks, brushes, colors; use of dots, lines to express whole moods, etc. 220 illus. 132pp. 6⅛ x 9¼.
T30 Paperbound **$1.95**

HANDBOOK OF ORNAMENT, F. S. Meyer. One of the largest collections of copyright-free traditional art: over 3300 line cuts of Greek, Roman, Medieval, Renaissance, Baroque, 18th and 19th century art motifs (tracery, geometric elements, flower and animal motifs, etc.) and decorated objects (chairs, thrones, weapons, vases, jewelry, armor, etc.). Full text. 3300 illustrations. 562pp. 5⅜ x 8.
T302 Paperbound **$2.00**

THREE CLASSICS OF ITALIAN CALLIGRAPHY. Oscar Ogg, ed. Exact reproductions of three famous Renaissance calligraphic works: Arrighi's OPERINA and IL MODO, Tagliente's LO PRESENTE LIBRO, and Palatino's LIBRO NUOVO. More than 200 complete alphabets, thousands of lettered specimens, in Papal Chancery and other beautiful, ornate handwriting. Introduction. 245 plates. 282pp. 6⅛ x 9¼.
T212 Paperbound **$1.95**

THE HISTORY AND TECHNIQUES OF LETTERING, A. Nesbitt. A thorough history of lettering from the ancient Egyptians to the present, and a 65-page course in lettering for artists. Every major development in lettering history is illustrated by a complete alphabet. Fully analyzes such masters as Caslon, Koch, Garamont, Jenson, and many more. 89 alphabets, 165 other specimens. 317pp. 5⅜ x 8.
T427 Paperbound **$2.00**

LETTERING AND ALPHABETS, J. A. Cavanagh. An unabridged reissue of "Lettering," containing the full discussion, analysis, illustration of 89 basic hand lettering tyles based on Caslon, Bodoni, Gothic, many other types. Hundreds of technical hints on construction, strokes, pens, brushes, etc. 89 alphabets, 72 lettered specimens, which may be reproduced permission-free. 121pp. 9¾ x 8.　　　　　　　　　　　　　　　　　　　T53 Paperbound **$1.25**

THE HUMAN FIGURÉ IN MOTION, Eadweard Muybridge. The largest collection in print of Muybridge's famous high-speed action photos. 4789 photographs in more than 500 action-strip-sequences (at shutter speeds up to 1/6000th of a second) illustrate men, women, children—mostly undraped—performing such actions as walking, running, getting up, lying down, carrying objects, throwing, etc. "An unparalleled dictionary of action for all artists," AMERICAN ARTIST. 390 full-page plates, with 4789 photographs. Heavy glossy stock, reinforced binding with headbands. 7⅞ x 10¾.　　　　　　　　　　　T204 Clothbound **$10.00**

ANIMALS IN MOTION, Eadweard Muybridge. The largest collection of animal action photos in print. 34 different animals (horses, mules, oxen, goats, camels, pigs, cats, lions, gnus, deer, monkeys, eagles—and 22 others) in 132 characteristic actions. All 3919 photographs are taken in series at speeds up to 1/1600th of a second, offering artists, biologists, cartoonists a remarkable opportunity to see exactly how an ostrich's head bobs when running, how a lion puts his foot down, how an elephant's knee bends, how a bird flaps his wings, thousands of other hard-to-catch details. "A really marvelous series of plates," NATURE. 380 full-pages of plates. Heavy glossy stock, reinforced binding with headbands. 7⅞ x 10¾.　　　　　　　　　　　　　　　　　　　　　　　　　　T203 Clothbound **$10.00**

THE BOOK OF SIGNS, R. Koch. 493 symbols—crosses, monograms, astrological, biological symbols, runes, etc.—from ancient manuscripts, cathedrals, coins, catacombs, pottery. May be reproduced permission-free. 493 illustrations by Fritz Kredel. 104pp. 6⅛ x 9¼.　　　　　　　　　　　　　　　　　　　　　　　　　　　T162 Paperbound **$1.00**

A HANDBOOK OF EARLY ADVERTISING ART, C. P. Hornung. The largest collection of copyright-free early advertising art ever compiled. Vol. I: 2,000 illustrations of animals, old automobiles, buildings, allegorical figures, fire engines, Indians, ships, trains, more than 33 other categories! Vol II: Over 4,000 typographical specimens; 600 Roman, Gothic, Barnum, Old English faces; 630 ornamental type faces; hundreds of scrolls, initials, flourishes, etc. "A remarkable collection," PRINTERS' INK.

Vol. I: Pictorial Volume. Over 2000 illustrations. 256pp. 9 x 12.　　T122 Clothbound **$10.00**
Vol. II: Typographical Volume. Over 4000 speciments. 319pp. 9 x 12.　T123 Clothbound **$10.00**
　　　　　　　　　　　　　　　　　　Two volume set, Clothbound, only **$18.50**

DESIGN FOR ARTISTS AND CRAFTSMEN, L. Wolchonok. The most thorough course on the creation of art motifs and designs. Shows you step-by-step, with hundreds of examples and 113 detailed exercises, how to create original designs from geometric patterns, plants, birds, animals, humans, and man-made objects. "A great contribution to the field of design and crafts," N. Y. SOCIETY OF CRAFTSMEN. More than 1300 entirely new illustrations. xv + 207pp. 7⅞ x 10¾.　　　　　　　　　　　　　　　　T274 Clothbound **$4.95**

HANDBOOK OF DESIGNS AND DEVICES, C. P. Hornung. A remarkable working collection of 1836 basic designs and variations, all copyright-free. Variations of circle, line, cross, diamond, swastika, star, scroll, shield, many more. Notes on symbolism. "A necessity to every designer who would be original without having to labor heavily," ARTIST and ADVERTISER. 204 plates. 240pp. 5⅜ x 8.

　　　　　　　　　　　　　　　　　　　　　　　　　　T125 Paperbound **$1.90**

THE UNIVERSAL PENMAN, George Bickham. Exact reproduction of beautiful 18th century book of handwriting. 22 complete alphabets in finest English roundhand, other scripts, over 2000 elaborate flourishes, 122 calligraphic illustrations, etc. Material is copyright-free. "An essential part of any art library, and a book of permanent value," AMERICAN ARTIST. 212 plates. 224pp. 9 x 13¾.　　　　　　　　　　　　　　　　T20 Clothbound **$10.00**

AN ATLAS OF ANATOMY FOR ARTISTS, F. Schider. This standard work contains 189 full-page plates, more than 647 illustrations of all aspects of the human skeleton, musculature, cutaway portions of the body, each part of the anatomy, hand forms, eyelids, breasts, location of muscles under the flesh, etc. 59 plates illustrate how Michelangelo, da Vinci, Goya, 15 others, drew human anatomy. New 3rd edition enlarged by 52 new illustrations by Cloquet, Barcsay. "The standard reference tool," AMERICAN LIBRARY ASSOCIATION. "Excellent," AMERICAN ARTIST. 189 plates, 647 illustrations. xxvi + 192pp. 7⅞ x 10⅝.　　T241 Clothbound **$6.00**

AN ATLAS OF ANIMAL ANATOMY FOR ARTISTS, W. Ellenberger, H. Baum, H. Dittrich. The largest, richest animal anatomy for artists in English. Form, musculature, tendons, bone structure, expression, detailed cross sections of head, other features, of the horse, lion, dog, cat, deer, seal, kangaroo, cow, bull, goat, monkey, hare, many other animals. "Highly recommended," DESIGN. Second, revised, enlarged edition with new plates from Cuvier, Stubbs, etc. 288 illustrations. 153pp. 11⅜ x 9.　　　　　　　　　　　　　　T82 Clothbound **$6.00**

ANIMAL DRAWING: ANATOMY AND ACTION FOR ARTISTS, C. R. Knight. 158 studies, with full accompanying text, of such animals as the gorilla, bear, bison, dromedary, camel, vulture, pelican, iguana, shark, etc., by one of the greatest modern masters of animal drawing. Innumerable tips on how to get life expression into your work. "An excellent reference work,' SAN FRANCISCO CHRONICLE. 158 illustrations. 156pp. 10½ x 8½.　　　　　　　　　　　　　　　　　　　　　　　　　　T426 Paperbound **$2.00**

DOVER BOOKS

THE CRAFTSMAN'S HANDBOOK, Cennino Cennini. The finest English translation of IL LIBRO DELL' ARTE, the 15th century introduction to art technique that is both a mirror of Quatrocento life and a source of many useful but nearly forgotten facets of the painter's art. 4 illustrations. xxvii + 142pp. D. V. Thompson, translator. 6⅛ x 9¼.　T54 Paperbound **$1.50**

THE BROWN DECADES, Lewis Mumford. A picture of the "buried renaissance" of the post-Civil War period, and the founding of modern architecture (Sullivan, Richardson, Root, Roebling), landscape development (Marsh, Olmstead, Eliot), and the graphic arts (Homer, Eakins, Ryder). 2nd revised, enlarged edition. Bibliography. 12 illustrations. xiv + 266 pp. 5⅜ x 8.　T200 Paperbound **$1.65**

STIEGEL GLASS, F. W. Hunter. The story of the most highly esteemed early American glassware, fully illustrated. How a German adventurer, "Baron" Stiegel, founded a glass empire; detailed accounts of individual glasswork. "This pioneer work is reprinted in an edition even more beautiful than the original," ANTIQUES DEALER. New introduction by Helen McKearin. 171 illustrations, 12 in full color. xxii + 338pp. 7⅞ x 10¾.　T128 Clothbound **$10.00**

THE HUMAN FIGURE, J. H. Vanderpoel. Not just a picture book, but a complete course by a famous figure artist. Extensive text, illustrated by 430 pencil and charcoal drawings of both male and female anatomy. 2nd enlarged edition. Foreword. 430 illus. 143pp. 6⅛ x 9¼.　T432 Paperbound **$1.45**

PINE FURNITURE OF EARLY NEW ENGLAND, R. H. Kettell. Over 400 illustrations, over 50 working drawings of early New England chairs, benches, beds cupboards, mirrors, shelves, tables, other furniture esteemed for simple beauty and character. "Rich store of illustrations . . . emphasizes the individuality and varied design," ANTIQUES. 413 illustrations, 55 working drawings. 475pp. 8 x 10¾.　T145 Clothbound **$10.00**

BASIC BOOKBINDING, A. W. Lewis. Enables both beginners and experts to rebind old books or bind paperbacks in hard covers. Treats materials, tools; gives step-by-step instruction in how to collate a book, sew it, back it, make boards, etc. 261 illus. Appendices. 155pp. 5⅜ x 8.　T169 Paperbound **$1.35**

DESIGN MOTIFS OF ANCIENT MEXICO, J. Enciso. Nearly 90% of these 766 superb designs from Aztec, Olmec, Totonac, Maya, and Toltec origins are unobtainable elsewhere! Contains plumed serpents, wind gods, animals, demons, dancers, monsters, etc. Excellent applied design source. Originally $17.50. 766 illustrations, thousands of motifs. 192pp. 6⅛ x 9¼.　T84 Paperbound **$1.85**

AFRICAN SCULPTURE, Ladislas Segy. 163 full-page plates illustrating masks, fertility figures, ceremonial objects, etc., of 50 West and Central African tribes—95% never before illustrated. 34-page introduction to African sculpture. "Mr. Segy is one of its top authorities," NEW YORKER. 164 full-page photographic plates. Introduction. Bibliography. 244pp. 6⅛ x 9¼.　T396 Paperbound **$2.00**

THE PROCESSES OF GRAPHIC REPRODUCTION IN PRINTING, H. Curwen. A thorough and practical survey of wood, linoleum, and rubber engraving; copper engraving; drypoint, mezzotint, etching, aquatint, steel engraving, die sinking, stencilling, lithography (extensively); photographic reproduction utilizing line, continuous tone, photoengravure, collotype; every other process in general use. Note on color reproduction. Section on bookbinding. Over 200 illustrations, 25 in color. 143pp. 5½ x 8½.　T512 Clothbound **$4.00**

CALLIGRAPHY, J. G. Schwandner. First reprinting in 200 years of this legendary book of beautiful handwriting. Over 300 ornamental initials, 12 complete calligraphic alphabets, over 150 ornate frames and panels, 75 calligraphic pictures of cherubs, stags, lions, etc., thousands of flourishes, scrolls, etc., by the greatest 18th century masters. All material can be copied or adapted without permission. Historical introduction. 158 full-page plates. 368pp. 9 x 13.　T475 Clothbound **$10.00**

* * *

A DIDEROT PICTORIAL ENCYCLOPEDIA OF TRADES AND INDUSTRY, Manufacturing and the Technical Arts in Plates Selected from "L'Encyclopédie ou Dictionnaire Raisonné des Sciences, des Arts, et des Métiers," of Denis Diderot, edited with text by C. Gillispie. Over 2000 illustrations on 485 full-page plates. Magnificent 18th century engravings of men, women, and children working at such trades as milling flour, cheesemaking, charcoal burning, mining, silverplating, shoeing horses, making fine glass, printing, hundreds more, showing details of machinery, different steps in sequence, etc. A remarkable art work, but also the largest collection of working figures in print, copyright-free, for art directors, designers, etc. Two vols. 920pp. 9 x 12. Heavy library cloth.　T421 Two volume set **$18.50**

* * *

SILK SCREEN TECHNIQUES, J. Biegeleisen, M. Cohn. A practical step-by-step home course in one of the most versatile, least expensive graphic arts processes. How to build an inexpensive silk screen, prepare stencils, print, achieve special textures, use color, etc. Every step explained, diagrammed. 149 illustrations, 8 in color. 201pp. 6⅛ x 9¼.　T433 Paperbound **$1.45**

MATHEMATICS, MAGIC AND MYSTERY, Martin Gardner. Astonishing feats of mind reading, mystifying "magic" tricks, are often based on mathematical principles anyone can learn. This book shows you how to perform scores of tricks with cards, dice, coins, knots, numbers, etc., by using simple principles from set theory, theory of numbers, topology, other areas of mathematics, fascinating in themselves. No special knowledge required. 135 illus. 186pp. 5⅜ x 8.
T335 Paperbound **$1.00**

MATHEMATICAL PUZZLES FOR BEGINNERS AND ENTHUSIASTS, G. Mott-Smith. Test your problem-solving techniques and powers of inference on 188 challenging, amusing puzzles based on algebra, dissection of plane figures, permutations, probabilities, etc. Appendix of primes, square roots, etc. 135 illus. 2nd revised edition. 248pp. 5⅜ x 8.
T198 Paperbound **$1.00**

LEARN CHESS FROM THE MASTERS, F. Reinfeld. Play 10 games against Marshall, Bronstein, Najdorf, other masters, and grade yourself on each move. Detailed annotations reveal principles of play, strategy, etc. as you proceed. An excellent way to get a real insight into the game. Formerly titled, "Chess by Yourself." 91 diagrams. vii + 144pp. 5⅜ x 8.
T362 Paperbound **$1.00**

REINFELD ON THE END GAME IN CHESS, F. Reinfeld. 62 end games of Alekhine, Tarrasch, Morphy, other masters, are carefully analyzed with emphasis on transition from middle game to end play. Tempo moves, queen endings, weak squares, other basic principles clearly illustrated. Excellent for understanding why some moves are weak or incorrect, how to avoid errors. Formerly titled, "Practical End-game Play." 62 diagrams. vi + 177pp. 5⅜ x 8.
T417 Paperbound **$1.25**

101 PUZZLES IN THOUGHT AND LOGIC, C. R. Wylie, Jr. Brand new puzzles you need no special knowledge to solve! Each one is a gem of ingenuity that will really challenge your problem-solving technique. Introduction with simplified explanation of scientic puzzle solving. 128pp. 5⅜ x 8.
T167 Paperbound **$1.00**

THE COMPLETE NONSENSE OF EDWARD LEAR. The only complete edition of this master of gentle madness at a popular price. The Dong with the Luminous Nose, The Jumblies, The Owl and the Pussycat, hundreds of other bits of wonderful nonsense. 214 limericks, 3 sets of Nonsense Botany, 5 Nonsense Alphabets, 546 fantastic drawings, much more. 320pp. 5⅜ x 8.
T167 Paperbound **$1.00**

28 SCIENCE FICTION STORIES OF H. G. WELLS. Two complete novels, "Men Like Gods" and "Star Begotten," plus 26 short stories by the master science-fiction writer of all time. Stories of space, time, future adventure that are among the all-time classics of science fiction. 928pp. 5⅜ x 8.
T265 Clothbound **$3.95**

SEVEN SCIENCE FICTION NOVELS, H. G. Wells. Unabridged texts of "The Time Machine," "The Island of Dr. Moreau," "First Men in the Moon," "The Invisible Man," "The War of the Worlds," "The Food of the Gods," "In the Days of the Comet." "One will have to go far to match this for entertainment, excitement, and sheer pleasure," N. Y. TIMES. 1015pp. 5⅜ x 8.
T264 Clothbound **$3.95**

MATHEMAGIC, MAGIC PUZZLES, AND GAMES WITH NUMBERS, R. V. Heath. More than 60 new puzzles and stunts based on number properties: multiplying large numbers mentally, finding the date of any day in the year, etc. Edited by J. S. Meyer. 76 illus. 129pp. 5⅜ x 8.
T110 Paperbound **$1.00**

FIVE ADVENTURE NOVELS OF H. RIDER HAGGARD. The master story-teller's five best tales of mystery and adventure set against authentic African backgrounds: "She," "King Solomon's Mines," "Allan Quatermain," "Allan's Wife," "Maiwa's Revenge." 821pp. 5⅜ x 8.
T108 Clothbound **$3.95**

WIN AT CHECKERS, M. Hopper. (Formerly "Checkers.") The former World's Unrestricted Checker Champion gives you valuable lessons in openings, traps, end games, ways to draw when you are behind, etc. More than 100 questions and answers anticipate your problems. Appendix. 75 problems diagrammed, solved. 79 figures. xi + 107pp. 5⅜ x 8.
T363 Paperbound **$1.00**

CRYPTOGRAPHY, L. D. Smith. Excellent introductory work on ciphers and their solution, history of secret writing, techniques, etc. Appendices on Japanese methods, the Baconian cipher, frequency tables. Bibliography. Over 150 problems, solutions. 160pp. 5⅜ x 8.
T247 Paperbound **$1.00**

CRYPTANALYSIS, H. F. Gaines. (Formerly, "Elementary Cryptanalysis.") The best book available on cryptograms and how to solve them. Contains all major techniques: substitution, transposition, mixed alphabets, multafid, Kasiski and Vignere methods, etc. Word frequency appendix. 167 problems, solutions. 173 figures. 236pp. 5⅜ x 8. T97 Paperbound **$1.95**

FLATLAND, E. A. Abbot. The science-fiction classic of life in a 2-dimensional world that is considered a first-rate introduction to relativity and hyperspace, as well as a scathing satire on society, politics and religion. 7th edition. 16 illus. 128pp. 5⅜ x 8.
T1 Paperbound **$1.00**

DOVER BOOKS

HOW TO FORCE CHECKMATE, F. Reinfeld. (Formerly "Challenge to Chessplayers.") No board needed to sharpen your checkmate skill on 300 checkmate situations. Learn to plan up to 3 moves ahead and play a superior end game. 300 situations diagrammed; notes and full solutions. 111pp. 5⅜ x 8.   T439 Paperbound **$1.25**

MORPHY'S GAMES OF CHESS, P. W. Sergeant, ed. Play forcefully by following the techniques used by one of.the greatest chess champions. 300 of Morphy's games carefully annotated to reveal principles. Bibliography. New introduction by F. Reinfeld. 235 diagrams. x + 352pp. 5⅜ x 8.   T386 Paperbound **$1.75**

MATHEMATICAL RECREATIONS, M. Kraitchik. Hundreds of unusual mathematical puzzlers and odd bypaths of math, elementary and advanced. Greek, Medieval, Arabic, Hindu problems; figurate numbers, Fermat numbers, primes; magic, Euler, Latin squares; fairy chess, latruncles, reversi, jinx, ruma, tetrachrome other positional and permutational games. Rigorous solutions. Revised second edition. 181 illus. 330pp. 5⅜ x 8.   T163 Paperbound **$1.75**

MATHEMATICAL EXCURSIONS, H. A. Merrill. Revealing stimulating insights into elementary math, not usually taught in school. 90 problems demonstrate Russian peasant multiplication, memory systems for pi, magic squares, dyadic systems, division by inspection, many more. Solutions to difficult problems. 50 illus. 5⅜ x 8.   T350 Paperbound **$1.00**

MAGIC TRICKS & CARD TRICKS, W. Jonson. Best introduction to tricks with coins, bills, eggs, ribbons, slates, cards, easily performed without elaborate equipment. Professional routines, tips on presentation, misdirection, etc. Two books bound as one: 52 tricks with cards, 37 tricks with common objects. 106 figures. 224pp. 5⅜ x 8.   T909 Paperbound **$1.00**

MATHEMATICAL PUZZLES OF SAM LOYD, selected and edited by **M. Gardner.** 177 most ingenious mathematical puzzles of America's greatest puzzle originator, based on arithmetic, algebra, game theory, dissection, route tracing, operations research, probability, etc. 120 drawings, diagrams. Solutions. 187pp. 5⅜ x 8.   T498 Paperbound **$1.00**

THE ART OF CHESS, J. Mason. The most famous general study of chess ever written. More than 90 openings, middle game, end game, how to attack, sacrifice, defend, exchange, form general strategy. Supplement on "How Do You Play Chess?" by F. Reinfeld. 448 diagrams. 356pp. 5⅜ x 8.   T463 Paperbound **$1.85**

HYPERMODERN CHESS as Developed in the Games of its Greatest Exponent, ARON NIMZOVICH, F. Reinfeld, ed. Learn how the game's greatest innovator defeated Alekhine, Lasker, and many others; and use these methods in your own game. 180 diagrams. 228pp. 5⅜ x 8.   T448 Paperbound **$1.35**

A TREASURY OF CHESS LORE, F. Reinfeld, ed. Hundreds of fascinating stories by and about the masters, accounts of tournaments and famous games, aphorisms, word portraits, little known incidents, photographs, etc., that will delight the chess enthusiast captivate the beginner. 49 photographs (14 full-page plates), 12 diagrams. 315pp. 5⅜ x 8.   T458 Paperbound **$1.75**

A NONSENSE ANTHOLOGY, collected by **Carolyn Wells.** 245 of the best nonsense verses ever written: nonsense puns, absurd arguments, mock epics, nonsense ballads, "sick" verses, dog-Latin verses, French nonsense verses, limericks, Lear, Carroll, Belloc, Burgess, nearly 100 other writers. Introduction by Carolyn Wells. 3 indices: Title, Author, First Lines. xxxiii + 279pp. 5⅜ x 8.   T499 Paperbound **$1.25**

SYMBOLIC LOGIC and THE GAME OF LOGIC, Lewis Carroll. Two delightful puzzle books by the author of "Alice," bound as one. Both works concern the symbolic representation of traditional logic and together contain more than 500 ingenious, amusing and instructive syllogistic puzzlers. Total of 326pp. 5⅜ x 8.   T492 Paperbound **$1.50**

PILLOW PROBLEMS and A TANGLED TALE, Lewis Carroll. Two of Carroll's rare puzzle works bound as one. "Pillow Problems" contain 72 original math puzzles. The puzzles in "A Tangled Tale" are given in delightful story form. Total of 291pp. 5⅜ x 8.   T493 Paperbound **$1.50**

PECK'S BAD BOY AND HIS PA, G. W. Peck. Both volumes of one of the most widely read of all American humor books. A classic of American folk humor, also invaluable as a portrait of an age. 100 original illustrations. Introduction by E. Bleiler. 347pp. 5⅜ x 8.
                      T497 Paperbound **$1.35**

Dover publishes books on art, music, philosophy, literature, languages, history, social sciences, psychology, handcrafts, orientalia, puzzles and entertainments, chess, pets and gardens, books explaining science, intermediate and higher mathematics mathematical physics, engineering, biological sciences, earth sciences, classics of science, etc. Write to:

Dept. catrr.
Dover Publications, Inc.
180 Varick Street, N. Y. 14, N. Y.